Early Mississippi Records

- 1827-1900 -

Volume #1

Washington *and* Issaquena Counties

Compiled by:
Katherine Clements Branton

Southern Historical Press, inc.
Greenville, South Carolina

This volume was reproduced
from a personal copy located in
the Publishers private library

Please direct all correspondence and book orders to:
SOUTHERN HISTORICAL PRESS, Inc.
1071 Park West Blvd.
Greenville, SC   29611

Originally printed Leland, MS 1982
ISBN #978-1-63914-323-8
Printed in the United States of America

EARLY RECORDS OF MISSISSIPPI

Issaquena and Washington Counties

WASHINGTON COUNTY, Mississippi, was formed 1827 out of Warren and Yazoo Counties, and is not to be confused with an earlier Washington County (located on the South Alabama and Mississippi line) which no longer exists.

Early records in Greenville, the county seat of the present Washington County, are a mixed bag. The Yankees grew weary of being shot at by snipers from the banks of the Miss. River, and burned "Old" Greenville to the ground, including the courthouse and what records that could be found. Luckily a lot of these records were salvaged by being removed and hidden away. Devastating floods took their tolls, plus yellow-fever epidemics. Some of the volumes are faded, water-marked, and nearly illegible. Packets are practically nonexistant...many are missing, especially the early ones.

ISSAQUENA County Records are included here, since it was formed from Washington County in 1844, amid the wild land speculation that swelled behind the Indian Treaties. The records in Mayersville are intact, but many of the packets are also missing there.

The Index to these records reads like a glimpse into the current phone book. The people arrived here, most stayed, multiplied. Some say they got their feet mired in the Mississippi mud, and never got out.

Collected and abstracted by Katherine Branton
Indexed by Alice Wade
1982

TABLE OF CONTENTS

Vol. I

Washington County, Mississippi

Circuit Court, "Records", 1839-1840	1 - 16
List of Early Records in Circuit Clks. Office	17
General Chancery Docket: Bk.1 (Begins 1856)	18 - 53
List of Early Lawyers; Law Firms	54
Marriage Records: Bk."A", White (1891-1892)	55
Marriage Records: Bk.1, White (1892-1896)	56 - 58
Records of Wills: Bk.1 (1839-1872) to be cont.	59 - 97
Random Listing of Greenfield Cemetary	98
Census 1870: Random Listing	99 - 105

Issaquena County, Mississippi

Index to Will Bks. A.B.C. (1846-1926)	106 - 125
Census 1850	126 - 133
Census 1860: Random Listing	134 - 145
Medical Licenses (1882-1907)	146 - 147
Marriage Bk."A"	148
Index to Estate Packets: to be cont.	149 - 152
Surname Index:	153 - 189

Page 1, Wash.Co.

Circuit Court Clerk's Office
Early Record book entitled simply "Records"
Begins - December Special Term 1839 - Presiding Judge - George Coalter
Unindexed

P. 1,2,3, Thomas J. Leigh vs Nancy Dillingham

P. 4,5, Thomas J. Payne vs John Turnbull, Jr. & William Walker (written Jan 1833) States that Turnbull, then in Rodney, Ms. Thomas Payne accuses them of owing him $100. The Defendants forfeited.

P. 6,7,8 Robert B. Mayes vs Stephen Arrington & Charles G. Walker. Plaintiff claims they owe him $440, to be paid Daniel Mayes. Result of suit - Stephen Arrington & C.G. Walker agree to pay Robert N. Russell $440 - (25 Dec. 1837), Robert N. Russell assigns to J.L. Nelson, who assigns the "within" to D. Mayes (24Nov. 1838) Danl. Mayes assigns the "within" to Robert B. Mayes (Apr. 28, 1839)

P. 8,9,10 Wm. H. Lawson vs Isaac Beall (Apr. 1839)

P. 11,12 Arrington vs Chas. G. Walker (he didn't pay) Case cont. Meany & Sutton, Atty.

P. 13,14 Martha Clarke vs G.W. Reynolds - Webster & Smith, atty.
15,16 Case states that on 8 Dec. 1838 at Bellville, Washington Co. Ms. G.W. Reynolds made a prom. note for $5025. Found in favor of Plaintiff.

P. 16,17 John B. Davis vs John H. Cocke - Davis complains Cocke, form-
18 erly partner of Rowland M. Whitman under name and style of "R.M. Whitman & Co" intered into prom. note, Vicksburg, Ms Warren Co. - 1838 - for $250. John F. Purson, Plaint. aty. Found for the defend.

P. 19,20 Sims & Reading vs F.G. Turnbull, in Warren Co. Ms 21 Aug. 1839, William H. Sims & Abraham B. Reading, partners in trade, accuse Frederick G. Turnbull of entering a prom. note in Warren Co 28 Dec 1837 for $535. John F. Pierson, Plain. Atty..W.S. Wills, Sheriff, Thomas M. Endicott, Clerk, Smith atty for defend....Turnbull pays.

P. 21,22 A. Fisk, Watt, &Co. vs F.G. Turnbull: Alvarez Fisk, JohnWatt,
23 Glendy Burke, merchants and partners in firm Fisk, Watt & Co. say that Frederick G. Turnbull did on 1Jan. 1836 at Lake Washington, Ms. (Washington Co. Ms) made prom. note $2562.50 payable 2 yrs later at Union Bank of Louisiana New Orleans Plaintiffs recovered.

P. 24, 25 Wilson Farr vs John H. Blanton ; Farr says Blanton made prom. note on 2 Jan. 1833, Washington Co. for $61.25 - Elbridge G. Walker Plain. atty. Plain. collected.

P. 26,27 Doremas, Suydams & Nixon vs Samuel R. Dunn: Thomas C.
28 Doremas & John M. Nixon merchants and partners in firm "Doremas Suydams & Nixon" declare that Samuel R. Dunn of Bachelors Bend, Washington Co. Ms. did on 18 July 1836 at New York by one Thos. B. Warfield, promise to pay $309.

P. 28,29,30 William H. Sims by his attorney Thomas Greenwood vs Council R. Bass: Plaint. states that Defend. on 8 Mar. 1836 at Washington Co. made prom. note for $205.65..H. Short Plaint. Atty.

P. 30,31 Yerger Chaffin & Co. vs Robert Hinton, Featherstone Bland;
32,33 On Sept 1839 John K. Yerger, John Kirk, Edward H. Chaffin,
34,35 Absolom Van Wicke & John M. Bell - merchants and partners in firm called "Yerger Chaffin & Co." complain of Robert

December Term 1839, cont.

Hunter and James Bland, Richard Featherstone & Edward S. Shannon, merchants & partners in firm called "Featherstone Bland & Co." did on 1 Dec.1837 at Vicksburg,Ms., give prom. note of $1183.67. Taylor & Johnson, Plaint.atty.

P.35,36:DeLa F.Roysdan vs Andrew Carson;Plain.states that on 22 Apr.1835 defend. made a prom.note of $204. Jurors serving for this term of court were the following "good and lawful men":Alfred G.Carter,Wm.C.Barrett,Wm.J.Penrice,Robt. McCullough,Thos.W.Morris,Philip Ault,James G.Herald,Calvin Belcher,Theodorick H.Jackson,Wm.Woods,Andrew Turnbull, Adam Shirley.

P.37,38,39;Wm.Miller & Co.vs Wm.Watson: States that in Sept. Term 1838,Anderson Miller & Wm.Miller merchants and partners in a firm called "Wm.Miller & Co." complain of Wm.Watson making a prom.note on 9 Jan.1838 at Princeton(Wash.Co.Ms. since sluffed off into the Ms.River)

P.39,40,41,42,43:Anderson Miller vs J.V.Hollingshead:Anderson Miller states that on --Oct.1836 Jeremiah, alias J.V. Hollingshead of Louisville,State of Ky.promised to furnish all material except sills, do all carpenter work of a storehouse to be built at Princeton. Hollingshead,now of Wash. Co.Ms...Detailed description of the building follows,then the final agreement. Depositions given by Wm.T.Miller taken before A.W.Samuel,Justice of the Peace: Jurors for March Term - Wm.W.Collins,Jos.Pervis,Samuel N.Sullivan,Jeffrey James, Abram Hyner,Thos.M.Tucker,Jas.B.Jackson,Andrew Turnbull,Jonathon Ballard,Parley Hill,Francis Penrice,Frederick Case...couldn't agree, mistrial declared. Another jury - Alfred G.Carter,Wm.C.Barrett,Wm.PenriceRobt.McCullough,Thos. W.Morris,Theodore D.Elliott,Jas.G.Herald,Calvin Belcher, John MCCullough,Theodorick H.Jackson,Wm.Woods,Stephen Arrington...found for the Defendant.

PP.43 - 46:John S.Penrice vs James Johnson

PP.46,47: Robt.H.Russell vs C.G.Walker & Stephen Arrington: J.H.Hay, Atty. for the Plaintiff.

P.47-50:Rood Wells & Co.vs Wm.A.Dromgoole:(sometimes spd. Dromgool,Drumgul) of Princeton,Wash.Co.Ms.; Harvey S.Rood & Cornelias Haring,partners of Eleaser H.Wells,formerly trading under the name of "RoodWells & Co.",state that on 1 Jan.1838 in Wash.Co.,defendant is in debt for $332.86. J.V.Hallam is Atty. for Plaint. Rood and Haring are surviving partners of"Rood Wells & Co". Jury:Thos.Grimes,Thos. H.Buckner,Green B.Long,Walter C.Lofton,Wm.S.Scott,Alfred Longley,John B.Pelham,Jos.B.Penrice,Robt.Wilkerson,John Carter,Gabriel James,Geo.W.Reynolds. Found in favor of Plaintiff.

Page 3, Washington Co.

Circuit Court, December Term 1839 cont.

P.51,52 George Cosett & Co. vs (Major) William A. Dromgoole: George
53,54   Cosett & Frederick A. Cossit claim the defendant owes them
55,56 $500 for itemized bill on page 52 - 53...Thos. B. Firth, J.P.
         of Lagrange, Lafayette Co., Tenn. examines Pearl S (L?)
         Cossitt of Lafayette Co. Tenn. (she was a clerk for the
         Cossitt"s) They say she is about 22 yrs. old, and she states
         she has known plaintiffs for about 7 years in Lagrange,
         Tenn. and met William A. Dromgoole in 1833. The Cossett's
         collected part of the claim.

P. 57,58 Birne & House vs Robert P. Shelby: In May Term 1837 Geo.
59,60   P. Birne & George W. Horne late merchants and partners under
61   name of Birne & House State that Robert P. Shelby on 1 Jan.
          1836 in Wash. Co. Ms. was indebt for $390.67...Rives, Hughs,
          & Clifton Atty. for Plaintiff. Bill itemized on pages 58 -
          59...The Sheriff of Warren Co. is instructed to seize Robert
          P. Shelby. In 1839 Robert P. Shelby back in Washington Co.
          Anderson & Brien attys. for Defendant. Jury found for Plain..

P.62,63   George Smedes & Co. R.M. Whitman: George Smedes & Nickolas
          W. Ford merchants complain that Rowlin (spelled Rolan, Row-
          land) M. Whitman did on 1 Jan 1837 in Vicksburg make a
          prom. note for $304.61.

P.64,65   Thomas Ragan & Hugh Kunan vs John H. Cocke & James Cocke

P.65,66   Edward Dunn vs George W. Reynolds

P. 67   William M. Gwin vs Samuel Saxton & Erasmus Saxton

P.67,68   Robert Tate & John A. Tate vs Benjamin R. Bookout
69
P.70   William W. Gwin vs George Sigler

P.70,71   Thomas I. (J?) Goodman & James L. Mayfield for the use of
72   John A. Sane vs John H. Cocke: N.D. Coleman atty for Plaint
          In Vicksburg J.H. Lane says Cocke paid.

P. 72,73 Zachariah Biggs, Daniel Ingles & George Speer vs Calvin
          Belcher: Zechariah Biggs and Daniel Ingles in firm of
          Zechariah Biggs & Co. Webster & Smith atty for Plaint.

P. 74   John H. Cocke adminstrator of Thomas I. Cocke vs George W.
          Reynolds...Plaint. sues for return of slave Alfred..Found
          for Plaint.

P.75,76   Thomas M. Green vs George W. Reynolds
77
P.77,78   Abram Spears, William Talbott & James M. Arnold (firm of
79   Spears Talbott & Co.) vs Matthew Bridges & William L.
          Ellis (firm of Bridges & Ellis)

Page 4, Wasington Co.

Circuit Court, December Term 1839 cont.

P.79,80 Andrew Turnbull vs Thomas Kershaw: Andrew Turnbull states that on 1 Aug 1830 Washington Co. Thomas Kershaw made note for $177.

P.81   William D. Holt & Joseph H. Holt vs Alfred G. Carter: states that on 5 Apr. 1839 Defendant in Columbia, Ark. made note for $181.50. Carter appears in Washington Co. Ms in December 1839.

P.82,83 Claibone Steed & Harvey M. Jenkins vs Benjamin R. Bookout

P.84,85 William D. Holt & Joseph D. Holt for the use of Charles Alling & Jeremiah C. Carthwait & John A. Vanderpool & Beech Vanderpool: (Plaintiffs trade under the name of C. Alling & Co.) vs Benjamin Jackson & Alfred G. Carter.

P.86,87 William D. Holt & Joseph Holt who sue for the use of A.C. & W Squire & Co. vs Alfred G. Carter

P.88,89 Charles H. Webb for the use of Thomas Ware vs Benjamin Jackson & Alfred Carter

P.89,90 Turpin Daughters vs Alfred G. Carter

Circuit Court, April Term 1840, Presiding Judge George Coalter

P.91   Egbert I (J?) Sessions vs George W. Reynolds: Plaintiff states that in 1839 at Pecan Grove, La. Defendant made a bill of exchange in writing to a certain Hobson & Gooch of New Orlean - must pay James Locke $6037.75 - who in turn pays John H. Cocke - who endorses said bill to Adam Shirley who then endorses said bill to Plaint.

P.92   Egbert Sessoins vs Adam Shirly

P.93,94 William R. Campbell vs Francis Penrice: Plaint. states that in Jan. Term 1835, Wash. Co., Francis Penrice, together with one William Penrice who is not sued in this action entered into prom. note on 9 Apr. 1831 in Washington Co. for $1000. McNutt & Paxton, Plaint. Atty.

P.94   W.R. Campbell vs F. Penrice

P.95   Egbert I. Sessions vs James Cocke

p.96,97 98,99 James J. Chewning & Henry S. Dawson vs Alias Philips

P.100   Robert W. Keating vs John Robb surviving partner of Patterson S. Bain in firm Bain & Robb

P.101,102 William S. Wells vs Jesse T. Rucker

Page 5, Washington Co. Ms.

<u>Circuit Court, April Term 1840</u> cont.

P.103,104 <u>John W.Davis & Adam S.Summers vs Samuel R.Dunn & Harriet B.Blanton adm.</u>: Plaint. states that in Mar. Term 1839 Samuel Dunn & Harriet B.Blanton adm of William W.Blanton who died intestate: One John P.Overton who in 1836 made a note to said W.W.Blanton. Plaint. files claim against estate for $800. Delaney & Frost Atty. for Plaint.

P.105,106 107 <u>William S.Bennett & William Ferriday</u> surviving partners of William Bullitt & William Shipp dec. vs <u>Rolin (Rowland) M.Whitman</u>

P.107,108 <u>William C.McMahan vs William Arrington</u>

P. 109,110 Passmore Hoops &John Clark (Firm named <u>Hoops &Clark</u>) <u>vs Davis Montgomery</u>

P.111 <u>Robert Keating vs William Bain & John Robb</u> (Firm - Bain & Robb)

P.112,113 114 <u>Joseph Pratt vs Cyrus M.Driskeld</u>

P. 115,116 <u>John W.Davis & Adam S.Summers vs John P.Overton & William W.Blanton</u> - Atty W.A.Lake & Delaney & Frost.

P.117,118 119 <u>Harvey S.Rood</u> - surviving partner of Harvey S.Rood, Eleazer, H.Wells, & Cornelius Harring (Firm named Rood Wells & Co.) <u>vs (Mrs.) Nancy Dillingham</u>

P.119,120 John P.Overton for the use of <u>John I. Guion vs Stephen M.Jackson</u>: Guion Smedes & Marshall Atty for Plaint., Meany & Sutton atty. for Def.

P. 121,122 <u>Philip A. Cocks vs Joseph Robertson</u>

P.123 Hugh R.Austin for use of <u>William Lewis vs George W. Reynolds</u>

P. 124,125 126,127 <u>Thomas W.Endecott</u> (who is the Clerk) <u>vs R.W.Keaton</u> Attachment

P. 127,128 129,130 131,132 <u>Philip Ault vs Robert H. Hunter</u>

P. 132,133 134,135 Alexander G.McNutt, successor of Charles Lynch, Gov. of State of Ms. useof <u>James E.Fenton vs Alfred G. Cox</u> & Frederick G.Turnbull surviving "obligars" of William F.Jeffries dec.: John Turnbull, President of the Board of Police (Governing Board of the County, later called Board of Supervisors) of Washington Co accepts bond -

Page 6, Washington Co. Ms.

Circuit Court, April Term 1840, cont.

in exhibit dated 13 Nov. 1837 (Jeffries living then). Sheriff W.L.Wells left the supeona for F.G.Turnbull with his overseer Mr. Ross Sept.2, 1839...Found for Def.

P.135 Nathaniel Seymour vs Virgil V. Skiene: attachment Nathan Seymour who appeared in Warren Co. in 1839 & Robert D. Miller swear an attachment against Virgil V. Skiene

P.136 Thomas W. Endicott (Clerk) vs (Mrs.) Nancy Dillingham

P. 137,138 Williams S. Wells adms. James Miller dec. vs Thomas Ward: A.F.Smith Plaint. Atty, signed Thomas W. Endicott, Clerk by M. Endicott DC

In 1840, Feb. the Sheriff of Washington Co. is Wm. W. Collins.

P.139 Nathan Seymour vs Benjamin Skrine: attachment

P.140 Philip A.Cock vs Calvin Belcher: an assumpsit

P.141 William M.Gwin vs George Sigler

P.142,143 William M.Gwin vs Samuel Saxton & Erasmus Saxton

P.144 Oren H. Hill vs Benjamin Dulaney; in debt

P.145,146 Samuel Folkes & Miles C. Folkes who sue for the use of Thomas L. Booraine vs Samuel Gustine

P. 147 The Preseident Directors & Company of the Planters Bank of Miss who sue for the use of John R. Llewellyn vs William P. Stone & John E. Richardson

P. 148,149 The Miss. & Ala Rail Road Co. vs George W. Reynolds, 150 James Glass, Claiborne Steele & Adam Shirley; Plaint. claims def. owe the banking firm in Brandon, Ms. $40,605

P.151 Egbert I. Sessions vs Geroge W. Reynolds

P. 152,153 James Stockman vs Thomas Kershaw

P.154,155 Egbert Sessions vs George W. Reynolds, Jmaes Cocke & Adam Shirley

P.156,157 John Fisher adm. of Sidney Fisher dec. vs Frederick G. Turnbull & John L. Chapman; John Fisher & Emily Fisher, adm. of Sidney Fisher of Princeton (Town in Washington Co. that has since sluffed off into the Miss. River)

P.158 Erasmus Towsey & William T. Price vs Nancy Dillingham

Page 7, Washington Co. Ms

Circuit Court, April Term 1840 cont.

P.159	Nimrod L. Lindsay & Henry F. Wilson vs William L. Ellis & Franklin Hutchinson
P.161	Erasmus Towsey & William T. Price vs Calvin Belcher
P.162	Philip A. Cocks vs John P. Cunningham
P.163	" " " " John O. Sanders
P.165	" " " " Francis Penrice
P.166	" " " " "
P.167,168	Thomas W. Endicott (Clerk) use of Cornelius Baker & Freeman Parmele vs Calvin Belcher
P.169	Thomas W. Endecott use of Cornelius Baker & Freeman Parmele vs Nancy Dillingham
P.170,171 172	Erasmus Towsey & William T. Price vs Jeremiah Y. Daschiele
P.173,174	Bank of Miss. vs Davis Montgomery & Alexander B. Montgomery
p.175	Alexander Montgomery vs Thomas Mason
P.176	William R. Brooks & Stephen W. Tibbets who sue for the use of Stephen M. Tibbet vs John Turnbull: Say John Turnbull made prom. note in Natchez Aug 1, 1839 for $400. Def. defaulted.
P.177,178	James I. Chewning vs D. Hardeman
P.179	Thomas W. Endecott vs George Joor
P.180,181	Miss. Union Bank vs William S. Scott, Alfred Cox, & John B. Coleman
P.182	Miss. Union Bank vs Alfred Cox, John G. Cox, & Andrew Knox
P.183	Elijah F. Atcheson vs Vincent W. McMurtry
P.184,185	David Bush vs Robert P. Shelby (1839 - R.P.Shelby is at Grand Gulf)
P.186	Thomas B. Warfield & William P. Warfield vs Robert Turnbull
P.187,188	Alfred G. Carter vs George W. Hunter
P.189, 190 191,192	John S. Penrice vs John O. Sanders; an attachment
P.193	Anderson Miller & William Miller vs Abram W. Samuels

Page 8, Washington Co. Ms

Circuit Court, April Term 1840, cont.

P.194,195　Alexander Montgomery vs Vs Davis Montgomery & John Snodgrass: Plaint. says def. made prom. note 21 Apr. 1838 in Natchez (Adams Co. Ms.)...Snodgrass owes Alexander Montgomery, And Davis Montgomery owes Snodgrass..$904.

P. 196　Thomas M. Green for use of Samuel Templeton & Wm. B. Belknap vs John H. & James Cocke

P.197,198 199,　The Bank of Miss. vs Thomas H. Buckner, Andrew L. Wilson & David W. Connerly et al merchants trading under name Buckner Wilson & Co. & John H. Robb & Thomas J. James

October Term 1840

P.200,201　Bank of Miss. vs David Suggett, Henry Johnson, Manluis V. Thomson: David Suggett prom. to ship 100 bales of cotton to W. Bogart at New Orleans for sale or reshipment to Liverpool for a/c Lake Washington & Deer Creek Rail Road & Banking Co...Feb 1838 - Princeton (Town in Washington Co that has since sluffed into the Miss. River)

P.202,203　Bank of Miss. vs Davis Montgomery: Def. made a bill of Exchange with Joseph Egg in 1837 at Princeton, Ms. Jury list: Augustus W. McAllister, Joseph Pervis, Theoderick H. Jackson, James Mayes, Richard Grant, Henry Slater, Joseph Holden, John James, Walter C. Lofton, William Talbot, James Johnson, and Joseph Pratt.

P. 204　John E. Richardson vs John H. & James Cock

The Hon. Charles C. Cage Judge of 3rd Dist acts in place of Hon. George Coalter, who is absent.

P. 205,206　Thomas W. Endicott (Clerk) vs Adam Shirley

P. 207　"　"　"　"　" Thomas Lyne

P.208　William Jenkins vs Andrew Knox

P. 209,210 211　William Jenkins vs Andrew Know, Ambrose Knox, John G. Cocks, Thomas Grimes

P.212　Abner M. Sawyer use of Edward A. Wright, Henry A. Nelson, & William E. Randall vs George W. Reynolds

P. 213,214 215,　Willis Allsbrook for use of Robert J. Campbell vs Frederick P. Plant: Jury: Frederick James, William H. Boswell, Alexander Montgomery, George M. Pinckard, Thomas Kershaw, John Hester, Albert W. Dunbar, Gabriel James, Adam Shirley

Page 9, Washington Co. Ms.

Circuit Court, October Term 1840 cont.

    John Fulton, Daniel McMahan and George G. Cregan.

P. 216,217 Keran Bows vs George W. Reynolds

P. 218 Chapman Coleman, Robert J. Ward & Robert A Moffett (Trade name Coleman Ward & Co.) vs Alfred Cox

P. 219,220 Robert Cooper vs Aron Chamberlain: Plaint. says Def. along with Silas R. Gilmore since dec. (dec. 1836) at Lake Providence (La. ?)

P.221,222 223 Thomas T. Stephens use of Chapman Coleman, Robert J. Ward, & Robert A. Moffett (Trade name Coleman Ward & Co.) vs Robert F. Shelby

P.224 Benjamin C. Buckley use of Richard Buckley vs Andrew Know

P.225,226 Evan W. Shelby use of Philip A Cock vs Walter C. Lofton

P.227 George Ward & Thomas T. Stephens (Trade name Ward & Stephens) vs Josiah P. Woofalk

P.228,229 Thomas P. Boyd vs John G. Cox (spelled Cocke, Cocks) & Thomas Grimes (Trade name John Cox & Grimes)

P. 230,231 John Fulton adm. Henry Crow dec. vs Isaac W. Arthen & Zenas K. Fulton (Trade name Arthen & Fulton Co.)

P.232 Erastus Towsey & William T. Price (Trade name Towsey & Price) vs John M. Campbell surviving partner of Horace Carpenter & Co. (A Planting Co.) Jas. D. Hallam Atty for Plaintiff.

P.234,235 Francis Penrice vs Alfred Cox

P. 236 George McMurchey & John McMurchey vs George W. Reynolds

P. 237,238 Parks B. Long use of John S. Penrice vs Thomas Kershaw

P. 239,240 John W. Williams vs James Cocke

P.241,242 James Guy vs George W. Reynolds

P. 243 Samuel E. Jones assignee of Alexander Tasley vs Thomas Stephens

P.244 William R. Verser vs Ann J. Singleton

P. 245,246 Harvey L. Rood surviving partner of Eleazer H. Wells & Corneluis Harring (Firm of Rood Wells & Co.) vs Thomas W. Endecott

Page 10, Washington Co. Ms.

Circuit Court, October Term 1840 cont. Judge C.C. Cage acting Judge

P.247 Robert Tate & Henry Poindexter (Firm name Tate & Poindexter) vs John H. Cocke & James Cocke (Firm name Cocke & Cocke)

Here the page numbers are duplicated
(2nd) 246 Lunsford P. Yandle vs Josiah P. Woolfolk

" 247 Miss. Union Bank vs Thomas Kershaw, F.G. Turnbull & John Turnbull

P. 249,250 David H. Threlkeld vs Daniel Bradford

P. 251,252 Claiborne Steele & Harvey M. Jenkins who sue for use of John Dulana & James Whiting vs James Cocke

P. 253 William M. Boice for use of Stephen Arrington vs James Cocke

P. 254,255 John F. McKinney vs Stephen Arrington, George W. Reynolds

P. 256,257 258 Thomas Dixon vs John H. Cocke & James Cocke

P. 259,260 The Agriculture Bank of Miss. for use of the United States of America vs Willm A. Dromgool, Andrew Knox, John Turnbull, F.G. Turnbull

P. 261,262 President Director & Co. of the Commercial & Rail Road Bank of Vicksburg for use of William W. Frazier, Thomas E. Robins & William S. Bodley, assignees of C & RR Bk. Of Vicksburg vs James Cocke

P. 263,264 All of the above for the Bank vs James Cock, Stephen Arrington, George W. Reynolds, & John H. Cocke

P. 265,266 Bank of Miss. vs Anderson Miller, Alfred Cox, John G. Cocks

P. 267 Alfred Cox vs Cyrus Dreiskill

P. 268 Felix A. Davis vs Frederick G. Turnbull

P. 269,270 Frederick P. Plant vs Thomas L. Stephens & John S. Chapman

P. 271,272 James B. Gascoigne & Charles Gascoigne vs Robert P. Shelby

P. 273,274 Morris Emanuel vs Adam Shirley

P. 275 "   ", Richards Barnett vs John H. Cocke & James Cocke

Page 11, Washington Co. Ms.

Circuit Court, October Term 1840, cont.

P.276,277   Fred P. Plant vs Thomas L. Stephens

P.278   Abram F. Smith vs Adam Shirley, James Cocke

P.279,280   Samuel B. Harwood, Isaac Webster & Alexander F. Newman (Trading under name of Harwood Newman & Co) use of Samuel P. Webster vs James Cocke

P.281   John Tarbe use of William W. Howell vs Samuel R. Dunn Adm. & Harriet B. Blanton ad, of William W. Blanton dec. William B. Howell surviving partner of Sprague & Howell

P.282,283   Harvey L. Rood surviving Partner of Eleazer Wells & Corneluis Harring vs Abram W. Smauel

P.284   Philip A. Cocks vs Charles Turnbull

P.285,286   Malachi B. Hamer & Daniel Blue vs Soloman Wolfe

P.287,288   Erastus Towsey & William T. Price (Trading under the
P.   name of Towsey & Price) vs Cyrus M. Driskell

P.289,290   William J. Prince vs John G. Cocks : Commands Sheriff
291,292   of Washington Co. Ms to keep $500 from estate of Loman
293   Brashaw (Brasher?) for a judgement in favor of John G.
            Cocks...Witness: Hon. Alexander Montgomery, Judge of 1st
            Judicial Dist...1832.

            In 1831 William Penrice was a Clerk of the Court of Washington Co. Ms.

P.294,295   John T. Wright & John H. Thomas (Trading under the name
296,297   Wright & Thomas) vs Richard E. Hammett: Many pages of
298,299   depositions follow...Some of the names mentioned:
300,301   W.S. Wells, Sheriff of Washington Co.; Dr. James Clarke
302,303   a citizen of the State of Arkansas; James M. Estill who
            bought a plantation and slaves in Arkansas from Dr. Clarke;
            Archibald W. Goodlow a citizen of Chicot Co. Ark.; E.A.
            Meany atty. for Plaintiff; W.W. Collins Sheriff (of where?)
            signed by JJno. R. Downing D.S.; William Henry Johnson of
            Chicot Co. Ark.; Jesse Jones Citizen of Louisiana (Parish
            of Carrol); M.B. Rogers citizen of La.; William Coleman
            Commissioner in and for the Parish of Carrol, La.; Tully
            Sawyer Commissioner in and for the Co. of Chicot, Ark.;
            William Collins Commissioner in and for the Co. of Chicot
            Ark.; James Blaine a witness

P.304   Morgan Morgan use of Calvin M. Rutherford vs Benjamin R. Bookout

P.305,306   Benjamin Bailey vs Samuel R. Dunn & William S. Wells
307,308   (In debt)

Washington Co.Ms.

CIRCUIT COURT, October Term 1840, cont.

P.309-310: Matthew R.Day vs Samuel R.Dunn & Thos.B.Warfield

P.311-312: James Coleman vs Robert Hunter

P.313-316: Samuel Craig, Treasurer of Miss. use of State of Miss. vs the Bank of Mississippi: Names mentioned - D.F.Blackburn (payment on a note due him); Lake Washington & Deer Creek Rail Road & Banking Co.; C.W.Muncaster, cashier; Andrew Knox, President; L.P.Plant (note payment due him); J.A.Miller (Note payment due him); T.K.Fulton president 1837; Thomas Kershaw; F.H.Collins, Atty.General for State of Miss.; John D.Freeman, District Attorney.

PP.317 - 320: David H.Turpin vs George W.Reynolds: & Lawrence P.Maxwell, Jas.A. Maxwell, Atty. for Plaintiff. George W.Reynolds states that he promises to pay Maxwell $800 with negotiables on the Grand Gulf R.R.Bank...Follows a certificate of Probate, U.S.of A., State of Miss, Claib. Co.Ms. 4 Jan 1838 by Louis Cronly, J.P. who says there were no funds in that bank for payment of Reynold's note.

PP.320-321: Thomas J.Scott vs Mordecai Powell: (with one John G.Singleton, since decd.)

PP.322-323: Philip A.Cocks vs Ann J.Singleton

PP.324-325:   "   "   "   "   Robert P(rince)Shelby

PP.326-327: Samuel R.Dunn & Wm.S.Wells vs Thos.B.Warfield

PP.328-329: Erastus Towsey & Wm.T.Price vs Robt.P.Shelby

PP.330-331: Vicksburg Water Works & Banking Co., use of Mark Valentine vs Robert P.Shelby (also with Henry D.Smede & V.S.Booth.

P.332: Philip A.Cocks vs John H.Blanton

PP.333-334: Philip A.Cocks vs John L.Chapman & Manluis V. Thomson.

PP.335-336: Philip A.Cocks vs John L.Chapman

P.337: Philip A.Cocks vs Council R.Bass

PP.338-339: Joseph Holt & John M.Chilton who sue for the use of Jos.Holt vs Alfred G.Carter.

P.340-341: Abram F.Smith vs Thomas Lyne

P.342: Philip A.Cocks vs Thomas Kershaw

PP.343-344: Philip A.Cocks vs Walter C.Lofton

Page 13, Washington Co. Ms

Circuit Court, October Term 1840, cont

P.345	Philip A. Cocks vs Macklin Evans
P.346	" " " " Willaim A. Dromgoole
P.347,348	Frederick P. Plant vs William A. Dromgoole
P.349,350	Robert H. Warren & Thomas D. Fisher vs Robert Hunter & George W. Hunter
P.351	Thomas W. Endicott use of Corneluis Baker & Truman(Trueman?) Parmele vs F.G. Turnbull
P.352,353	Thomas W. Endecott - use of Corneluis Baker & Truman Parmele vs John S. Chapman
P.354	Thomas W. Endecott (Cler) - use of Corneluis Baker & Truman Parmele vs Walter C. Lofton
P.355,356	Erastus Towsey & William T. Price vs William A. Dromgoole
P.357,358	James O. Harrison & Joseph Holt vs Thomas T. Stephens & John S. Chapman
P.359	Thomas W. Endecott vs Turner & Jones (Samuel S. Turner & Samuel Jones, partners)
P.360,361	James O. Harrison & Joseph Holt vs James Cocke & A.F. Smith
p.362	Towsey & Price (Erastus Towsey & William T. Price) vs John T. Penrice
P.363,364 365	Towsey & Price (see above) vs John T. Penrice & William T. Penrice
P.366,367	Towsey & Price (see above) vs Thomas Kershaw
p.368	E.D. Hydes & Co. vs Robert P. Shelby of Princeton, Ms.
p.369,370	Tandy & Price vs William A. Dromgoole, Jr. (18 Feb. 1840)
p.371,372 373	Frederick P. Plant vs Robert P. Shelby (15 Feb 1840)
p.374,375	Harrison & Holt vs George W. Reynolds
p.376	" " " Cocke & Reynolds
p.376	David F. Blackburn vs Nancy Dillingham
p.378,379	Dunn & Wells vs Adam Shirley & Fisher
p.380	William S. Scott vs William L. Rusk
p.382	The Bank of Mississippi vs John G. Singleton

Washington Co.

CIRCUIT COURT, Records, cont.

P.384: The Bank of Miss. vs Wm.A.Dromgoole, Council R.Bass, Frederick P.Plant.

P.387: The Bank of Miss. vs John M.Carpenter, Vans M. Sullivan.

P.390: The Bank of Ms. vs John M.Carpenter, Thos.Kershaw, Charles W.Mancaster.

P.391: The Bank of Miss. vs Jeremiah B.Dashiell, John Turnbull, and Frederick P.Plant.

P.395: The Bank of Miss. vs Joseph Egg.

P.397: The Bank of Miss. vs David Suggett

P.399: John R.Downing vs Samuel R.Dunn: Saml.R.Dunn is Adm. of Est. of Wm.L.Wells; Wm.W.Collins is Sheriff; Thos. W.Endecott is Clerk of the Court; M.Endecott - Dep.Clerk.

P.401: Samuel Cotton vs Samuel Saxon

P.402: Bank of Miss. vs Wm.E.Hall: States that Hall, together with H.G.Holmes, who lives out of the State, and Jno. Turnbull, since decd., did in 1838 at Princeton, make a prom.note for the Rail Road.

P.403: William B.Ross vs Frederick Turnbull

P.404: Vicksburg Water Works & Banking Co. vs Isaac B.Beall

P.406: John S.Penrice vs John O.Sanders

P.408: John L.Wright & John H.Thomas vs Richard E.Hammett entered into 23 Jan.1839.

P.411: Rolin M.Whitman vs James Cocke & John H.cocke; entered into 28 Mar.1838.

P.414: Bank of Miss vs Thoams Kershaw, Frederick Turnbull and John L.Chapman.

P.415: Bank of Miss. vs Frederick Turnbull

P.417: Bank of Miss. vs James C.Wilkinson & Andrew Turnbull Dealing with the Rail Road.

P.4---NEXT FEW PAGES BLANK

P.428: Thomas E.Endecott vs Frederick P.Plant, Wm.L.Price, Council R.Bass, Wm.W.Collins, Theodorick H.Jackson, Wm.J. Penrice, Albert S.Miller. Entered into 26 July 1839.

Circuit Court, Records, cont.

- p. 431 James Trippe & John F. Trippe vs Neesom Lambe & Charles Turnbull (entered into 19 June 1839)
- p. 432 Bank of Vicksburg vs Robert P. Shelby & Miles C. Folkes
- p. 435 James M. Harris vs Alfred G. Carter
- p. 436 Alexander G. McNutt use of Mott & Bryson vs Walter C. Loftin
- p. 438 John O. Sanders vs Thomas Kershaw
- p. 441 Erastus Towsey & William L. Price vs Joshia P. Woolfolk
- p. 443 Bk. of Miss. vs William A. Dromgoole, Council R. Bass, Frederick P. Plant
- p. 446 Bk. of Miss. vs Vans M. Sullivan & John M. Carpenter
- p. 448 John R.W. Dunbar vs Samuel R. Dunn (States: Thomas W. Dunn now of Baltimore, Md., had Samuel R. Dunn to cosign a note. John R.M. Dunbar is identified as an M.D., and Dean of the Medical Faculty of the Washington University of Baltimore)
- p. 450 Richard G. Davenport use of Alexander P. Peite vs William L. Rusk
- p. 452 Joseph Pratt vs John L. Chapman vs Manilius V. Thomson
- p. 454 Frederick P. Plant vs William P. Stone & William H. Robard
- p. 455 Thomas W. Endecott vs James Cocke
- p. 457 Crockett Peery, John W. George, Thomas B. Shields use of James M. White vs John Turnbull
- p. 459 Mississippi Union Bank vs Andrew Knox, John S. Chapman, & Frederick G. Turnbull
- p. 460 Miss. Union Bank vs Robert P. Shelby, D. Hardeman & Seargent J. Prentiss
- p. 463 Ms. Union Bk. vs Robert P. Shelby, D. Hardeman, Albert G. Creath
- p. 465 Ms. Union Bk. vs T.G. Turnbull, Thomas Endecott, A.W. Samuel, & Anderson Miller
- p. 467 Alexander G. McNutt, William R. Campbell, vs John H. Cocke
- p. 469 Laven Kimball vs Robert P. Shelby
- p. 471 Nelson Shelton & Samuel Anderson vs James Cocke
- p. 473 Sameul Hildeburn vs William R. Campbell & Charles R. Campbell

Washington Co.

CIRCUIT COURT, Records,1840,cont.

P.475: Oliver Hull & Samuel Bowne vs Nelson Lambe & Charles Turnbull.

P.476: JURY LIST: Greer B.Lonh,Joseph W.Robertson,McLin Evans,John H.Blanton,James Godbolt,James B.Jackson,Thomas H.Buckner,David Suggett,Thomas J.Likens,H.T.Carlin,Green S.McCarroll - 12 April 1840

P.480: Samuel F.Dorr,Francis F.Dorr & Wm.C.Allen vs Wm. Rushing and Thomas W.Endecott - 25 July 1840.

P.483: James Redhamer vs Thomas S.Penrice and Andrew Knox - 12 Aug.1840

P.485: President Director & Co. of Agriculture Bank of Miss. for the use of the Unithed States of America Bank at Natchez vs John Turnbull,Thomas Kershaw,Samuel R.Dunn - entered into 1838.

P.487: Joseph Bragg and Benjamin Jones vs Frederick G. Turnbull.

P.488: Thomas Armstrong vs Reding B.Herring and Samuel Herring.

P.489: JURY LIST: Emedicus Murphy,Isaac Worthington,Wm. Hunt,Jackson M.Haun,Wm.Myers,D.C.Page,Wm.Jenkins,W.C. Jackson,John S.Knox,Evan W.Shelby,James Johnson,David F.Briggs - April Term 1840.

P.491: Andrew G.Carpenter vs John L.Chapman & Manluis V.Thomson.

P.493: Bank of Miss. vs Robert P.Shelby, Andrew Knox, and David F.Blackburn - 17 Sept.1840.

P.494: Bank of Miss. vs Robert P.Shelby and Alfred Cox 17 Sept.1840

P.496: Bank of Miss. vs Robert P.Shelby

P.498:   "   "   "   "   "   "   "

END OF ENTRIES

Page 17, Washington Co.

Other Early Records in the Circuit Clerks Office

<u>Minute Bk.1</u>: April 13, 1840 - March 28, 1850

<u>Minute Bk.</u> 3: May 13, 1861 - Nov. 21, 1868

<u>Minute Bk.</u> 4: May 10, 1869 - May 30, 1872

<u>Minute Bk.</u> 5: Nov. 18, 1872 - April 1876

<u>Minute Bk.</u> 2: May 9, 1876 - Nov 15, 1879

No Minute to cover the time period 1850 - 1861. This apparently explains why the sequence of numbers is irregular. Supposedly the original docket was burned.

Some of these earlier records are not on microfilm, and are unindexed. k.b.

Washington County Records

GENERAL CHANCERY DOCKET: Book 1 (begins 1856)

This book is handwritten, unindexed, and water marked. The first number is the page number, the second number is the case number. The date is the date the suit was first filed. Some of the cases listed names opposite, in which case I have copied them. K.B.

1. (1) Yerger & Rucks vs F.B. Case, Thos. Kershaw, & R.M. Cunningham
   Bill of Interpleader   Filed 13 Feb. 1856

   (2) Andrew Turnbull vs John L. Chapman, et al
   Bill of Foreclosure   Filed 13 Mar. 1856
   (names George Haig, Thomas D. Condy, Robert F. Allston, Mary Allen & Claudia Tucker, Sarah Allen, Joseph Tucker, Brander McKinny & Hubbard Mordecai Abrams, John Churchman. All but Sarah Allen and Joseph Tucker non-residents of the state)

2. (3) Ambrose Knox vs David Hunt & George F. Blackburn
   Injunction   Filed 22 May 1856

   (4) Louisa M. Young vs Jacob Barker & S.B. Newman
   Bill of Foreclosure   Filed Apr 18, 1856

3. (5) Benjamin F. Finlay vs Mary Ann Hood, Wm. H. Hood, Elizabeth W. Hood and Thomas H. Hood
   Filed 26 Apr. 1856

   (6) Robert H. Carter adm Alfred G. Carter vs A.B. Montgomery & John L. Finlay Treas. of C.
   Bill of Injunction   Filed 7 May 1856

4. (7) James T. Matthew & Eliza A. Matthews vs Margaret Campbell exec. of Wm. R. Campbell
   4 July 1856

   (8) John D. Rodewald, Henry Rodewall, Eliza Rodewall, Frederick W. Rodewall, & Henrietta R. Rodewall vs B.R. Bookout & Thos. Penny
   Filed 26 Sept, 1856

5. (9) Henry R. Beall vs Absolom Shart
   Bill to Perfect Title   30 Sept, 1856
   (10) Morris Ash & Michaelis Horwitz vs John S. Penrice
   Injunction   Filed 10 Oct. 1856

6. (11) John M. Bott vs William Finney, R.D. Garrett, N.G. Nye & J.W. Barnett
   Bill to Perfect Title   Filed 11 Oct, 1856

   (12) John A. Miller vs Mary I. Jackson, Andrew Jackson, & Elizabeth Jackson
   Pet. for division   20 Oct.1856
   (Andw. & Elizabeth are minor heirs...1859 Mary marries R.H. Hord)

GENERAL CHANCERY DOCKET: Bk. 1

7 (13) Samuel N. Canghey (Caughey ?) vs Benjamin Kunningham,
        Wm. I. Ellis, Wm. H. Bryan, Shepherd Brown & Joseph H.
        Johnson
        Bill to perfect Title   Filed 13 Oct. 1856
   (14) Alexander Rudd, Wesley Maulding & Henry Smith vs Wm.
        Bacon & C.S. Moore
        Bill to Perfect Title   Filed 13 Oct. 1856

8. (15) Henry Smith vs James Folks & Henry W. Vick
        Bill to Perfect Title   Filed 13 Oct. 1856

   (16) Henry Smith vs James T. Harper, Jesse Harper, Benjamin
        Roach, David Roach, James Wilkins Roach, Eugene Roach
        Bill to Perfect Title   Filed 13 Oct 1856

9. (17) Alexander Rudd, Wesley L. Maulding & Henry Smith vs
        Henry Johnson, George W. Ward
        Bill to Perfect Title   Filed 13 Oct 1856

   (18) Henry Smith vs Lewis W. Thompson
        Bill to Perfect Title   Filed 13 Oct. 1856

10 (19) Benj. Cason & Henry Smith vs the unknown heirs of Alfred
        Longley decd. & Andrew Carson
        Bill to Perfect Title   Filed 13 Oct 1856

   (20) William Bailey vs D. Hardaman, Volney Thompson & the
        other heirs of M_____ V. Thompson
        Bill to Perfect Title   Filed 28 Oct 1856

11 (21) William Bailey vs Planters Bank of Tennesee & H.W.
        Pejroneau (?)
        Bill to Perfect Title   28 Oct 1856

   (22) William Bailey vs Gabriel W. Denton, N.G. Nyes & Jeff-
        erson J. Hughes
        Filed 28 Oct 1856

12 (23) The President Directors & Company of the Planters Bank
        of Tennessee vs John H. Dunlap, Sarah Virginia Dunlap,
        Susan Virginia G. Dunlap & Henry Peyronneaux, John A.
        Craig, Susan F. Craig
        Filed 3 Nov. 1856
        (Susan Virginia Gilliam Dunlap)

   (24) Henry H. Morris vs John Henderson & John Black
        Bill to Perfect Title   Filed 4 Nov 1856

13. (25) Out of sequence..see next page

   (26) Mary Ann Hood & William N. Hood vs Sidney R. Smith,
        Elizabeth W. Hood & Thomas H. Hood
        Filed 1 Mar. 1857
        (W.R. Fleming, guard. of T.H. Hood)

Wash. Co. Records

General Chancery Docket: Bk. 1 cont.

14 (25) Moses Ashbrook vs James Marstin & John Isaacs
     Injunction 22 Dec 1856
     (Out of sequence in the book)

   (27) Jane W. Campbell, Washingtonia Campbell, Nedham Campbell vs Margaret Campbell, exec. W.A. Campbell decd., Daniel Perkins, Caroline Perkins, Wm. R. Campbell, Martha G. Campbell, Stella Campbell, Joseph H. Campbell, and Margaret S. Campbell
     Bill of Complaint 9 Apr. 1857
     (Minor heirs & heirs scattered into Bolivar Co, also)

15 (28) Aaron Wickliffe
     On Exparte Petition 13 May 1857
     (Petition making Aaron Wickliff Worthington heir of Aaron Wickliffe)

   (29) Aaron W. Worthington
     On Exparte Petition   13 May 1857
     (Petition to change name of Aaron Wickliff Worthington to Aaron W. Wickliffe)

16 (30) James W. Browder, Elizabeth Browder, Henry C. Fields and Harris J. Fields, George W. Faison (?) and Ellen R. Faison
     An Exparte Petition 13 May 1857

   (31) A.W. McAllister Treas. of Washington Co. vs John L. Chapman, et al
     13 May 1857

17 (32) Nicholas R. Marr, Sallie P. Marr & Claudia V. Marr who sue by next friend R.H. Marr, Agatha S. Inge, Thomas D. Carson & Sarah V. M. Carson his wife, N. (?) Venables and Tennesse E. Venable his wife, R.H. Marr and Jane E. Marr his wife, Samuel E. McLemon, Price P. McLemon, and Jefferson McLemon who sue by their next friend John D. McLemon
     On Exparte Petition 5 Oct 1857

   (33) Sarah Anderson vs Lewis H. Anderson
     Bill for Divorce 29 Oct 1857

18 (34) W.B. Shearer & Letitia J. his wife & Ann L. Fitzpatrick, who sues by next friend W.B. Shearer vs J.E. Fitzpatrick & John W. Robinson, Robert W. Burney & Mary F. his wife, James S. Hampton & Octavia his wife, James W. Phillips & (blank) his wife, Charles L. Buck & Alfred Murdock
     Bill of Complaint 2 Nov 1857
     (Writs issued to Sunflower, Hinds, and Warren Cos. Robinson & Phillips in Hinds Co.)

Wash. Co. Records

General Chancery Docket: Bk 1 cont.

    (35) Jacob Rath vs Henry Clore & David L. Clore
        Injunction 10 Nov. 1857

19 (36) Ambrose J. Foster and Elizabeth A. Foster his wife,
        formerly Elizabeth A. Harris, Laura D. Harris, and
        Daniel Harris a minor who sues by next friend Ambrose
        J. Foster vs James Wallace & Robert Wallace
        Bill of Complaint 5 Dec 1857
        (James Wallace found in Holmes Co. Ms)

    (37) Ambrose J. Foster and Elizabeth A. Foster his wife
        formerly Elizabeth A. Harris, Laura D. Harris, and
        Daniel Harris a minor who sues by next friend Ambrose
        J. Foster vs J.H.C. & W.R. Sims & A.C. Holt
        (Subp. served to Holt in Wilkinson Co. Ms., also
         Charles Sims and John H. Sims)
        5 Dec 1857

20 (38) William P. Barton & Lucy H. Barton his wife vs Charles
        E. Smedes & Martha L. Smedes his wife, Abram K. Smedes
        & Thomasine L. Smedes his wife, Mary T. Brodnax, W.E.
        Brickell And Helen Brickell his wife, Adele Brodnax &
        Roberta Brodnax (minors) William Brodnax and Edward
        Brodnax
        5 Dec 1857

    (39) Stewart W. Fisk exec. of Alvarez Fisk decd. vs Andrew
        J. Paxton
        5 Dec 1857

21 (40) Joseph McGuire and Rosind McGuire his wife vs Lewis G.
        Galloway, Henry Peebles, and James F. Talleferro
        14 Jan 1858

    (41) Thomas S. Redd vs John L. Chapman
        Bill of Complaint 15 Feb 1858

22 (42) Sarah Black vs John Burton & William Burton
        15 Feb 1858

    (43) William J. Franklin vs James A., Ellen E., and Joseph
        J. Cooper
        Bill to Foreclose 12 Apr. 1858

23 (44) C.F. & W. Hampton vs C.T. Howell
        16 Apr 1858

    (45) Sarah V. Dunlap & Susan V.G. Dunlap vs Charles M.
        Hart and the President Director of the Planters Bank
        of Tennessee
        12 May 1858

24 (46) President Director of the Bank of State of South Carolina
        vs C.F. Howell
        24 July 1858
        Marked off as Error

Wash. Co. Records

General Chancery Docket: Book 1 cont.

  (47) C.F. Hampton, C.F. Hampton adm. of Wade Hampton Sr.
    decd. & Wade Hampton vs Charles T. Howell
    29 July 1858

25 (48) Mary Morris vs Henry H. Morris
    Writ to pay Alimony 20 Aug. 1858
    (Deposition taken of Mary Dobbins of La. & of Jo
     Hobson of Ark. 30 Apr 1860)

  (49) Franklin K. Beck vs John L. Finlay & A.P. Bagley
    28 Aug 1858
    (Transfer of Ala. Records filed 1860..Death of A.P.
     Bagley in 1859 proves problem)

26 (50) William A. Percy vs J. Walker Percy, L.P. Percy,
    Thomas G. Percy, Ellen Percy, Josiah M. Percy, Charles
    P. Percy and Henrietta Percy
    6 Sept 1858

  (51) David Hunt vs Ambrose Knox, D.F. Blackburn, Elijah
    Pealy, William H. Davis, Andrew Knox
    8 Nov 1858

27 (52) Brown Brothers & Co. vs Bank of Mississippi
    12 Nov 1858

  (53) Bank of Ky. vs Merchant Bank of New Orleans

28 (54) Jacob Roth vs John A. Biddle
    4 Jan 1859

  (55) John J. Grant agent for Daniel Grant vs Freeman
    Walker & James S. Walker 10 Jan 1859

29 (56) Daniel Grant vs James S. Walker, et al
    Injunction

  (57) John S. Penrice vs E.A. Wallis, et al
    Injunction 4 Feb 1859

30 (58) George H. Buford & wife vs Annie Fulton & A.J.H. Crow
    Bill of Complaint 9 Mar 1859
    (Death of Annie Fulton suggested 1859)

  (59) L.L. Herndon vs John L. Chapman
    19 Mar 1859

31 (60) Guigniard Scott vs John A. Scott, et al
    21 Mar 1859

  (61) Arnold Lashley vs James Zunts and Thomas Blackmore
    Bill of Complaint 31 Mar 1859

32 (62) A.B. Montgomery et al vs John H. Likens et al
    15 Apr. 1859

Wash. Co. Records

General Chancery Docket: Bk. 1 cont.

    (63) Virginia L. Brooks vs John T. Buckner et al
        26 Apr. 1859

33 (64)*Board of Police of Washington Co. vs John Dayley
        12 May 1859
        (*Afterward renamed Board of Supervisors)

    (65) Exparte Petition of Michaelis Horwitz
        May 1859
        (Shall Shrimpski appointed Trustee in place of Mr.
        Horwitz in '86)

34 (66) John S. Penrice Guardian & a/c vs Robert Marsh
        31 May 1859

    (67)*Board of Police of Washington Co. vs Gabriel W. Rabb
        9 June 1859

35 (68) President Director & c Bank of the United States vs
        Andrew Knox & wife

    (69) William L. Nugent vs David Harrison, et al
        1 Aug 1859
        (Subpoena issued for David Harrison, Emily C. Briscoe,
        Sidney B. Briscoe, Lizzie S. Briscoe, Emma & James
        P.*Harrison to Jefferson (Co. ?) Henry Shaefer &
        Clarissa Shaefer issued to Claiborne Co.
        *James Parmenas Harrison)

36 (70) Lewis Hord, Jr. et al vs Willis L. Robards et al
        8 Sept 1859

    (71) Joseph McGuire vs Benjamin Roach
        29 Sept 1859

37 (72) Francis A. Burgess et al vs Margaret Campbell
        8 Oct 1859

    (73) Robert Marsh vs Thomas Kershaw
        4 Nov 1859

38 (74) Joseph R. Williams et al
        to..Exparte Petition
        Chancery Court
        8 Nov 1859

    (75) Arnold Lashley and James A. McHatton on agreement
        16 Nov 1859

39 (76) R.H. Hord et al vs John A. Miller
        Feb 1860

Washington Co.

General Chancery Docket: Bk. 1 cont.

 (77) Thomas Kershaw vs Ann Kershaw, et al
  28 Feb 1860
  (Subpeona s for Ann & George T. Kershaw, and deposition
  of A.F. Smith filed)

40 (78) William L. Nugent vs Lewis Hord, et al
  5 Mar 1860

 (79) Francis Griffin vs High Knox et al
  5 Mar 1860
  (Order of Publication taken against High and Andrew B.
  Knox, copies sent to Hinds & Tallehatchie Cos., also
  against Tallula & Green P. Sharkey same day...Petition
  against S. Livingston.)

41 (80) Charles G. McHatton vs A. Lashley & J.A. McHatton
  12 Mar 1860

 (81) Guignard Scott vs James S. Guignard et al
  27 Mar 1860
  (Subp. for Calhoun Scott)

42 (82) Bank of Miss. by C.A. Lacoste use & c vs Andrew Knox
  & wife
  20 Mar 1860

 (83) Wm. F. Smith vs J.S.&Freeman Walker, et al
  28 Mar 1860

43 (84) Sarah E. Scott vs F.E. Scott & J.S. Guignard
  30 Mar 1860

 (85) Charles L. Buck & Jas. H. McRaven Exparte
  2 Apr 1860

44 (86) Margaret Campbell vs unknown heirs at law of Thomas
  James, decd.
  21 Apr. 1860

 (87) Wm. W. Stewart et al vs Jno. R. & J.L. Woodburn
  15 May 1860

45 (88) William P. Mellen vs A. Gibson & others
  30 Apr 1860
  (Subp to Hinds Co. for A. Gibson. Demurrer of G.W.
  Ball)

 (89) Francis A. & John R. Burgess to Chancery Court
  Exparte petition for sale of land
  12 May 1860

46 (90) Arnold Lashley vs James McHatton
  16 May 1860
  (very lengthy)

 (91) Andrew Carson, Sr. vs E.J. Carson
  16 May 1860

Washington County

General Chancery Docket: Bk. 1 cont.

47 (92) John S. Penrice vs Charles L. Robards & Jane T. Rucks
16 June 1860

(93) C.G. McHatton vs Arnold & Robert Lashley
3 July 1860

48 (94) Elijah A. Wallis vs Edward P. Byrne
31 July 1860

(95) J.S. Clarke vs W.H. Bunn adm. & others
17 Sept 1860
(Subp. issued for Bunn in Issaqueena Co. & for W.S. Collins in Wash. Co.)

49 (96) James & John Patterson
Exparte for tax 26 Sept 1860

(97) J.W. & S.G. Parks
Exparte Bill Tax 26 Sept 1860

50 (98) Margaret Campbell vs A.B. Burgess et al
27 Sept 1860

(99) Marcus F. Johnson vs A.J.H. Crow
20 Oct. 1860

51 (100) James T. Rucks vs Mary M. Ruck_ et al
23 Oct 1860

(101) Arnold Lashley vs Charles G. McHatton & James A. McHatton
23 Oct 1860

52 (102) Mary Morris vs Henry Morris
12 Nov 1860

(103) E.F. Lowe vs Levee Commission et al
20 Nov 1860

53 (104) Margaret Campbell et al vs Levee Commission et al
28 Nov 1860

(105) Henry H. Morris vs Wm. StJohn, Elliot Henderson
5 Feb. 1861
(Subp. to Harrison & Jackson Cos. Both returned, "not found")

54 (106) Daniel Grant decd. vs J.S. & F. Walker et al
5 Feb 1861

(107) George Shall vs Penrice & McGrath
11 Feb 1861

55 (108) Robert Marsh vs John S. Penrice et al
23 Feb 1861

Washington County

GENERAL CHANCERY DOCKET: Bk. 1 cont.

[109] Edwin G. Cook vs George C.Waddell et al 26 Feb 1861
[Subp. issued Hinds Co. for Aberta Creath]

56 [110] Andrew Carson vs E.J.Carson
27 Feb 1861

[111] Martha T. Baker et al vs Thomas B.p. Ingram
2 mar 1861

57 [112] William F. Smith vs Duff Greene et al [Subp. names
Crump, A.K. Smedes, R.Randolph]
4 Mar. 1861

[113] G.B.Graham to Chancery Court
Application to confirm tax title
4 Apr 1861

58 [114] Mary Morris vs Henry Morris
Decree of Divorce...[Final 20 May 1861]
4 Apr. 1861

[115] John S.Penrice vs C.L.Robards, et al
1 Apr. 1861

59 [116] G.M Pinckard vs J.S.Yerger
8 Apr. 1861
[Names; Wm.M.& Sarah Ann Pinckard exec.,Sarah Ann
Pinkard widow of G.M.Pinkard, decd., J.S.Yerger decd.
W.G.Yerger adm. & E.J.Comstock appionte Guardian Ad
litem of Campbell Yerger, minor. 13 May 1868]

[117] Jane Wray Campbell et al vs Arnold Lashley et al
9 Apr. 1861

60 [118] J.B.Bailey vs R.M.Carter & A.R.Carter
17 Apr. 1861

[119] J.B.Bailey vs Jno.S.Penrice & A.Wickliff
17 apr 1861

61 [120] L.L.Taylor vs W.H.Lee Adm. et al
19 Apr.1861

[121] W.L.Campbell vs W.H.Lee Adm. et al
19 Apr 1861 [names Kate Lee, Math Lee]

62 [122] E.G.Cook & William P. Mellen vs A.F.Smith
22 Apr 1861 [Death of Wm.P.Mellen,1866 also Abram
F.Smith. W.F.Mellen Adm. of WM.P.Mellen]

[123] Samuel T. Taylor vs William Hardeman. receiver et al
3 may 1861[Subp.issued Hinds & Claiborne Cos.]

Washington Co.

General Chancery Docket: Bk.1 cont.

63 (124) John L. Finlay vs Andrew B. Carson, et al
16 May 1861

64 (90) (A continuation of previous #90, final date 23 Aug 1870)
Arnold Lashley vs James A. McHatton

65 (125) Mary Morris vs Henry Morris
4 July 1861

(126) Ward Saunders & Hunt vs Charles G. McHatton et al
7 Sept 1861

66 (127) Ward Saunders & Hunt vs James A. McHatton, et al
7 Sept 1861

(128) Evelina M. Hammet vs Edward Hammet et al
28 Oct. 1861

67 (129) Nannette Abell vs W.A. Haycraft
29 Oct 1861

(130) Ro.B. Carter exec. vs R. H Carter Adm
12 Nov 1861

68 (131) V.W. Wilson et al vs Joseph Lovell et al
5 Dec 1861

69 (132) H.F. Lemmon vs John A. Biddle
10 Apr 1862
(133) Orsamus Winn et us vs T.F. Royall
25 Sept 1862

70 (134) Case & Colburn vs John Norwood
7 Feb 1862

** ———————————————————
(135) Christopher Gillespie vs M.H. Walker et al
28 Nov 1865

71 (136) John J. Smith vs Charles Vernon
25 Dec. 1865

(137) James Cammack vs Walter L. Campbell, William F. Smith et al
29 Dec. 1865

**A Three year break in the records occur here. The Yankees were in control of the Miss. River from Spring of 1862 until after the Civil War. There were gunboats up and down Deer creek, and skirmishes about the Delta during this time. Vicksburg fell 4 July 1863. In the Spring of 1864, the Yankees burned Greenville, including the courthouse. Legend tells the story of a slave named Martin Marble, owned by Sheriff Andrew Carson, who loaded all the County papers on a wagon and hid them in a canebrake. Thus some of the early records survived.

P.28
Washington Co.

General Chancery Docket: Bk.1, cont.

72 (138) A.F. Alexander Adm vs Wm.F. Smith
30 Jan 1866

   (139) Benjamin Andrews vs Charles Vernon
31 Jan 1866

73 (140) Abat & Generes vs Wm.H. Lee, J.R. Groves, John S. Groves, J.T. Sims, Ed Bridge
17 Feb 1866 (filed also Coahoma Co., Ms.)

   (141) Margaret Campbell vs Robt. M. Carter
22 Feb 1866

74 (142) James T. Rucks vs Benj. Hardaway et al
28 Mar 1866 (Also to Warren Co.,Ms & Wilk. Co.,Ms. Names; T.G. Stockett, W.A. Haycraft appointed Guard. of Emily White & Vandke White, minors; Intermarriage of Lucy Hamilton with Hamilton Wright proved; Sup. to Warren Co. for Wright and wife 1868)

   (143) Bartley Johnson & Co. vs T.D. Elliott et al
30 Mar 1866

75 (144) Thos. H. Johns vs R.C. Kershaw et al
16 Apr. 1866 (Names: R.C., J.P.C., GEorge, & Thos. Kershaw....others not found)

   (145) Jane M. Moore vs Lewis G. Galloway & Harvey Latham
17 Apr. 1866 (Subp. to Bolivar C.Ms for L.G. Galloway; to Warren Co.Ms. for Latham)

76 (146) Emily White Adm. of Franklin White, decd. vs Charles E. Smedes and Edward H. Dabney
12 May 1866 (Subp. to Hinds Co.Ms for Chas. E.Smede 1866; to Pike Co.Ms for him May 1869)

   (147) Bartley Johnson & Co. vs Jos. Bertinattie & Eugene P. Bertinattie * et al
20 Apr 1866 (Subp. E.P. Bertinatti, E.P. Tyrel, H.C. Bate)

77 (148) Ellen A. Conway et al vs James A. McHatton et al
20 Apr 1866 (Affidavit filed against Geo Ward, R.H. Chinn, Wm.C. Graves, Archibald Edgar, J.M. Williams, M.B.R. Williams, Jno. Viley, & Fenelon McHatton)

   (149) Benjamin Roach vs F.P. Alexander & others
23 Apr 1866

*"Papers of Wash. Co. Ms. Historical Soc." :p.115; "Council R. Bass married a Miss Bate from Tenn. who after his death marr. an Italian Count and visited Greenville as Countess Bertinatti"

Washington Co. Ms.

GENERAL CHANCERY DOCKET: Bk.1, cont.

78 (150) Jeremiah S. Robinson vs Christopher Gillespie & Margaret H. Walker, Adm. of Est. P.M. Walker, et al - 25 Apr. 1866.

(151) P.B. Swan vs John M. Batt et al 26 Apr. 1866 (Answer of Josephine M. Worthington filed 14 May 1867)

79 (152) Benjamin Roach vs V.P. Alexander & Albert Mellen 3 May 1866

(153) W.E. & G.B. Hunt, Execs. et al vs W.F. Smith, et al 14 May 1866. Answer of W.F. Smith, Demurrer of Jas. S. Walker.. unknown heirs of Freeman Walker, decd. 21 Nov. 1866. Answer of Sarah F. Walker, A.J. Paxton.

80 (154) Samuel Smith & Co. vs C.J. & Eugene P. Bertinatti 22 June 1866

(155) Wm. P. Sanders & R.P. Hunt, surviving partners vs Chas. G. McHatton, et al. 12 Sept. 1866

81 (156) Farley Turey & Co. vs L.S. & S.P. Taylor 12 Nov. 1866

(157) John A. Scott vs Wm. Little, et al 28 Sept. 1866 - Names; Wm. Little, John Little, Samuel Little, Emily Little and her husband Alfred Little, Patsy Chick, (also sp. Chiele) and her husband Alfred Chick, Elizabeth Taylor, Rebecca Davis and her husband Joseph Davis - heirs at-law of Benjamin Montgomery Little, decd. Publication notices sent to <u>Vicksburg Weekly Times</u>; Shelbyville, Tenn; Fayetteville, Tenn; Fayetteville, Ark.

82 (158) A.B. Carson Adm. vs Junius L. Johnson, et al - 28 Sept. 1866. Unknown heirs of George Downing. Wm. Haycraft is the guardian of Betty Erwin, J.S. & E.P. Johnson & N.F. Lonsdale. Betty Erwin comes of age 1875.

(159) S.P. Bailey and wife vs Grant A. Bowen 8 Oct. 1866.

83 (160) Wm. P. Montgomery and William Montgomery vs John W. Hughes - 10 Oct. 1866

(161) A.D. Kelly vs J.T. Andrews - 16 Oct. 1866

The first number is the Chancery Docket Book page number. The second (#) is the packet number, many of which are missing. (See Vol. II of this series for Abstracted Packets)

Washington Co. P. 30

General Chancery Docket: Bk. 1, cont.

84 (162) Z.C. McGinty vs T.F. Royall et al
17 Oct 1866
Filed also Warren Co. & Yazoo Co.

(163) Thomas Reed vs S. Myra Smith et al
23 Oct 1866

85 (164) Richard S. Drone vs Jacob S. Yerger
26 Oct. 1866

(165) Harvey W. Walter & M. Fredonia Walter vs John T. Courtney
surviving partners & c
8 Nov 1866

86 (166) L.P. Percy vs W.A. Percy et al
6 Nov 1866
(Answered..Fannie E. & W.A. Percy and Maria W. Percy by
her Guardian Fannie E. Percy)

(167) Sarah Davis et al vs Sterling Neblett et al
13 Nov 1866

87 (168) James A. King vs Charles Vernon & Joseph Tinker
16 Nov 1866

(169) Abat & Generes vs A.J. Phelps & Mary B. Phelps his wife
17 Nov 1866

88 (170) John R. Blanchard vs Edward P Byrne
22 Dec 1866

(143) Cont. from the earlier listing
Bartley Johnson & Co. vs T.D. Elliott et al

89 (171) Edward T. & William W. Worthington vs A.C. Caperton
29 Dec 1866

(172) Thornhill & Richardson vs Junius L. Johnson et al
17 Jan 1867

90 (173) Richard Ten Croeck, Patsy D. Ten Brick, Thomas J. Kennedy
Kate M. Kennedy, Mary Martin Anderson vs John T. Courtney
21 Feb 1867

(174) Agnes F. Warren vs William Warren Adm & a/c et al
18 Mar 1867
(Answ. of W.L. Nugent who was Trustee to take over
premises in controversy filed 11 May 1867, Answ. of
A.B. Carson filed 13 May 1867, Answ. of Wm. Warren
filed 17 June 1867)

Washington Co.

General Chancery Docket; Bk. 1, cont.

91 (175) Oliver T. Morgan vs William Warren adm. et al
2 Mar 1867
(names: Phil Warren)

(176) James Ginguard, Adm vs O. M. Blanton
25 Mar 1867

92 (177) J.S. Ginguard Adm. vs Thomas Shelby
4 Mar 1867
(19 May 1868 death of J.S. Ginguard suggested)

(178) Chas. L. Robards vs Jno. S. Penrice
13 Mar 1867

93 (179) Alfred B. Carter vs C.A. Brown & C.H. Tupper
18 Mar 1867

(180) William W. Worthington vs Dean Adams & Gaff
22 Mar 1867

94 (181) Jacob Bricker Exec. & a/c vs R.L. Sims exec.
1 Apr 1867
(Sup. sent to Wilkinson Co., Warren Co. to E.A.Sims & Nancy Sims - W.R. Sims Decd.)

(182) Wm. F. Smith & E.P. Johnson vs M.A. May & Andrew B. Carson, Sheriff
2 Apr 1867
(Sup. to Bolivar Co. Returned because of high water)

95 (183) Wm. F. Smith vs F.P. Alexander adm. & a/c & A.B. Carson
2 Apr 1867

(184) Wm. F. Smith vs P.T. Bailey & wife & A.B. Carson
19 Apr 1867

96 (185) Wm. F. Smith & E.P. Johnson vs H.C. Lindsay et al
2 Apr 1867

(186) Birkhead & Hoffman vs T.G. Walcott et al
29 Mar 1867

97 (187) Tufts & Cooley et al vs Morris Ash et al
16 Apr 1867

(188) Ann Matthews vs Thomas Kershaw et al
16 Apr 1867

Page 32
Washington Co.

GENERAL CHANCERY DOCKET: Bk.1, cont.

   98 (189) B.& G.B.Macklin vs Thomas G.Polk
         16 Apr.1867

      (190) Edward McCales et al vs Junius S.Johnson, et al
         17 Apr.1867

   99 (191) B.M.Lee vs Thomas Kershaw, et al
         18 Apr.1867

      (192) Hewitt Norton & Co. vs E.A. & G.R.Fall
         22 Apr.1867

100 (193) Philip Singert & F.K.Hunt, exec. of the Est. of John H.Hanna, decd. vs Junius L. Johnson, et al. 22 Apr.1867

      (194) Wm.M.Lee vs E.G.Cook
         22 Apr.1867

101 (194½) M.S. & S.E. Ruse & Bank of Kentucky vs William Yerger, et al - 24 Apr.1867 - (the et al: Mary M(argaret) Rucks, Amanda Rucks, James Rucks, Grant B(Bowen) Rucks, Sally Rucks, James T.Rucks, Henry Rucks, Alexander Rucks, Elizabeth B.Yerger, Frank Valliant, Marion (Rucks) Valliant, & L.T.Rucks, _____ William Yerger, Malvina H.(Rucks) Yerger, Maria L.(Louise Rucks) Yerger, William S.(Swan) Yerger, Henrietta (Rucks) Yerger, & R.W.Scott. Subp. sent to Washington Co., Hinds Co., Yazoo Co.**

      (195) Alfred D.Offutt, et al vs James A.McHatton
         24 Apr.1867

102 (196) Leroy B.Valliant vs O.B.Blanton, et al - 26 Apr. 1867 - O.M.Blanton, M.R.Blanton, W.C.Blanton, H.B.Theobald, Samuel Theobald, and J.M.Smith.

      (197) Elihu B.Kilpatrick Adm. de Bonis non of Ebenezer Kilpatrick, decd. vs Fred N.Macklin & Samuel T.Taylor.

103 (198) Margaret Campbell vs M.H.Litchford & Co. & A.B. Carson, Sheriff - 9 May 1867

      (199) Aaron Wickliff vs J.B.Bailey - 4 May 1867

104 (200) Thomas Hinds vs M.H.Litchford, et al - 4 May 1867

      (201) John P.Dillingham vs T.M. & D.Shannahan and A.B. Carson, Sheriff - 10 May 1867

** From Papers of Washington County Historical Papers: p.251 "Four of Judge James Rucks daughters married Yergers - Malvina marr. Judge W, Yerger, Bettie marr. Alex.Yerger, Maria Louise marr. James Yerger, Henrietta marr. Wm.Swan Yerger...Arthur Rucks marr. Mary Margaret Yerger.

Washington Co.

GENERAL CHANCERY DOCKET: Bk.1, cont.

105 (202) Wm.F.Smith vs John A.Miller & A.B.Carson, Sheriff
    1 June 1867

  (203) An error

106 (204) John A. Miller vs Eugenia D.Bertinatti, et al.
15 June 1867 - Names: E.P.Tyre, Eugenia P. and Joseph Bertinatti at Washington Co.,Ms. and Constantinople, Turkey; Cornelius Fellows, Daniel P.Logan, Thompson Greenfield, Sheppard Brown, Philip Rotchford at New Orleans, La; Wm.Fraziers Kelly & Zin (?) Hardaway, A.B.Carson, Sheriff.

  (205) Ann B.Finlay Adm., et al vs Y.S.Mosley
    8 July 1867

107 (206) Sam T.Taylor vs Andrew B.Carson, Sheriff & Tax Collector - 26 July 1867

  (207) Ann Poindexter vs Henry T.Lonsdale
    19 Aug.1867
Publication sent to A.Foster Elliott and Henry T.Lonsdale at New Orleans...F.W.Lonsdale to Wash.Co.Ms...others not found.

108 (208) Thos.H.Hill vs A.B.Carson, Sher.
    21 Aug.1867

  (209) Wm.H.Lee vs Andrew B.Carson, Sher.
    21 Aug. 1867

109 (210) Lewis T.Rucks, et al vs Frank Valliant, et al.
11 Sept.1867 - Subp. to Coahoma Co, Hinds Co, Wash.Co.

  (211) Thomas R.Warfield vs Samuel T.Taylor
    25 Oct. 1867

110 (212) Endarguire (?) & Co. vs Christopher Gillespie and J.S.Robinson - 26 Oct. 1867

  (213) Toof, Philips & Co. vs Weatherbee & Philips, et al
    23 Nov.1867

111 (214) Planters Bank of Tenn. vs Haney Latham & Thomas J.Martin, Jr. - 28 Oct. 1867

  (215) Given Watts & Co. vs N.M.Meriweather & Watt F. Johnson - 19 Nov.1867

112 (216) C.R.Estill vs William Gant
    3 Nov.1867

GENERAL CHANCERY DOCKET: Bk 1, cont.

    (217) E.R.Kimball & Co. vs Harvy Yerger et al
         30 Nov. 1867 (names: Harry & Sallie Yerger)

113 (218) Thos. H.Johns vs Andrew B.Carson, shrf. & Davis Apple
         7 Dec 1867

    (219) Shipp Burgess & Co vs R.H.Carter, R.H.Carter adm,
         19 Dec. 1867

114 (220) G.H. Kennedy & Co vs W.F.Randolph et al
         23 Dec 1867 Supreme Court (Ordered property seized
         & sold; Bankruptcy of Randolph "suggested"; final
         entry 21 Nov. 1877)

    (221) Given Watts & Co. vs J.C.Jones receiver et al
         2 Jan 1868

115 (222) Gustave Greenwood vs Lawson Rouse et al
         9 Jan 1868

    (223) John D.Gouter vs N.B.Johnson
         14 Jan 1868

116 (224) C.R.Estill vs Given Watts & Co., Given Brown & Co.,
         Ann D. Halsey*
         23 Jan 1868

    (225) S.H.Kenedy & Co. A.W.McAllister,Sr. et al

117 (226) Wm.Montgomery et al vs Summers & Brammie(?) et al
         23 Jan 1868

    (227) Morris Weiss surviving partner vs Ludwig Alexander
         29 Jan 1868

118 (228) Given Watts & Co vs T.J.Moss
         30 Jan 1868

    (229) Given Watts & Co vs Thos H.Johns, Jos.C.Jones &
         Arche Baugh
         8 Feb 1868

119 (230) Howell Hinds et al vs H.B.Theobald & Wm.C.Blanton
         2 Mar 1868. (May 1869; Death of compl. H.Hinds "suggest.)

    (231) S.H. Kennedy & Co. vs Jno.A.Scott & Sarah E.Scott
         7 Mar 1868

* Ann Dunn Hill was married to Stephen Mason Jackson, who dec.
    Wash.Co.Ms 1847. She marr. 1851 Dr.Seymour Halsey
    and they lived in Vicksburg, Ms.

P. 35
Washington Co.

General Chancery Docket: Bk. 1, cont.

120 (232) J.S. Bradford vs Stuart White
9 Mar 1868

(233) Board of Levee Comm. vs Mary H.R. Yerger
18 Mar 1868

121 (234) Jurey & Harris vs R.H. Hord et al
30 Mar 1868

(235) H.G. Blackmon vs R.H. Hord et al
30 Mar 1868

122 (236) Brandis & Crawford vs Geo. Torrey
2 Mar 1868
(Subp. sent to Wash., Sunflower, Jefferson, Cos)
(Washington Co.'s not found due to high water)

(237) John T. Foote vs Sallie Yerger & her husband Hal Yerger, Maggie Miller, Malvina Miller, Harvey Miller heirs at law of Harvey Miller, decd, E.T. Johnson exec. of Harvey Miller, decd., A.C. Bullet & Irene Smith & George W. Ward
4 Apr 1868
(E.J. Comstock, Commissioner, appointed Guardian to minor Pullen heirs & minor heirs of A.C. Bullett)

(236) Brooke & Smedes Vs Wm. F. Smith & A.L. Gaines
10 Apr 1868

(237) Jno. H. Nelson Tres. vs Thomas Shelby
13 Apr 1868

(238) Jno H. Nelson Treas. vs N.J. Nelson, John T. Courtney, A.P. Montgomery, A.M. Kirk, W.P. Montgomery
13 Apr 1868

(239) James G. Brown, surviving partner of Cummings Brown & Co. vs Sarah F. Buckner, Sarah F. Buckner, exec., Lomax Anderson, Nellie Anderson, Kate Buckner, John Parker, Roberta Parker, Lon DeN. Evans, Emma Evans
13 Apr 1868
(Supb. issued in Washington, Claiborne, Bolivar Cos.)

25 (240) John N. Nelson, Treas. of Wash. Co. vs W.P. Montgomery
21 Apr 1868

(241) John N. Nelson, Treas. of Wash. Co. vs S. Myra Smith, A.C. Smith, E.H. Comstock, E.J. Comstock, E. Nugent, W.L. Nugent
21 Apr 1868
(19 May 1869 - death of A.C. Smith & Evil H. Comstock "suggested".)

126 (242) John H. Nelson vs Wm. Hunt exec. et al
21 Apr 1868

(243) John H. Nelson Treas. vs R.L. Dixon
21 Apr 1868

P. 36
Washington Co.

General Chancery Docket: Bk. 1, cont.

127 (244) John H. Nelson vs O.M. Blanton & M.R. Blanton
           22 Apr 1868

    (245) John H. Nelson vs A.B. Carson adm. of Robt. Marsh decd
           W.A. Haycraft adm. of James Abell decd.
           22 Apr 1868

128 (186) Cont. from case (186) on p. 96 in Docket Bk. 1
           Binkhead & Hoffman vs T.G. Walcott et al
           2 Dec 1867   Final entry 12 May 1909

129 (246) John H. Nelson Tres. vs Sarah F. Buckner
           26 Apr 1868

    (247) John H. Nelson, Treas. vs W.B. Montgomery, et al

           (SKIPS TO P. 140 (248) Page no. out of sequence)
140 (248) S.F. White vs R.G. Sims et al
           29 Apr 1868

    (249) Farley Jurey & Co. vs R.H. Hord et als
           29 Apr 1868

141 (250) S.W. Ferguson adm. vs Thomas H. Buckner
           29 Apr 1868

    (251) E.W. Jack & E.H. Porter vs Wade Hampton
           29 Apr 1868
           (Bankruptcy of Hampton)

142 (252) E.J. Flournay exec. & c vs C.W. Dudley et als
           29 Apr. 1868

    (253) A.W. Newman vs John H. Nelson
           4 May 1868

143 (254) T.B. Warfield vs A. Willis & T. Greasy, Shrff.
           19 May 1868

    (255) E.G. Booth vs E.W. Ferguson & E.P. Byrne
           5 May 1868

144 (256) E.J. Bowens vs N.C. Orrick & wife et al
           30 Apr 1868

    (257) Stephan Duncan vs Christophe F. Hampton et al
           5 May 1868

145 (258) S.J. Henderson vs W.A. Haycraft exec. et al
           5 May 1868

    (259) Geo. W. Burch & Jas. D. Smith vs Sidney R. Smith
           14 May 1868

Washington Co.

General Chancery Docket: Bk. 1, cont.

146 (260) Jno. R. Viley vs Junius R. Ward
           12 May 1868

    (261) Larz Anderson Trustee vs T.B. Warfield
           19 May 1868

147 (262) Matilda French by next friend vs Saml. G. French et al
           20 May 1868

    (263) Thomas H. Hood vs William N. Hood, et al
           23 May 1868

148 (264) Wade Hampton vs E.W. Jack et al
           17 June 1868

    (265) Wade Hampton vs E.N. Apperson surviving Partnr. et al
           26 Aug 1868

149 (266) R.P. Carrico vs Robt. H. Lowry & David Hollis
           22 Sept 1868

    (267) Thos. W. Hill vs Nelson T. Warren et al
           25 Sept 1868

150 (268) E.L. Carter vs Ro. H. Carter et al
           31 Oct 1868
           (Names: Mary E. Carter)

    (269) Shipp Bourgess & Co. vs Robert H. Carter
           14 Oct 1868

151 (270) Shipp Bourgess & Co. vs A. Grayson/Carters Heirs at Law
           14 Oct 1868

    (271) Dixon & Percy vs John James et al
           14 Oct 1868

152 (272) Jno. Doyle vs Margaret Nary
           23 Oct 1868

    (273) Jos. T. Matthews vs R.M. Lashley et al
           22 Oct 1868

153 (274) F.A. Metcalfe vs A.T. Stewart
           27 Oct 1868

    (275) E.P. McDowell vs L.D. McMeekin   27 Oct 1868

154 (276) " "   "   "   R.H. Sutton   "   "   "

    (277) " "   "   "   Harry St. John Dixon 27 Oct 1868

155 (278) Alex Newman vs A. Worthington et al
           29 Oct 1868

Washington Co.

General Chancery Docket: Bk. 1, cont.

      (279) E.P. McDowell vs Andrew B. Carson
             30 Oct 1868

156 (280) W.B. Portman use & c vs Wade Hampton
             31 Oct 1868

      (281) N.T. Warren vs Robert W. Walcott et al
             31 Oct 1868

157 (282) C.W. Wolfe vs C.W. Dudley exec. & c et al
             31 Oct 1868
             (Writing very difficult to read! Names: John Erwin
              & William Erwin Daniel (?) - Johnson & William Erwin
              & Emma Morgan, Victor Erwin)

      (283) W.L. Nugent vs B.F. Comegy et als
             11 Nov 1868

158 (284) Mary W. Rives (Rines?) & O.C. Rives vs Jno. Desouthern
             1 Dec 1868

      (285) Annie M. Foster exec. vs M.L. Yerger et al
             1 Dec 1868

159 (286) S.W. Thompson vs Edmond Winn et al
             1 Feb. 1869

      (287) Alexander N. Beck vs Joseph M. Brooks, adm. & heirs
             8 Feb 1869

160 (288) Huntington & Levally vs Board of Levee Comm.
             24 Feb 1869

      (289) Julia R. Worden by next friend vs George Worden
             20 May 1869
             (Decree of Divorce - care and custody of child awarded to
              Julia R. Worden)

161 (290) William Marshall vs Florence Marshall
             13 May 1869

      (291) W.J. Henderson vs S.S. Taylor et al
             11 Mar 1869

162 (292) Jefferson W. Moore vs J. Livingston Surviving partner
             6 Apr. 1869

      (293) John T. Foote vs Hal Yerger et al
             6 Apr 1869

Washington Co.

General Chancery Dockett: Bk.1, cont.

163 (294) John M. Bell vs Hal Yerger, et al
       6 Apr. 1869

   (295) Farmers Bank of Ky. vs Jno.B.& James P.Poynt(?) et al
       7 Apr. 1869

164 (296) E.L. Carter vs Board of Comm. to liquidate & collect
       Levee Purpose - 15 Apr. 1869

   (297) Sallie J. Buford use & a/c vs T.J. Craig
       15 Apr. 1869

165 (298) Hewitt Norton & Co. vs A.J. Phelps & wife
       11 May 1869
       (States: to take deposition in Shelbyville, Ky. Filed
       depos. of Jona Peirce; Depos. of Capt. Johnson filed;
       "   " James Comodore, et al filed.)

   (299) E. Wilkerson, et al vs Z.C. Offutt
       24 Apr. 1869

166 (300) N.J. Nelson vs Jn.T. Courtney & wife
       26 Apr. 1869

   (301) Norton & Tarleton, assignees & a/c vs A.D. Halsey
       20 May 1869

167 (302) Wm. Grimes & Louisa D. Hickman vs Wm.H. Bolton, assignee
       & a/c et als - 29 Apr. 1869

   (303) E.E. Norton Assignee &a/c vs Wm. Montgomery et al

168 (304) H.St.John Dixon & James P. Dixon vs R.L. Dixon
       19 May 1869

   (305) Kate D. Buckner vs Liq. Levee Board
       30 Apr. 1869

169 (305½) C.R. Estill vs E.P. Byrne et al
       4 May 1869

   (306) C.R. Estill vs Lewis & Geoghegan et al
       13 May 1869
       (Bill of attachment on Wm.& E.A. Montgomery)

170 (307) C.R. Estill vs M. Selig & Co. et al
       4 May 1869

   (308) C.R. Estill vs Cox & Everman et al
       4 May 1869

171 (309) C.R. Estill vs Jos. Hay & Co. et al
       4 May 1869

   (310) H.P. Lee et al vs Liq. Levee Board
       18 May 1869

172 (311) C.M. Lewis vs C.T. Geoghegan
       4 June 1869

P. 40
Washington Co.

General Chancery Docket: Bk. 1 cont.

  (312) Grant A. Bowen vs S.P. Bailey et al
     2 July 1869

173 (313) W.B. Wheatley vs C.E. Morgan Shrf. & Tax Coll.
     28 July 1869

  (314) Wilton Bine vs Edwin G. Cook, et al
     19 Aug 1869

174 (315) Henry Harris vs Martha Harris
     27 Aug 1869 Decree of Divorce

  (316) Payne Huntington & Co. vs Jones S. Hamilton et al
     19 Nov 1869

175 (317) Payne Huntington & Co. vs E. Mount et al
     Sept 1869

  (318) Payne Huntington & Co. vs J. Dillingham et al
     15 Sept 1869

176 (318½) Clarinda Martin et als vs Mrs. Willie Willis et al
     4 Oct 1869

  (319) S. Drabelle et al vs Cox & Everman et al
     8 Oct 1869
     (J.R. Cox, Ellen M. Cox, S.W. Ferguson, Adm. of est of Wm
     C.C. Smith, Aaron Mann, Isaac Mack, & W.A. Everman

177 (320) W.E. Hunt exec. vs W.A. Haycraft exec. et al
     27 Oct 1869

  (321) H.S. Buckner vs S.G. & B.A. Aldrich
     28 Oct 1869

178 (322) E.D. Morgan & Co. vs P.W. & P. Gregory
     28 Oct. 1869

  (323) Columbus Insurance & Banking Co. vs Geo. R. & E.A. Fall
     28 Oct 1869

179 (324) Harry Verdelet et al vs Elizabeth A. Fall & Geo. R. Fall
     1 Nov 1869

  (325) W.H. Bolton Tres. & c vs G.G. Sims
     20 Nov 1869

180 (326) B. Hamway & Co. vs N.T. Nelson et al
     21 Nov 1869

  (327) Jno. H. Evans vs S.H. Kennedy & Co. et al
     28 Nov 1869

Page 41
Washington Co.

General Chancery Docket: Bk. 1 Cont.

181 (328) Geo. D. Fischer et al vs S.T. Taylor et al 11 Nov 1869

    (329) J. Radjesky vs Wm. Johnson et al 24 Nov 1869

182 (330) Jno. H. Nelson & Co. vs Henry Banett & Catharine Banette 25 Nov 1869

    (331) C.B. Hundley vs Wesly Brown et al 25 Jan 1870

183 (332) " "   "   " Cornelius Wilson   "   "   "

    (333)

184 (334) F.Y. Ulen vs E.G. Peyton & C.E. Morgan 29 Jan 1870

    (335) Jeremiah S. Johnson vs Margaret H. Walker adm. of P.M. Walker, et al 1 Feb 1870

185 (336) R.S. Buck vs Jos. J. Matthews et al 25 Jan 1870

    (337) J.T. Taylor vs Jno. A. Miller et al 4 Feb 1870

186 (338) C.M. Lewis vs Thomas Hinds & E.P. Byrne 5 Feb 1870
(E.P. Byrnes files Bankruptcy Nov 4, 1872)

    (339) Gwyn & Wallis vs Thomas Powell 7 Feb 1870

187 (340) R.D. Howe et al vs all persons & c 22 Feb 1870
(Answ. of Milton Bailey filed)

    (341) Edward P. Byrne vs Carson & Gay, Richardson & May 23 Feb

188 (342) Robert Pugh vs Mary A. Hinds et al 18 Feb 1870

    (343) W.S. Frank Trustee vs President Director Farmers Bank of Ky. 30 Mar 1870

189 (344) Wyndham R. Trigg vs James A. McHatton et al 31 Mar 1870

    (345) Rebecca S. Shannon vs Elizabeth J. Flournoy exec. et al 31 Mar 1870

190 (346) Thos. R. Lee vs J.J. Cox et al 31 Mar 1870

    (347) John W. Heath vs Margaret V. Tamplin et al 21 Apr 1870

191 (348) Seelig & Co. vs John Jackson 13 Apr 1870

Page 42
Washington Co.

General Chancery Docket: Bk.1, cont.

191 (349) S.W.Ferguson, Adm. & a/c vs Wm.Warren, Adm.et al 12 Mar.1870 - Names Demurrer filed by Agnes F.Warren. Note of A.G.Frazier against A.Lashley, a/c of Mrs.A.C.Benson - $8060; Agnes F.Warren - $46040; Note of T.F.Porter for $1500; W.L.Nugent - $100; Shepherd & Blackburn $453 + $36... against the Est. of John F.Warren. Decree vs A.Lashley in favor of R.L.Dixon for $2500; Theodore Phillipson vs Arnold Lashley - $297; Nugent & Yerger $23; against the Est. of Arnold Lashley.

192 (350) J.W.Handlzer vs E.P.Byrne - 16 Apr.1870

(351) H.P.Hollenbeck, Adm. & a/c vs Elizabeth Bott, Adm. et al.

193 (352) Robert Pugh vs Robert Davenport - 18 Apr.1870

(353) N.Fontanie & N.Hill, surviving a/c vs Mansfield Wilmot, et al - 18 Apr.1870

194 (354) Thomas Hinds vs E.P.Byrnes, et al - 18 Apr.1870

(355) Wm.Marshall & Co. vs Peter Manning, et al

195 (356) Seelig & Co. vs Gisso Desavier - 23 Apr. 1870

(357) Wm.A.Hopkins vs Robert Ford and all persons a/c/ 19 Mar.1870

196 (358) Appleton Noyes & Co. vs C.T.Geoghegan, et ux 25 May 1870

(359) H.R.Putnam vs J.R.Murphey - 13 June 1870

197 (360) Joseph Smith vs Ellen Smith - 27 June 1870
         Divorce

(361) Charles G.Dablegreen Adm. a/c vs Frank Valliant, et al - 27 June 1870

198 (362) C.W.Lewis vs C.T.Geoghegan - 27 June 1870

(363) Daniel Williams vs S.T.Taylor, et al - 2 July 1870

199 (364) Jones S.Hamilton vs W.& A.R.Dillingham, et al - 8 July 1870 - E.J.Elder, Trustee of H.S.Van Eatton. The death of Huntington admitted and case revived in name of surviving partners...Dec.1871

(365) T.C.Bedford vs Samuel Raney - 20 July 1870

200 (366) T.C.Bedford vs Phil.B.Thomson, et al 20 July 1870

(367) Joseph Radjesky vs C.E.Morgan, Sheriff & Tax Collector - 18 July 1870.

P. 43
Washington Co.

General Chancery Docket: Bk 1, cont.

201 (368) Pollock & Trigg vs J.J.A.McHatton et al 19 July 1870

(369) W.A.Pollock vs D.B.Whitney 22 July 1870

202 (370) Andrew Abson surv. vs. Mary James et al 23 July 1870

(370½) W.A.Pollock vs F.A.Dawson 22 July 1870

203 (371) Ed.T. Worthington vs John C. Calhoun 3 Aug 1870

(372) Wm. Wallace vs Andrew J.Turnbull 3 Aug 1870 (Subp. filed Issa.Co.Ms..."Not found in my county". Death of Turnbull suggested and proved 21 Feb 1871. Heirs-at-law in case #658..Subp. for Gracia Turnbull, case #666. Subp. to Issa.Co.Ms for R.J. Turnbull.)

204 (373) John M.McGinnis vs Norman McLeod et al 25 July 1870

(374) Josephine M.Worthington vs John T.Courtney 25 Aug 1870

205 (375) Nancy Dorson vs Soloman Alexander 16 Aug 1870

(376) Wm.Scott vs Pamelia Emeline Scott 16 Aug 1870

206 (377) J.B.M.Lawson vs E.A. Lawson 16 Aug 1870 (Alimony; also filed Issa. Co.Ms.)

(378) F.A.McGregor & J.E.Harris vs unknown heirs of James Brown, decd. 26 July 1870

207 (379) Mother Colombo Carroll vs Robt. H.Hord, Guard. et al (Jno. Davis app. Guard. ad litem 23 July 1872; death of Hord "suggessted" & cause revived vs Lizzie A. Partee & her husband)*

(380) Geo. B.Hunt exec. et al vs A.S.Gaines, L.T.Webber & P.B.Starke, Sherf. 30 Sept 1870

208 (381) N.A. & M.L. HEard vs Wm.Taylor et al 22 Oct 1870

(382) Catherine Egg etal vs Brd. of Superv. Wash.Co. 23 Oct 1870

209 (383) S.Picard vs Jacob Adeson et al 27 Oct 1870

(384) H.B.Theobald vs Town Council of G'ville 31 Oct. 1870 (Harriet Blanton Theobald)

*Lizzie A.Partee was Dau. of Jas.B.Jackson & Mary I.Askew. Jas.B. Jackson déc. Wash.Co.Ms 1854. Mary I.Askew marr. 2nd 1858 Robt. H.Hord. Lizzie A. & Andrew Jackson were minors when their father died. Lizzie A.Jackson marr. Chas. Partee.

Page 44
Washington Co.

GENERAL CHANCERY DOCKET: Bk.1, cont.

210 (385) Lengsfield & Co. vs Steven Scott, et al - 3 Nov. 1870

(386) J.J.McMurray, et al vs S.T.Webber, Sherf. - 3 Nov. 1870

211 (387) John H.Nelson & Co. vs Herndon & Selby - 4 Nov. 1870 - In Dec.1871 the death of W.H.Hunter admitted & suit revived in name of John H.Nelson - p.5 Minute Bk.2.

(388) Marshall & Co. vs Robert Johnson 5 Oct. 1870

212 (389) John H.Nelson & Co. vs John M.Briscoe and Harry Percy Lee - 8 Nov. 1870

(390) Cully & Bolly (Boll?) vs C.B.Hundley & John W. Ward. - 8 Nov. 1870

213 (391) E.M.Sprague, Adm. & a/c vs John T.Courtney, et al 9 Nov. 1870

(392) B.Bunn vs J.T.Courtney, et al - 9 Nov. 1870

214 (393) Everman & Wilson vs H.W.Buckley, et al 15 Nov. 1870

(394) Susan P.Taylor vs Wm.Montgomery, et al 16 Nov. 1870

215 (395) Everman & wilson vs P.W.Holley, et al 19 Nov. 1870

(396) A.D.Aldridge & Co. vs J.J.Simpson 9 Dec. 1870

216 (397) Jos.Hay & Co. vs Taylor & Mobley 9 Dec. 1870

(398) Lengsfield & Co. vs J.E.Rogers, et al 27 Dec. 1870 Deposition of J.I.Lengsfield.

217 (399) D.G.Cook & Co. vs Joel Jones, et al - 6 Jan. 1871 Bankruptcy of Cook "suggested" and admitted.

(400) Sarah D.Crenshaw, et al vs W.B.Murdock 7 Jan. 1870

218 (401) D.G.Cook vs H.P.Muir, et al 23 Jan. 1871; Answer of Ed.Hammett filed 20 Feb. 1871...Death of E.Hammett suggested 27 Apr. 1872.

(402) Calhoun Haile, next friend & a/c vs Amanda Haile 13 Jan.1871. Published in <u>Greenville Republican</u>. (Ed. This is the first mention of a newspaper in this area used for citations)

219 (403) J.Radjesky vs Perry & Julia Giles 16 Jan. 1871 Order land to be seized

(404) Everman & Walker surviving partners & a/c vs Henry Taylor - 17 Jan. 1871.

Washington Co., Ms.

GENERAL CHANCERY DOCKET: Bk.1, cont.

220 (405) S.Picard vs Dick Addison et al 19 Jan.1871

   (406) A.L.McRae vs Julius Milton, et al 24 Jan.1871

221 (407) Wm.Marshall vs Saml.Lampkins 27 Jan.1871
   (408) N.W.Wilson, et al vs C.S.Stone, et al 28 Jan.1871
      (Subp.to Everman, Kate Stone, W.W.Stone, Dr.Walter
      and J.W.Stone, Caleb and Oliver Stone. Answers of
      D.L., Kate and Oliver Stone filed 20 July 1871)

222 (409) J.Radgesky vs Robt. and Jane Reed 31 Jan.1871

   (410) A.J.Phillips et ux vs Geo.C.Harris et ux 8 Feb.1871
      (Depos.of Chas.E.Smedes, Jno.Dover, L.W.Thompson,
      C.Q.Andrews. Transcript made out by W.G.Phelps. Depos.
      by W.T.Barnard.)

223 (411) S.Picard vs R.B.Murphy et al 8 Feb.1871
      (Answer of J.W.Murphy)

   (412) Lengsfield & Co. vs Sam Partee et al 8 Feb.1871

224 (413) M.Ginsburger vs Bail Rievson (?) 9 Feb.1871

   (414) H.S.Buckner & H.L.Baker vs Nancy Williams et al 14
      Fe.1871 - (John Fawn, Comm.Appointed Guard.for M.A.
      & J.C.Williams in Case #652. Pro Confesso as to Nancy
      Thos.J., Henry J. & J.B.Williams in Case #653. Comm.Deed
      rec. Deed Bk."G2,p.602,603.)

225 (415) James Stone et ux vs Amanda Worthington et al 15 Feb.

   (416) Everman & Co. vs Willis Hubbard & Sidney Lamkin
      15 Feb.1871

226 (417) W.W.Stone vs Ned Davis 15 Feb.1871
   (418) W.W.Stone vs Wm.Smith   "   "   "

227 (419) J.Radgesky vs John Williams et al 15 Feb.1871

   (420) D.Y.(G?)Cook vs Jas.Buchanan et al 20 Feb.1871

228 (421) D.Y. "   " vs Griffin Buchannan et al 20 Feb.1871

   (422) J.Radgesky vs Robt.Franklin et al 21 Feb.1871

229 (423) Richardson & May vs W.A.Clary et al Mar.1871

   (424) W.A. & F.Clarey vs Richardson & May et al 3 Mar.
      1871. (Subp.to R.M.Carter, Trigg & Buckner, Wm.
      Carter, Eleanor Carter, Mrs.E.Carter, W.F.Randolph,
      F. and L.B.Valliant.)

Washington Co. Ms.

GENERAL CHANCERY DOCKET: Bk.1, cont.

230 (425) S. Picard vs Wm. Thompson et al 16 Mar. 1871

(426) Wm. A. McPhilters vs John A. Miller & L. L. Webber, Sheriff 30 Mar. 1871

231 (427) D. G. Cook vs Jas. Long, et al 3 Apr. 1871

(428) John J. Smith vs McLemore, et al 10 Apr. 1871

232 (429) H. R. Merchant vs Frank Valliant, assignee, et al 12 Apr. 1871.

(430) J. Q. Wills vs Fitz Wm. Lonsdale, et al 12 Apr. 1871 (Fawn appointed Guard. of Nannie J. Lonsdale, T. Lonsdale, H. H. Lonsdale, Martha O. & Saml. B. Newman, Jane T. Lonsdale...case in Pkt. #652)

233 (431) Alex. & Marshall vs Harry Harrison, et al 15 Apr. 1871

(432) Jno. H. Nelson & Co. vs S. B. Weems 15 Apr. 1871

234 (433) L. D. Aldrich vs Bettie A. Aldrich, et al 15 Apr. 1871

(434) Maria S. & C. E. Morgan vs Heirs of R. T. Archer, decd. et al 20 Apr. 1871

235 (435) F. H. Boyce vs D. M. Buckner, Adm., et al 21 Apr. 1871 (Lucy and Bettie Brooks, minors, defendants)

(436) M. Ginsburger vs Newman Turner 8 May 1871

236 (437) Everman & Co. vs Sam Railey 11 May 1871

(438) "   "   "   " C. W. Standard   "

237 (439) "   "   "   " Asa Storms & Dawson Clark "

(440) "   "   "   " W. N. Johnson 12 May (cont. on p. 313)

238 (441) Louis Goodman vs Danile Brown, et als 15 May 1871

(442) D. G. Cook vs Carroll, Terrard, et al 16 May 1871

239 (443) "   "   "Wm. Johnson, et al   "

(444) Wills, Buckner, & Robbs vs Ella Wall   "

240 (445) "   "   "   Jerome Cross   "

(446) Harrow & Johnson vs Fielding Buckner (J. W. Harrow & C. W. Badger...also deposition of John Calahan, F. Buckner filed.)

241 (447) Harrow & Johnson vs Loyd Grubbs 19 May 1871

Page 47
Washington Co.

General Chancery Docket: Bk.1, cont.

241 (448) Jefferson Davis et al exec. & a/c vs Mary M. Rucks et al
10 June 1871 (Subp. issued to Washington Co., Hinds,
Coahoma, 10 June 1871. Subp. issued to Jas. Rucks.)

242 (449) John A. Miller vs N.T. Nelson et al 23 May (cont. p. 314)

(450) Wills & Buckner vs Robb, Worthington et al 10 July 1871

243 (451) Margaret Campbell vs E.W. Brown & E.E. Morton assignee
12 July 1871

(452) John Allen vs Ellen M. Johnson et al 19 July 1871
(Subp. issued to Thos. Shelby & Bettie Shelby; Ellen
M. Johnson & Wm. H. Johnson not found in Washington Co.)

244 (453) Wallace & Co. vs Amelius C. West et al adm & a/c 10 Aug

(454) Rachel Kempt vs Wesley Kempt 15 Aug 1871
(Supb. issued to Bolivar Co.)

245 (455) M.B. Portman vs Lucy V. Semple Ames 18 Aug 1871

(456) Wm. Johnson et al vs Wm. B. Murdock et al 19 Aug 1871

246 (457) Frederick Hall et al vs The Board of Levee Comm. et al
29 Aug. 1871

(458) James L. Brown et al vs " " " " " " "

247 (459) Joseph Hart et al vs Mary A. Hinds et al 22 Aug 1871

(460) Davidella Montgomery vs Alexander Montgomery 26 Sept. 1871

248 (461) J.C. Pierce vs J.D. & W.A. Jewell 17 Oct. 1871

(462) Dock Porterfield vs Nellie Porterfield 18 Oct 1871

249 (463) Theo. G. Walcott vs C.S. Whitcomb et al 25 Oct. 1871

(464) James R. Yerger et al vs Jesse I. Duncan et al 3 Nov 1871

250 (465) Jno. H. Nelson surviving Partner vs Dailey Searcy et al

(466) D.C. Robinson vs W.W. Worthington et al 8 Dec. 1871
(Answer of W.W. Worthington, P. Thomson, & S.R. Thomson
filed & Elizabeth P. Worthington granted 30 days to
file her answer.)

251 (467) Jno. R. Cameron vs Board of Supervisors of Washington
Co. & Philip Hanser 30 Nov 1871

(468) A.M. Vanarsdale vs E.(??) P. Crane et al 26 Nov.
(Supb. sent to Issaquena Co.)

Washington Co.Ms.

252:(469) E.Richardson vs Spencer Carter 21 Dec.1871
    (470) Wm.Cook vs Wm.Gillespie,et al 23 Dec.1871
253:(471) Wash Tyrner vs Houston Farmer & Thos.Hinds 31 Dec.1871
    (472) V.L.Saunders vs H.H.Elliott 8 Jan.1872
254:(473) J.& J.J.Lengsfield vs J.L.Griffin 10 Jan.1872
    (474) Moses Seilig vs J.P.Ball 12 Jan.1872
255:(475) Frank Valliant vs Board of Supervisors of Wash.Co.Ms.17 Jan.1872
    (476) D.G.Cook vs Will H.Stephens 19 Jan.1872
256:(477) C.& A.E.McGrath vs Sam Perry 8 Feb.1872
    (478) A.D.Aldridge & Co. vs Hortin Thomas & Aaron Wright 13 Feb.1872
257:(479) A.D.Aldridge & Co. vs Ed.Canty,et al 13 Feb.1872
    (480) L.D.Aldridge vs G.M.Bailey 15 Feb.1872
258:(481) J.L.Harris vs R.G.Sims, et al 7 March 1872
    (482) John L. & Amelia E.Penrice vs W.B.Wheatley et al 16 March1872
259:(483) W.H.Letchford & Co. vs R.G.Sims, et al 20 March 1872
    (484) J.D.Webster vs Elizabeth Webster 29 Mar.1872
260:(485) Rueben Johnson vs Martha Johnson 30 Mar.1872
    (486) Marietta Reisinger vs Jacob Reisinger 12 Apr.1872
261:(487) Johnson & Goodrich vs J.D.Jewell & W.A.Jewell 15 Apr.1872
    (488) T.Greary (Sp.?)vs N.T.Nelson, et al 15 Apr.1872
262:(489) John A.Scott vs Virgil F.P.Alexander 16 May 1872
    (490) Harriet Peoples vs Levi Peoples 7 June 1872
263:(491) V.P.F.Alexander vs Callin White & Stewart White 11 June 1872
    (492) S.Picard vs B.A.Offult, et al 14 June 1872
264:(493) William F.Smith vs Abner L.Gains, et al 15 June 1872
    (494) J.S.Buck & George S.Kausler vs All Persons a/c 17 June 1872

General Chancery Docket: Bk.1, cont.

Washington Co.

General Chancery Docket: Bk. 1, cont.

265 (495) Archie Nelson & Co. vs N.B. Johnson & Co. 21 June 1872

    (496) Winnie A. Fulton & G.A. Fulton vs J.W. Parberry 29 June

266 (497) Richard Burdett vs George P. Beirne et alll persons 1 July (Oct.1874, deposition of G. Andrews & copy of will of Andrew Beirne filed. Petetion of Miss Nancy McFarland filed.)

    (498) W.E. Hunt vs W.W. Robinson adm. & a/c 8 July 1872

267 (499) Evansville National Bank et al vs E.J. & Mat F. Johnson 8 July

    (500) T.M. Shanahan vs Margaret Roach, exec. et al 10 July 1872

268 (501) H.S. Buckner vs Math. F. Johnson et al 10 July 1872

    (502) Jos. Hay & Co. vs Johnson & Shelby (W.H. & Ellen Johnson, Thos. Shelby & Bettie Shelby)

269 (503) C.L. & R.W. Gibbs vs D.B. O'Bannon 11 July 1872

    (504) W.L. Jackson adm. vs R.G. Sims adm. et al 23 July 1872

270 (505) Bettie H. Nelson vs T. Greany & L.T. Webber 24 July, 1872

    (506) J.L. McNeily vs J.P. Ball et al 8 Aug. 1872

271 (507) " " " " " " " 9 " " (ProConfesso /Ball, Lucas, Berry, Jewell, Harrison, Winslow
    (508) J.L. McNeily vs J.D. Welles, Jr. & Jas Ball et al 13 Aug

272 (509) Saml. C. Harbison et al vs E.G. Booth 19 Aug. 1872

    (510) Richard Ten Broeck et al vs John T. Courtney et al 29 Aug

273 (511) Julius J. Lingsfield vs J.W. Murphy 5 Sept. 1872

    (512) Yeatman & Co. vs H.C. Miller 14 Oct. 1872

274 (513) Jno. Chaffe & Bro. vs Jno. S. Fisher et al 18 Oct. 1872

    (514) Board of Levee Comm. for the counties of Bolivar, Wash., Issaqueena vs all persons 24 Oct. 1872

275 (515) Mary Clark vs Jno. Clark 26 Oct. 1872

    (516) Yeatman & Co. vs H.C. Miller 16 Nov. 1872

Washington Co.Ms.

General Chancery Docket: Bk.1,cont.

P.276:(517) S.W.Ferguson vs Fulton & Childs 18 Nov.1872
( ) Entry marked error

277:(518) Napoleon Jourdan vs Lydia Jourden 20 Nov.1872
(519) Nelson Trugg & Co. vs Alfred Swansey 29 Nov. 1872

278:(520) Glen Augustis vs George Gourville 3 Dec.1872
(521) Rachel Dawsey vs John Dawsey 9 Dec.1872

279:(522) E.Bourges vs Arkansas City & Grenada Rail Road Co.,et al 10 Dec.1872
(523) Lydia Hollis vs Alfred Hollis 13 Dec.1872 (Subp. sent to Bolivar Co.Ms.)

280:(524) Robert Davis vs Henry Barrett & Catherine Barrett 13 Dec.1872
(525) J.A.Goldman vs Thomas Renshaw 14 Dec.1872

281:(526) Susan Addison vs Caleb Addison 17 Dec.1872
(527) Richardson & May vs Peter Haslen 20 Dec.1872

282:(528) Amanda Brown vs James Brown 21 Dec.1872
(529) William Gray vs Hester Gray 1 Jan.1873

283:(530) Eugene A.Robb vs Thomas Briscoe,et al 4 Jan. 1873
(531) G.W.&D.T.Mouras (Momas?) vs S.F.White,et al 9 Jan. 1873

284:(532) Bank of Ky.,et al vs M.F.Johnson,et al 16 Jan. 1873

285:(533) W.A.Everman vs J.R.Cox, et al 16 Jan.1873 Cont. in Case #319.
(534) M.Ginsburger & Co. vs Dred Newsom & N.D. Skinner 16 Jan.1873

286:(535) E.G.Peyton vs Wm.Davis, et al 8 Feb.1873
(536) Lunelzy Standard & wife vs O.C.Rives & wife 17 Jan.1873

287:(537) Julius Lengsfield, Adm. vs Thomas Key & Merr- edith Houston. J.Lengsfield was Admin. of J.A.Goldman 18 Jan.1873
(538) Eliza Keone vs Emma Eastin, et al 20 Jan. 1873

288:(539) John Hanway vs Momas ------(Mournas?) Jan.1873
(540) Jane David & Catherine Murlell vs George W. Offult, Exec. 28 Jan. 1873

Page 51
Washington Co.

General Chancery Docket: Bk. 1, cont.

289 (541) Coote Lombard vs All Persons a/c 2 Feb.1873

     (542) Sallie White vs Abe White 6 Feb.1873

290 (543) Everman & Co. vs Lewis Thomas et al 4 Mar.1873

     (544)   "   " "   " S. Wilzinski et al 17 Mar.1873
            (cont. p. 315)

291 (545) & (601) John Williams & Sons & Thomas C. Ballou vs
            Winston E. West 14 Mar.1873

     (546) M.E.Hawes vs J.D. Jewell et al 22 Mar.1873

292 (547) A continuation of # (463) on page 249, now listed as
            Thos. G. Walcott vs C.S. Whitcomb et al. First entry
            on this page 27 Apr. 1873

293 (514) A contin. of #(514) from Page 274

     (547) S.T.Bay vs J.A.C. Shroder 27 Mar.1873

294 (548) C.W.Lewis vs O.D. Thomas 10 Apr.1873

     (549) Lenord Richardson vs John B. Cole 11 Apr.1873

295 (550) Eliza B. Emmons vs W.G. Holder 11 Apr. 1873

     (551) S.W.Ferguson vs Minnie A. And G.A.Fulton 21 Apr.1873

296 (552) Ellen. M. Johnson vs Peter Taylor et al 30 Apr.1873

     (553) Wortham and Kirk vs Bd. of Supervisors of Wash. Co. 29 Apr

297 (554) Ellen M. Johnson vs Peter Taylor et al 30 Apr.1873

     (555) C.A.Huntington vs J.W.Harrow & Stevenson Archer 31 May
            (Subp. to Jas. Archer in Jefferson Co.)

298 (556) Lucy V. Semple vs J.M.Howell et al 4 June
            (Power of Atty. to Farish from Thomas)

     (514) Cont. of #(514) from page 274

299 (557) Jno. W.Harrow vs D.B.Bell & L.T. Webber 23 June 1873

300 (557½) H.W.Foot et al vs E.M.Barwick et al 14 July 1873

     (558) Andrew B. Carson adm. & a/c vs Stevenson Archer Trust.
            16 July 1873 (Subp. to Hinds Co. for M.E.Richardson)

Washington Co.

General Chancery Docket: Bk.1, cont.

P. 301:(560) E.T.Bainbridge vs John R.Woodburn, et al
3 Sept.1873 - (Subp. for D.B.Bell,Bell &
John H.Nelson to Wash.Co.Ms. Subp. to E.
Richardson...Hinds Co.)

302:(561) Jacob Alexander and William Marshall vs J.P.
Ball 17 Sept.1873 (Subp. for Ball sent to
State Penitentiary at Jackson.)
(562) J.C.Febiger,Jr. vs Washington Jackson 26 Sept.

303:(563) E.Richardson vs John Boyd,et al 27 Sept.1873
(564) Union Bank of La.,et al vs Ann D.Halsey
13 Oct.1873

304:(565) Rucks and Scott vs Joe Wright 16 Oct.1873
(566) J.W.Piles, Superintendant of Education vs
Marshall Burdett 16 Oct.1873

305:(567) Emily Black vs Moses Black 24 Oct.1873
(568) Everman & Co. vs C.W.Standard,et al 17 Nov.

306:(569) William B.Wheatley, et ux Emma N.Wheatley
vs Tim O'Connor & Patrick McKeon 21 Nov.1873
(570) L.Picard vs Chas.Scott,et al 24 Nov.1873
(Subp. returned on Thos.J.Smith,S.G.Worthing-
ton, ------ Worthington, Chas.Scott)

307:(571) D.Morris,Trustee vs James Howard 26 Nov.1873
(572) Board of Levee Comm.vs Thomas Barnard 26 Nov.
1873.(Depositions of Helen Barnard filed.)

308:(573) Richard A.O'Hea vs H.H.Elliott,et al 1 Dec.
(574) C.W.Lewis vs Isaac Moore

309:(532) Bank of Ky., cont. from page 284
(514) Levee Bd., cont. from pgs.274,293,298.

310:(575) S.Picard vs Wm.Porterfield 9 Dec.1873
(576) Sallie West vs B.Cahn,et al 10 Dec.1873
(Mahala Scott,B.Cahn witnesses)

311:(577) L.Wilczinski & Co. vs Edward Dixon,et al
11 Dec.1873

Washington Co.

General Chancery Docket: Bk. L, cont.

311 (578) D. Hicks vs Granville & Betsy Norman 13 Dec. 1873

312 (579) Nelson, Trigg, & Co. vs Silas Iverson et al 27 Dec. 1873

    (580) O. Winslow, Clerk vs John D. Werles, et al 27 Dec. 1873

313 (581) Katie H. Stone et al vs Greenville, Columbus & Birmingham Rail Road Co. 29 Dec. 1873

    (440) Cont. from pg. 237 Everman & Co. vs W.N. Johnson (Depositions taken from G.W. Thomas in Madison Co., others from Hinds, Neshoba Cos.)

314 (449) Cont. from pg. 242 (First date on this page May 7, 1874. Order revising cause in names of M. Georgie Miller, adm.) Original suit: John A. Miller vs N.T. Nelson et al

    (349) Cont. S.W. Ferguson adm. vs Wm. Warren on p. 191

315 (459) Cont. from pg. 247: Joseph Hart et al vs Mary A. Hinds

    (544) Cont. from pg. 290: Everman & Co. vs L. Wilczenski

316 (319) Cont. from p. 285: S. Drabelle et al vs Cox & Everman

    (533½) W.A. Everman vs J.R. Cox

    (514) Board of Levee Comm. vs All Person etc. cont. from p. 309

317 (298) Hewit Norton & Co. vs A.J. Phelps et al (from p. 288)

    (539) John Hanway vs Thos. Greany et al 13 Jan. 1875 (Dep. of Jno. Hanway - Cert. copy of final a/c of Mary Hanway, adm. of B. Hanway dec. filed, motion to dismiss as to Jas. & Mary Robertshaw filed. Pro Confesso agst. Thos. Greany filed.

318 (476½) (From p. 255) Will H. Stephens vs E.J. & R.S. Cooper adm. of H.R. Merchant decd.

P. 54, Wash. Co.

List of Early Lawyers and Law Firms in Washington Co.

Yerger & Rucks
R.L.Dixon
A.F.Smith
W.C. & A.K. Smedes
Robards
Smedes & Robards
Nugent
Smith & Nugent
Brooke
H.C.Dunlap
F. & L.B.Valliant
Marshall & Miller
Dixon & Percy
R.S. & C.L.Buck
Yerger, Rucks, & Valliant (1860)
Nelson & Valliant
W.Yerger
A.C.Burwell & Cook
W.R.Trigg & Nelson
G.V.Moody
Moody & Baldwin
Harris & Harris
Clark & Montgomery
Morehead & Trigg
Reed & Jones
Walter & Scruggs
S.Ferguson
Jno. H.Nelson
Paxton
Stith Upshaw
Falconer
W.& J.R.Yerger
W.A.Percy
W. & J.K. Yerger, W.Yerger,Jr.
E.J.Bowers
Winchester
Mac Leman
T.A. & M.M.Marshall
Buck & Clark
Trigg & Buckner
Phelps
McNeely
Scarborough
Jeffords & Harris
Chas. W.Clarke
Clarke & Huggins
Danl. W.Adams
Huggins & Skinner
Foot & Foot
Wm.G.Phelps
Clarke & Shields
Y.Baker

Page 55, Wash. Co. Ms

Marriage Records, Book "A" White

	Groom	Bride	Date issued	Date returned
P.2.	Christopher Meade to Elizabeth Julia Hanway			8 Sept. 1891
3.	W.G. Jaynes (Jaquse?) to Maude J. Weber			18 May "
4.	Sam Blum	" Ruth Stein	2 June	3 June "
5.	J.J. Gibbs	" Miss L.A. Rossman	8 "	9 " "
6.	Henry Gottlich	" Etta Orgler	25 "	28 " "
7.	S. Davidow	" Freida Cohn	18 July	30 July "
8.	Joseph Kanatser*	" B.E. Jeter	27 Aug.	30 Aug. "
9.	W.W. Wiles, Jr.	" Lizzie C. Daniel	2 Sept.	10 Sept "
10.	R.T. Lamberson	" Mrs. T.T. Barrett		18 " "
11.	J.B. Harrison	" Miss Sarah C. Sutton	22 Sept.	23 " "
12.	H.C. Goldman	" Jennette Lemle (?)	26 "	27 " "
13.	James M. Rushing	" Miss Lenora Arnold	20 Oct.	21 Oct "
14.	Charles VanVecoven*	" Miss Pricilla Arnold		29 " "
15.	W.H. Cummings	" Miss L.J. Haring	29 Oct.	16 Nov. "
16.	A. Shaffer	" Miss Mattie Harden	10 Nov.	10 " "
17.	J.G. Webb	" Miss Carrie J. Worthington		25 " "
18.	Charles Axman	" Mrs. Rebecca L. Robinson		28 " "
19.	John Reed Pearson	" Miss Fannie M. Worthington		10 Dec "
20.	Sol Hahn	" " Rosa Hirsch	22 Dec.	22 " "
21.	R.E. Vannamer*	" " Mattie Murgee	1 Jan.	6 Jan 1892
22.	R.P. Williamson	" Miss F. Ida Lacey	25 Jan	27 " "
23.	C.F. Coursan (?)	" Geneiva Morgan	Certificate unsigned	
24.	L. Miller Brickell (Brickwell) to Minnie C. Harrison			2 Feb. "
25.	J.R. Porter	" Mrs. W.D. Burus	28 Jan.	28 Jan. "
26.	Alphonse Moyse	" Ms Belle S. Vexter*	Certificate unsigned	
27.	Blank			
28.	Alphonse Moyse	" Miss Belle S. Hexter*	22 Feb.	
29.	J.B Clarke	" " Abby Mayfield	28 Mar	28 Mar "
30.	Joseph N. Ring	" Miss Lura Coffall (Lena Caffall)		20 Apr. "
31.	E.W. Miller	" Miss Elizabeth Hood	1 June	2 June "
32.	Josuah Ede	" Nina Vannerman		20 July "
33.	Ephraim Brouson*	" Lula Armall		2 Aug. "
34.	Charles D. Bass	" L.F. Grunwell*		28 July "
35.	Lee Flouacher*	" Miss Josie Cahn	9 Sept	11 Sept "
36.	Charles LeSassur, Jr.	" " Elizabeth I. Rowan	27 Sept	28 " "
37.	R.P. Poole	" N.I. Brown	28 "	28 " "
38.	Jacob S. Weiss	" Miss Rachel Alexander	3 Oct.	4 Oct. "
39.	J.L. Johnson	" L.E. Day	12 "	12 " "
40.	Robert L. Willis	" Martha J. Weilenman	17 "	19 " "
41.	Luther Campbell	" Pinkey Graham	20 "	23 " "

Rest of Book "A" blank

* This hand written book was very difficult to read, so I am sure there are many mistakes in the spelling of the names. K.B.

Page 56, Wash. Co. Ms

Washington County Marriage Records
Circuit Clerk's Office
Marriage Record Book 1 White
Dec. 13, 1892 - Dec. 28, 1898

Page 1. C.J. Kelly to G. Lashley - Certificate returned 16 Dec. 1892
2. Sarah Isenbery to Joe N. Isenberg 16 " "
3. William H. Grammer to Mrs. Josephine Aiken 28 Sept 1893
4. Thomas H. Hood to Mary W. Sheilds 3 Jan. 1893
5. C.P. Neilson gives consent for Samuel P. Skinner to Marry Mary E. Neilson 9 " "
6. A.H. Bolling to P.C. Lankford, permission by Charles Axman 16 " "
7. Soloman Cahn to Sara Weinberg 24 " "
8. John Atkins to Miss Ella Coleman 18 Feb. "
9. R.M. Mullen to Miss Bertie Mullen 16 Mar. "
10. James L. Davis to Lula C. Davis 18 " "
11. W.B. Cannon to A.R. Clack 19 Apr. "
12. Stephenson Archer, Jr. to Miss Nat Lou Jackson 3 May "
13. J.S. Yerger to Sallie H. Ruck 3 " "
14. W.R. Eatherley to Annie P. Turner 10 " "
15. H.C. Brashear gives consent for Robert Wood McKee to marry Nanny Virginia Harrison 10 " "
16. L.A. Bell to Mrs. N.A. Lafoe 21 " "
17. Walter E. Oden to Gracis L. Walker 19 " "
18. Carneal Warfield to Mrs. Nannie B. Helm 1 June "
19. Philip Riter to Mary J. Jones 1 " "
20. W.W. Tillotson to Belle Oursler 5 " "
21. Emanuel B. Benjamin to Rachel Goldsmith 6 " "
22. Samuel C. Bull, Jr. by H.W. Ball to Miss Alice Archer 13 " "
23. P.B. Paterson to Parcena Lamb 24 Aug "
24. Leo Florentino to Mary Butera (certificate unreturned)
25. C.J. Serio to Rosa Cerniglia 10 Sept "
26. C. Burton to Minnie G. Roden signed by Sten Burton 13 " "
27. George McCaul to Addie Watt 28 " "
28. C.J. Lanerman to Mrs. Walter A. Lester 2 Oct "
29. E.C. Blackburn to Willie S. Scott 30 " "
30. J.A. (I) Waddell to L.S. Benson 12 Dec "
31. A.M. Quattlebaum to Annie Willie Harris 15 Nov. "
32. John L. Hebb to Mary Sterling 19 Dec. "
33. Peter R. Branton to Ada Quay Barry co-signed by J.E. Branton taken out 16 Jan 1894 not returned (see Page 45, below)
34. L.J. Parnell to Mattie A. Bromley 14 Dec. "
35. Arthur G. Dean to Georgianna Fryer 13 " "
36. Harvey Miller to Mary Valliant 19 " "
37. B.L. Gilman to Lou Lusk, permission by R.S. Rutherford 24 " "
38. J.T. Oglesby to Pauline Chisholm 25 " "
39. W.L. Lusk to Mrs. Kate Chisholm 26 " "

Wash. Co., Ms.

Marriage Record Book 1, cont

40.	M.B. Weiss (he signs his name as M.B. Wice, next section shows Vise) to Julia Hirsch	10 Jan. 1894
41.	C.E. Jordan to Mary E. Smith	9 " "
42.	Percy T. Hilzimn (?) to Georgia Lamb	15 " "
43.	S.S. Miller to Kate B. Morson	24 " "
44.	Charles Lewis to Mary E. Sanderling	17 " "
45.	J.E. Branton approves marriage of Peter R. Branton to Ida (Ada) Quay Barry. Ceremony performed by Rev. Stevenson Archer	16 " "
46.	Abe Green _____ gives perm. for Edgar B. Musgrove to marry Carrie Yerger (believe the date a mistake)	5 Feb. 1895
47.	Charles Pencoffs gives perm. for Robert Lemmon to m Jesse Elnora Law	4 Feb. 1894
48.	John T. Washington to Mary Kinchen	23 Feb. "
49.	W.G. Clouston to Annie Scott	7 Mar. "
50.	Waldemar Bauer to Lisette Schrick	20 " "
51.	Van Johnson to Alice Hunt Stone	1 Apr. "
52.	A.B. Calhoun to Eva K. Ingram; Mrs. M.C. Ingram gives her consent for her dau.	19 " "
53.	T.W. McCoy to Annie M. Archer	30 " "
54.	John Caswell gives perm. for Fred McCoy to m Ruth Caswell	7 May "
55.	Warren Davis to Annie Mae Warner	5 " "
56.	Houston B. Wood to Eugenia R. Lewis	16 " "
57.	_____ B. Cohn to Hattie Hirsch	8 July "
58.	John Stout to Katie Elnora Howard	3 " "
59.	Capt. John A. Webb to Willie Stewart	5 " "
60.	Julius C. Stokes to Carrie Rose Melton; W.C. Hope signs	8 " "
61.	Smith Harrod to Mrs. Emma Dunn	21 " "
62.	J.G. Larrine (Larriner, Larrinen) to B.A. Smith	15 Aug. "
63.	Robert C. Newman to Edna Earl Bronson	27 Aug. "
	Attached to page :Cold Lake, Washington Co. I, the mother of Edna Earl Bronson and the step-father Robert Livingston are willing for her to marry Robert C. Newman. Signed Mrs. Mattie Livingston	
64.	Ed G. Sawyers to Mattie B. Flowery	11 Sept "
65.	W.S. Myers to E.E. Jeter	10 Oct. "
66.	M. Gensburger signs for Louis Rotchild & Helen Grusberger	17 " "
67.	A.B. Willis to Phebbia Petman	14 " "
68.	R.J. Bishop to Sarah E. McKee	21 " "
69.	J. Rabun Jones to Alice Victor Bell	28 Nov. "
70.	Wm. W. Weeks to Miss Eva L. Barefield	16 Dec "
71.	Warner Friar to Miss Jennier Ingram	15 " "
72.	T.M. Lewellyn to Miss A.P. Coffman	19 " "
73.	David Horsch to Mrs. Mary Frnaces Kleiber	14 Jan. 1895
74.	F.C. Riechman to Mrs. Alice A. Smith	9 Feb. "
75.	Wm. L. Matthews to Mrs. Nannette Johnson	5 Mar "
76.	Harvey Miller signs for Mr. Van Buren Doddie & Miss Fay Shields	13 " "
77.	Alfred H. Stone signs for Edward C. Gilliland to Miss Jennie Smythe	13 " "
78.	T.W. Smart to Miss Lula Littleton	23 Apr. "

Marriage Record Book 1 cont.

79.	J. Scott signs for Joe Frame to Katie Jeter	1 May 1895
80.	Dan McLean signs for J.G. Lowrey to Miss Mattie Belle Baldwin	7 May "
81.	David Hagan to Miss Mollie Hatter	12 June "
82.	F.M. Tousiman to Hattie E. Eckford	31 July "
83.	W.R. Ball to Mrs. Mary Jane Passenger	16 " "
84.	Edgar Ellsworth Higgs to Anna Louise Salzizer	27 July "
85.	David Meyer to Mary G. Otis	30 " "
86.	E.E. Stevenson to Miss T.J. Jones (31 July-canceled) See next entry	
87.	T.J. Jones to Miss E.E. Stevenson	31 July "
88.	J.R. Green to Jennette Thompson	3 Aug "
89.	Willie R. Sims to Dottie C. Reed	15 " "
90.	Thomas J. Sem to Percie B. Wetherbee	18 Sept "
91.	F.W. Riggs to Ellen G. Trigg	20 Oct. "
92.	Frank M. Pepper to Edna Burton	10 Sept "
93.	A.L. Ellis signs for Eli Ellis to Dollie Boon	30 July "
94.	H.J. Jones to Neta Beardslee	10 Oct "
95.	J.F. Riviere signs for Thos. F. Dawson to Miss Margaret L. Sommers	28 Oct. "
96.	B.P. Floyd to Dillie May Morgan	30 " "
97.	Blank	
98.	J.H. Kieth to Mrs. Emma Patterson	31 " "
99.	John A. Gorman to Martha E. Lyons	3 Oct. "
100.	A.H. Rabhun to Nellie Ragland	5 Nov "
101.	Archer Williamson to Birdie Wise	12 " "
102.	J.H. Emerson to Minnie Davison	12 " "
103.	Joseph Uhl signs for Fred W. Gambal & Anna Kreger	20 " "
104.	F.J. White to Lucy A. Hammons	24 Dec. "
105.	Harley Metcalfe to Sallie Terry Jeffries	8 Jan. 1896
106.	E.M. Jordan signs for Mr. P.L. Mann & Nannie R. Banks	15 " "
107.	T.A. Burford to Katie E. Willis	15 Jan. "
108.	J.L. Lawler to L.J. Oursler	16 " "
109.	Sam Jacobs to Sara Genseberger	29 " "
110.	W.B. Aiken to Carrie Perry	29 " "
111.	Harry C. Robinson to Marian Dunn	12 Feb. "
112.	T.W. Tarum to Cora Pender	19 " "
113.	Geo. F. Phillips to Bessie Love	20 " "
114.	T.B. Van Norman to Emma H. Wheat	3 Mar. "
115.	O.S. Yerger to Florence Burton	16 Apr. "
116.	R.C. Garnett to Georgie Bookout	22 Apr. "
117.	Frank Oswald Reinhold to Della Elizabeth Dan	23 May "
118.	B.F. Wasson signs for R.L. Ratliff & Mrs. R.C. Matthews	15 June "
119.	Marks Eckstone signs for Alfred Holman & Clara Eckstone	24 " "
120.	J.A. Shall signs for Alfred Holt Stone & Mary Bailey Ireys	25 " "
121.	J.W. Bridges to Mamie C.A. Gorman	8 July "
122.	Canceled on top: M.P. Sturdivant to Miss Margaret Campbell Love (see below 126) on bottom reads: Frank C McCleish to Lillian May Buchanan	3 Sept "

RECORD OF WILLS - 1   Washington County, Ms.

P. 1: Adm. Bond; Henry Dawson, Andrew Knox, John G. Cocks, Wm. L. Scott, Abram F. Smith, all of Wash. Co., Ms. Est. of Rich. J. Hunley, decd. 1839+

P. 2. Adm. Bond; Charles Turnbull, Wm. W. Collins, Thos. W. Endecott. Est. of James Burnes, decd. 27 Dec. 1839+

P. (3: April Term 1840: Will of H.R. Dulaney, decd. (Written
  (4 29 Oct, 1825)
  (5 Henry Rojier Dulaney of Shutes Hill, Fairfax Co., Va.
      names: Dau. Rebecca to receive residence called "Sherters Hill" in Fairfax, Va., a cousin, the late Lady Hunter of England: States that his wife and daughter, Gertrude, are buried at "Sherters Hill": requests that Rebecca's husband take the name Henry Rozier Dulaney: Further states that he is great grandson of Daniel Dulaney, Esq. of Maryland, eldest son of Daniel Dulaney, Esq. ofag. a je je(?);
      Also has a son Grafton Shelton Dulaney, 2 brothers, Alfred and Benjamin, and sisters whmm he does not name: appoints Henry Dangorefield of Alexandrea, John P. Dulaney of Va., Grafton S. Dulaney of Baltimore, Eanora Dangerfield of Alexandria, Arthur Morson of Fredricksburg, Va., John A. Carter of Va. guardian of child Rebecca and of Grafton, and to serve as exec.
      Witnessed: Charles Murray, E,L, Carter, E. Generis
      Admitted for Probate: 17 June 1839 (Va.) Entered in Washington Co., Ms. 27 Apr. 1840

P.6,7; Will of John Turnbull, admitted at Nov. Term 1840
   8   Names: wife, Mary Ann; 2 brothers, Frederick G. & Charles; 2 ½ brothers William B. Turnbull and Robert J. Turnbull.
       Dated: Aug. 1837
       Probated: 23 Nov. 1840
       (Ed. In Probate Records; Andrew Turnbull is his son)

P. 8,9: Adm. Bond: William W. Collins, William L. Scott, Philip A. Cocks, John G. Cocks post $25,000. bond; William W. Collins app. guardian of Louisiana Cocke
        Entered 23 Nov. 1840

P.9,10; Will of John C. Miller, written at age 36 on 14 Sept. 1836:
   11   Admitted March Term 1841:
        Leaves the house he lives in in Georgetown, Ky. to his wife (unnamed); a dau. Agnes F. Miller, brother Harvey Miller; Exec. Harvey Miller
        Codicil (May Court 1840) (Written 2 May 1840)
        States that he now has a dau. Laura, and that he now has a plantation in Miss.

+: Dates documents were admitted

Washington Co.Ms.
RECORDS OF WILLS - 1

P.12,13: March Term 1841
Will: Francis Penrice of Wash.Co.Ms.
Wife,Elizabeth Penrice; Youngest dau.Susan E.Penrice; son,John L.(S.?)Penrice; granddau.Merian Aurora Collins; other children - William J; Cordelia A; Joseph H; Francis R. Appoints William L.Penrice,Francis R.Penrice, and Francis Smith,Exec.
Written: 26 Dec.1837
Wit: Thomas James, Thomas P.Boyd,William Boys
(Ed."Papers of Wash.Co.Hist.Soc."states that the Penrice's were kin to the Prince's)

P.14: Adm.Bond: James B.Jackson,Frederick P.Plant.
Est. of Samuel W.Sullivan, decd. of Claib.Co.Ms.
Dated 26 Apr.1841

P.15: Oct. Term 1841
Will of Augustus B.Faust,decd. of Wash.Co.Ms. names Sarah S.Faust,Adm. (Will is not recorded here)

Oct. Term 1841
Jane H.Miller,widow of decd.John C.Miller, late of Wash. Co.Ms, renounces all claims to terms of will and elects to take a dower instead.
Document dated 20 Mar.1841 (She appeared in Ky.24 Mar. 1841)

P.16: Dec. Term 1841:
Est. of James B.Maulding,decd. William R.Jones appt. Adm.

P.16,17:Dec.1841
Vicksburg: John Turnbull(Principal) and Andrew Turnbull (security) - promissory note to W.W.Frazier,Esq.
Several transactions follow between the above.

P.18,19: One of the transactions quoted from p.16,17, addressed to Robert J.Turnbull,Esq. at the counting Room of Samuel Donaldson,New York/
More loans negotiated, 1 co-signed John Turnbull,F.G. Turnbull.

P.20: Adm.Bond:for Est. of Alfred Cox,decd: Philip A. Cocks,John G.Cocks,David F.Blackburn of Wash.Co.Ms.
28 Feb.1842

P.21,22: Feb.Term 1842:
Will of Frances R.Kershaw,decd.(widow) State of S.C. Charleston: Names Dau. - Mrs. Ann Claiborne; son - Thomas Kershaw of Princeton,Wash.Co.Ms; leaves land in Union Dist. to children of John Kershaw; names a friend Mr.James Fife of Charleston; states "wife of son Thomas is Mary Jane";names Mrs.Newman Kershaw,widow of her late son-in-law Newman Kershaw - his children - Fanny,Charles, Henry,Mary,Emeline,Mattie.

RECORD OF WILLS - 1　　　　　　　　　　Washington County, Ms.

       Will of Frances R. Kershaw, cont.
       Names George Kershaw of Union Didt, S.C. (does not exp.
       the relationship); Robert Barnwell & Edward Barnwell, sons
       of Rev. Wm. H. Barnwell.
       Exec; James Fife of Charleston, S.C.
       Wit: Thos. D. Condy, Thos. Y. Simms, J.D. Dawson
       Written: 4 Oct 1840
       Codicil: to Charles Kershaw Robertson, son of Alexander
       Robertson of Charleston, S.C. 30 Oct 1840
       Probated: S.C. 15 Sept. 1841

P.23,24: March Term 1842
       Will: Thomas G. Percy, Decd.
       Probated 1 Nov 1841, Huntsville, Madison Co., Ala.
       Names: wife Maria Percy exec. and friend & relation
       Nathaniel A. Ware co-exec.
       States he has children but does not name them. Has a
       plantation in Washington Co. Ms.
       Written: 1 Nov 1832

P.24,25: Adm. Bond: Est. of Mrs. Frances R. Kershaw; John P.
       Cunningham, Anne Claiborne, by her attorney D.F. Blackburn
       June Tr. 1842

P.25: Adm. Bond: Est. of Richard L. Howel, decd.: Charles
       Turnbull & Council Bass. Approved 27 June 1842

P.26: Adm. Bond Est. John Stow, decd: Council Bass & Charles
       Turnbull
       27 June 1842

P.27,28: August 1842
       Adm. Bond: Est Samuel Tanner, decd. John H. Blanton,
       Charles Turnbull of Wash. Co. Ms.

P.28,29: Guardianship: _____ Thompkins has guardian George N.
       Parks, & Thomas Parks app. (all pertinent data blanks)
       Sept Term 1842

P.29,30: Adm. Bond: Est Wm. H. Dromgoole, decd.: Sarah (Sally)
       Dromgoole, exec., William Jas. Penrice, David I. Briggs,
       Robert J. Turnbull, adm.
       6 Sept. 1842

P.31: Nov. Term 1842
       Adm. Bond: Est. of John G. Penrice, decd.: David F.
       Blackburn, Willliam Hunt, John G. Cock of Wash. Co. Ms
       26 Dec. 1842

P.32: Nov Term 1842
       Adm. Bond: Est. of Daniel C. Page, decd.: Thomas I. Likens,
       Thomas Grimes of Wash. Co. Ms
       28 Nov 1842

RECORD OF WILLS - 1   Washington County, Ms.

p.33:   Philip A. Cocks, adm of est Alfred Cocks, decd. Other
        adm. John G. Cocks, Abram F. Smith

p.34:   Dec. 1842
        Adm. Bond: Est. of Francis Penrice, decd.: $90,000
        bond posted for adm. William J. Penrice, Frances R.
        Penrice, Elizabeth Penrice, John R. Downing, Jno. L.
        Chapman, John M. Powell, Thomas W. Endecott

p.35:   Verbal Will of Wm. M^e B Slemons, overseer, made 9 Dec
        1842; Wit; Mc L. Evans & D.F. Blackburn at Peru Plantation;
        Filed: 12 Dec. 1842

p.35,36: Will of William Ley, decd. admitted Jan. Term 1843,
   37   Montgomery Co. Ala.
        Written July 1, 1840 :(William Ley was a resident of
        of Washington Co., Ms.)
        dau. Florida Ley
        Exec: William Henry Taylor & James Hunt Taylor of Mont-
        gomery Co. Ala. They are also to be Florida's guard.
        Wit: Albert G. Goodwin, George W. Hails, Eleanor S. Gilmer

p.38:   Inventory of John G. Penrice: 31 Dec 1842

p. 39: Guardianship: of Evan J. Harvey, Belinda Harvey, James
        R. Harvey of Wash. Co. Ms to Joseph W. Robertson - 1851

p.40:   Adm. Bond: Est. John M. Ross, decd: William B. Ross,
        Andrew Carson
        27 Feb 1843

p.41:   Feb Term 1843
        Will of Thomas Sellers, decd: of Wash. Co. Ms.
        Written 17 Dec. 1842 - Probated 27 Feb 1843
        Eldest son, Silas Sellers, son David Sellers, only surv.
        dau. Ann Hill, sons Benjamin Menus Sellers, Wrenna
        Breathette Sellers, Isaac Sellers.
        Exec: Isaac Sellers (son)
        Wit: William R. Cochran, Joseph Cordell, George N. Parks

p.42:   Guardianship of Susan E. Penrice of Wash. Co. to Robert
        A. Johnson
        28 Mar 1843

p.43:   Adm. Bond: Est. of James H. Harwood, decd.; Thomas Harwood,
        Thomas J. Likens, William J. Penrice
        23 May 1843

p.44:   Adm. Bond: Est. of James Garrett, decd.; William Myers,
        R.A. Johnson, T.J. Likens
        23 May 1843

RECORD OF WILLS - 1   Washington County, Ms.

p. 45: July Term 1843
        Adm. Bond: Est of Thomas Sellers; decd.: Isaac Sellers,
        Benjamin M. Sellers, Isaac C. Hill

p. 46: Adm. Bond: Est. of Wernna B. Sellers (Spelling difficult
        to read) decd: Isaac Sellers, Benjamin M. Sellars, Isaac
        C. Hill
        24 July 1843

p. 47: Guardianship of Emily, Cornelia, Thomas, William and
        Edwin Ruthman Seller, infant orphans of Wernna B. Sellers,
        decd. Isaac Sellers appointed.
        24 July 1843

p. 48: Sept 1843
        Adm. Bond: Est. of James J. Chaney, decd: Ann L. Chaney,
        William Rushing, Mordecai Powell. Appointed Ann Chaney
        Guardian to Wood S. & Margaret N. Chaney, infant orphans
        of James J. Chaney, decd.
        25 Sept 1843

p. 49: Adm. Bond: Est of John Whitten, Jr.: Ann L. Chaney,
        William Rushing, Mordecai Powell. Guardian of Melissa C.
        Whitten, infant orphan of John Whitten, Jr., is Ann L.
        Chaney. 25 Sept 1843

p. 50: Adm. Bond: Est of Francis Penrice: William J. Penrice
        25 Sept 1843

p. 51: Adm. Bond: Est of George M. Thompkins, decd: George N.
        Parks, Thomas Parks
        23 Oct 1843

p. 52: Nov Term 1843
   53   Will: John A. Rowan, decd. of Lynchburg, Va.
   54   Names: Mother, Elizabeth Rowan
                Sister, Martha E., wife of William Crawford & her
                    children
                   "   , Margaret A., Sarah J., Eliza M., Ester A.
                Wife, unnamed
        Exec: friends, Samuel Garland & George Wl Turner
        Written: 13 April 1841
        Wit: J. Garland, Edmund Richards, Wm. T. Smith, Thomas Wright
        Probated: 5 June 1843, Lynchburg, Va.
        Probated: 27 Nov. 1843, Washington Co., Ms.

        Susan A. Rowan, widow of John A. Rowan, late of Miss.,
        renounces claim to bequest & elects to take a dower share
        27 Sept 1843
        Wit: William Barr, George B. Kinkead, Jas. H. Woolfolk
        13 Nov 1843 Signed by Clerk of Court Isaac Worthington
        Also filed in Commonwealth of Kentucky, Court of Appeals
        of Superior Court

RECORD OF WILLS - 1   Washington County, Miss.

p. 54: Adm. Bond: Est. of James F. Miller, decd: Bond for
William H. Gay, Dennis Griffin, Orin Hill
25 Sept 1843

p. 55: Adm. Bond: Est. of John A. Rowan, decd: Samuel Garland,
Joseph H. Johnston, Shepherd Brown, James D. Ware $50,000
Bond: 25 Dec. 1843

p. 56: Adm. Bond: Est of Zacariah Jayne: Robert C. Dinwiddie,
57: Henry H. Morris, John C. Berry
25 Dec 1843

p. 58: Adm. Bond: Est Wm. B. Ross, decd: Andrew Carson, Samuel
Carson. Feb. Term 1844

p. 59: Adm. Bond: Est. of John M. Ross decd: Andrew Carson,
Samuel Carson. 26 Feb 1844

p. 59: March Term 1844
60: Will: Christopher L. Bennett, Washington County, Ms.
Written: 10 April 1843
Names: Dau. Charlotte H. Adams, wife of Henry A. Adams of
U.S. Navy
Gr.Dau. Rebecca L. Bennett
Nancy Nutt & Virginia Nutt, step-dau. of son Albert
G. Bennett to get land in Madison Co., Ms.
Dau. Margaret S. Bennett
Son-in-law Henry Turner
Exec: Albert G. Bennett & Margaret S. Bennett
Wit: Char. J. Seales, Geo. W.Henderson, D.S. Bloom, John
Handy
Probated: 25 Mar 1844

p. 61: April Term 1844
62: Will: Robert M. Allan of Charleston, S.C.
Names: Children, Sarah, Claudia, Mary,
Brother, Richard Allan
Sister, Mary Allston, Susan Harg
Exec: Bother Richard Allan, bro-in-law Andrew Turn-
bull; Friend Thomas D. Condy
Written: 20 Feb 1839
Wit: H.P.Daves, George Buist, W.S.Elliott
Probated: 9 Mar 1844, Charleston Dist., S.C.
20 Apr 1844, Washington County, Ms.

p. 63: Adm. Bond: Est. of Robert M. Allen, decd: Thomas L. Condy
of City of Charleston, S.C., William J.Bull of S.C.
10 Apr 1844

p. 64: May Term 1844
Suit of Susan A. Rowan vs Samuel Garland, exec. of est.
of John A. Rowan, decd.
27 May 1844

RECORDS OF WILLS - 1   Washington County, Miss.

p. 65: Adm. Bond: **Est of Davis Montgomery**, decd: Thomas H. Buckner, Philip B. Thompson, Elizabeth Montgomery
28 Oct 1844 (Bond $60,000)

p. 66: Adm. Bond: **Est. of Denton H. Valliant**, decd: Elihui Kil-
67:    patrick, Samuel Wothington
28 Oct 1844

p. 67: Guardianship of Elihue R. Valliant, Franklin Valliant,
68:    Martha E. Valliant, Jane C. Valliant, Levy (Lewy ?)
Valliant, infant orphans of Denton A. Valliant, decd.
of Washington Co. Ms. Names Elihue Kilpatrick as G.
28 Oct 1844

p. 68. Nov 1844
Adm. Bond: **Est. of William Barr**, decd: George M. Pinckard, Jas. H.D. Bonnaan, Frances Griffin

p. 69: Adm Bond: **Est. George W. Clark**, decd: McLin Evans, William C. Barrett, Felix G. Gamble
25 Nov 1844

p. 70: Noncupative Will of Charles Henry Mitan of Washington Co.
"became ill while staying at house of William G. Tutt".
died 24 Oct 1844 in presence of Stephen Morris and Charles Hilton.
Names: ½ brother William G. Tutt
       ½ sister Henrietta H. Boyd (full sister to William G. Tutt)
Placed in writing 15 Nov 1844
Probated: 26 Nov 1844

p. 71: Est. of Thomas Infram, decd: Alfred G. Carter gives Power of Atty. to Endecott to sign as security to adm. William O. Chilton, exec.
14 Nov 1844

p. 72: Adm Bond: **Est. of John B. Holt**, decd. of Washington Co.
John R. Holt, Thomas J. Likens, John P. Cunningham
25 Dec 1844

p. 73: Adm. Bond: **Est. William B. Rucker**, decd.: Sarah H. Rucker,
74:    Abram F. Smith, Felix G. Gamble
28 Apr 1845

p. 75: Adm Bond: **Est. of James Phelps**, decd of Wash. Co. Ms
Thomas Bodley, Edward B. Church, A.W. McAllister
28 Apr 1845

p. 76: Nov 1845
Will: George (x) Downing "late of the town of Frankfort," now resident of state of Miss.
Partnership with E.P. Johnson. Names a brother John Downing; Mother - unnamed; decd. brother James Downing's children's share to be held by friend John Payne of Scott Co. Ky.; Neice, Nancy Gibson; Ann Johnson dau of Willa

RECORDS OF WILLS - 1   Washington Co., Miss.

p. 76: (Will of George Downing, cont.) Viley
77: Elizabeth Williams, wife of George Williams; friend Mrs.
    Penelope H. Wingate; 2 sisters Elizabeth Cammeron, Nancy
    Gibson; children of sister Nelly Lockland, decd.
    Exec: John Payne of Scott Co., Ky.
    Wit: H. Wingate, Thos. Theobald, John T. Pendleton
    Written: 28 Sept 1841
    Probated: 21 July 1845 Scott Co. Ky
              25 Nov 1845 Washington Co., Ms.

p. 78: Adm. Bond: Est. of George Downing, decd: John Payne,
       Edward P. Johnson
       24 Nov 1845

p. 79: Adm Bond: Est of Philip A. Gilbert, decd: Thos. W. Endecott
       Montague Endecott, Robt. A. Johnson
       24 Nov 1845

p. 80: Jan. 1845
       John Downing refuses to accept interest in plantation
       jointly owned by George Downing, decd. & Edward P.
       Johnson.
       25 Dec. 1845

p. 80: Will: Matthew Flournoy, of Fayette Co., Ky
81:    Names: Dau. Betsy Julia Johnson to receive land left to
82:           her grandfather and sold to Matthew Flournoy
              Dau. Louisa E. Sanders to receive land sold by
              exec. of David Flournoy in Scott Co. Ky + 2 lots
              in Georgetown, Ky.
              Dau. Emily M. Ward
              Son C. Marcellus Flournoy
              Son Victor Moriam Flournoy
       States: he has land on Cumberland River in Caldwell Co.
       Mentions heirs of Francis Flournoy
       Exec: C. Marcellus Flournoy, Victor Marian Flournoy
       Written: 5 Dec 1840
       Wit: Waller Rodes, Tho. A. Russell
       Codicil: 6th Dec 1840 names dau-in-law Betsy Flournoy
       Probated: June 1842, Fayette Co. Ky
                 23 Feb 1846, Washington Co. Ms

p. 83: Adm Bond: Est. of Matthew Flournoy, decd: Victor M.
       Flournoy, Robert A. Johnson, John R. Viley
       25 Feb 1846

p. 84: Adm Bond: est of Andrew Sellers, decd: Isaac B. Beall,
       William H. Gay, Dennis Griffin by his agent Willis L.
       Robards
       23 Mar 1846

RECORDS OF WILLS - 1   Washington Co. Ms.

p. 85: <u>Adm Bond</u>: <u>Est William Frazier,</u> decd: John Fulton, Thomas
       J. Likens
       27 Apr 1846

p. 86: <u>Guardianship</u> of Philip G. Cocke app. to John G. Cock<u>s</u>
       Adm. Bond: John G. Cocks, Philip A. Cock
       30 Mar 1846

p. 87: <u>Will</u>: <u>Henry T. Irish</u>, decd
             Adm: Jethro B. Bailey
       24 Nov 1846 admitted for Probate

p. 88: Henry T. Irish of New Port, R.I. appoints Jethro B.
   89   Bailey of New Orleans, La. and William Sillers of Port
   90   Gibson, Ms. exec. of his estate. (he owned @2000 acres
   91   called "Mound Plantation" in Washington Co. Ms: Also
        had land in Copiah Co., Carroll Co. Tallahatchie, Choctaw,
        Yallabusha Co. Ms & Bolivar Co. Ms.
        (Mound Plantation was Sec. 17 & 18; 5/8 of 19; ½ of 30
        tshp 19, rg. 8w) Asks that William Sillers be attorney;
        appoints Joseph I. Bailey of Newport, R.I. exec. of R.I.
        estate;
        Names: wife Hannah Mary Irish
               children (unnamed)
               decd. brother George Irish has dau. Josephine Irish
               of whom he is guardian
               decd. brother John Irish
        Written: 25 May 1846
        Wit: W.S.Purnell, A. Gilkey, J.B. Thrasher
        Probated Wash. Co. Ms 24 Nov 1846

p. 92: <u>Guardianship of Andrew J. H. Crow</u>, by Green S. McCarroll
       Andrew is infant child of Henry Crow, decd.
       28 Dec 1846

p. 93: <u>Adm Bond</u>: <u>Est William B. Bruise</u>, decd: Robert T. Davidson
       Francis Griffin
       25 Jan 1847

p. 94: <u>Will: Patterson L. Bain</u> of Frankford, Franklin Co. Ky.
       Names: son William E. Bain
              Thomas T. Theobald & wife Sarah W. Theobald and
              their dau. Adelia
       Exec: Thomas T. Theobald
       Wit: Thos. B. Stevenson of Frankford, Ky, A.C. Keene of
            Georgetown, Ky.
       Written: 7 Sept 1837
       Probated: 1 Mar 1847 Frankford, Ky
                 29 May 1847 Wash. Co. Ms

p. 96: <u>Adm Bond</u>: <u>Est Edward B. Church,</u> decd: Maria G. Church,
       Susan P. McCutchen
       28 Apr 1847

RECORD OF WILLS - 1

Washington Co.

p. 97: Guardianship of Catherine Church, William Church, Edward Church, infant children of Edward B. Church, decd; to Marcia G. Church
28 June 1847

p. 98: Guardianship of Alice E. Penrice of Washington County to John S. Penrice - Amelia Penrice security.

p. 99, 100: Adm. Bond: Est of Joseph Downing, decd: C.V. Rhoades, John L. Finklay
23 Aug 1847

p. 101: Sept Term 1847
Noncupative Will: Thomas Boyd, decd.
Wit: Joseph M. Brooks, Henry Houn
States he has 2 sisters (unnamed)
leaves rifle to Romades Poindexter
" horse to Wm. Ely
" watch to Thos. Poindexter
States he has 2 nephews (unnamed)

p. 101: Adm Bond: Est Thomas G. Percy: Charles B. Percy, James Rucks, Augustus W. McAllister ($50,000 bond)
25 Oct 1847

p. 102: Document states that Thomas G. Percy, decd. adm. was Maria Percy, who died 18 Aug 1847. Charles B. Percy app. adm
25 Oct 1847

p. 102, 103: Adm. Bond: Est of Stephen M. Jackson: Ann D. Jackson, John L. Findlay, William Mills
25 Oct 1847

p. 104: Guardianship of Milton G., Madison J., and Mary Frances Tidwell, infant children of Jesse Tidwell, decd. by Felix G. Gamble: Adm. F.G. Gamble, J.N. Sutton, Bawley Hudson
13 Dec 1847

p. 105: Adm. Bond: Est. of James B. Cottingin, decd: Thos. B. Shelby, Sheriff of Wash. Co. Ms.
5 Jan 1848

Adm Bond: Est William H. Green: Thomas B. Shelby
5 Jan 1848

p. 106: Adm Bond: Est of Samuel W. Adams: Robert M. Carter, A.G. Carter
4 Feb 1848

p. 107, 108: Estate of Florida Ley (infant under age of 14) of Montgomery Co. Ala.: William Taylor is her Guardian: Adm. William Taylor, Thos. Taylor, Jesse P. Taylor
29 Dec 1847

RECORDS OF WILLS - 1   Washington Co.Ms.

p.109:Adm.Bd:Est. of Frederick C.Clark,decd:Philip Cocks,
   111:A.F.Smith. Mar.1848

p.111:Adm.Bond:Est.Thomas Lacy,decd:Thomas Shelby -
      Sept.Term 1848

p.112:Adm.Bond: Est. of William H.Gay,decd.:Thomas Shelby
      Sheriff,Ad. Sept.1848.

p.112:Adm.Bond:Est. of William H.Pope,Decd: Charles B.
   113:Percy,Grant A.Bowen,John C.Clark.

p.114:Adm.Bond: Est. of Dennis Griffin: Abram F.Smith,
      Willis S.Robards,A.K.Smedes. 24 Jan.1849.

p.115:Adm.Bond: Est. of Joslin Ross,decd;Judge A.K.Smedes,
   116:Adm. signed by Andrew Carson,A.G.Carter. 28 Feb.1849

p.117:Adm.Bond: Est. of Macklin Evans: Mary A.Evans,Robert
      J.Fitz,James Prince,Alfred W.Mosley,Charles Turnbull.
      24 Sept. 1849.

p.118:Adm.Bond: Est. Alfred Langely,decd.

p.119:Adm.Bond:Est. of John Bucks:(Burk?) Eliza G.Burk,
      A.M.McAllister. 6 Dec.1849

p.120:Re Estate of George W.Man: examined witnesses Tenn.
   121:Man,S.S.,Louisa Cochran,Nancy G.Man,WilliamCochran
      of Tuscaloosa. 25 Aug.1849

p.121:Will of G.Man of Tuscaloosa,Ala
      Written: 7 Mar.1849
      Exec:Uncle Nicholas Perkins
           Brother Daniel P.Mann
      Wit:S.S.Louisa Cochran,G.E̅.Man,Nancy G.Man,William
           Cochran   Aug.1849

p.123:Adm.Bond:Est. of William Flagg,Decd.:Augustus Mc
      Allister,S.Theobald. 28 Jan.1850

p.124:Will of Starling Gorman of Pendleton Dist.S.C.
      "since 1812 of Perry Co.Ala;"son of Elijah & Mary
      Gorman and born a citizen of U.S......ill at house
      Donna Joseph Carbonaiflaza Viego in City of Havanna...
      Wit:J.W.Brown,William Chandler,Dr.Osgood,Wm.Johnson;
      Leaves land in Marengo Co.,Perry Co.Ala - Wash.Co.
      Ms. to brothers and sisters,only names the two youn-
      gest - Felix and Sarah.
      Written: 2 Aug.1839
      Recorded: 20 Sept.1840 in Marengo and Perry Cos.in Ala.
          "   : 27 Feb.1850 in Wash.Co.Ms.
      (Note: The brothers and sisters of Starling Gorman
      were: 1.Terrel, 2.Oliver, 3.Mary, 4.Artimecy,
      5.Elizabeth G., 6.Felix, 7.Sarah----Information
      taken from Public Notice in Vicksburg paper.)

RECORDS OF WILLS - 1   Washington Co. Ms

p. 127: Est of Eleanor Percy Lee
        Dec 1850

p. 128: Will: Jackson M. Ham
        Names: ½ sister Mary Ann Doyle (Dozer?) of Richmond, Ky
        Exec: Victor Fournoy (Flournoy)
        Probated 1850

p. 130: Guardianship of Robert H. Percy & William A. Percy, minor
        heirs of Thomas Percy, decd. G. is J. Walker Percy.
        Adm Bond: Charles B. Percy, Leroy P. Percy
        1850

p. 131: Est of Isaac Beall, decd:
        June Term 1850

p. 132: Est John W. Ward, decd:
        June Term 1850

p. 137: Adm Bond: Est of William B. Rucker, decd: Adm are Sarah
        H. Amos, formerly Sarah H. Rucker, William Amos her husband & John Cowden of Madison Parish, La.
        (Clerk states he made an error, John Cowden is from Ms.)
        28 Apr 1845

p. 139: Will of John W. Ward
        Asks Alonzo Lancaster to take his daughter Sarah Ann to
        a free state; States that no relative shall get 1 dime.
        Written: 5 July 1848
        Probated: 17 Feb 1850

p. 142: June Term 1850
        Est. of Isaac B. Beall, decd:

p. 143: Sept 1850
        Will: William M. Robertson
             Names: wife Elizabeth M. Robertson
             Written: 28 Oct 1847
             Prob: Sept 1850

p. 145: Adm Bond: Est James Johnson, decd: Guardian of James
        Ann Johnson, minor heir, is Isaac Worthington
        15 Nov 1850

p. 146: Est of Joseph C. Threkeld, decd
        1851

p. 147: Est of William Jenkins, decd; William W. Collins exec:
        1851

p. 149: Will: William H. Pope of Madison Co. Ala.
             Names: wife Frances Anne
                    my child (unnamed)
                    Brother, Leroy Pope, Jun. of Memphis, Tenn.
             Exec: Father-in-law Andrew Erwin of Bedford, Tenn
             Prob: 29 May 1848

RECORDS OF WILL - 1   Washington Co. Ms.

p. 153: Guardianship of Cartherine Williams and Edward Church, minor heirs of Edward B. Church, decd. to Maria I. Church.

p. 155: Will: William Jenkins of Chicot Co. Ark.
   Written: 31 Dec 1847
   Names: sister Frances Butler
          William W. Collins, Jr. Thomas Harwood
          William W. Collins, Sr. sole exec.
   States he is about 40 years old
   Wit: Theodora S. Alexander, Daniel H. Sessions
   Prob: 4 Jan 1848

p. 167: Will: Joseph B. Penrice
   Written: 28 June 1851
   Names: brother Thomas S. Penrice
          T.J. Likens dau. and "my" neice Catherine Likens
   Exec: "my relation" James Penrice of Wash. Co. Ms
   Probated: 26 Jan 1852

p. 167: Jan. Term 1852
   Adm. Bd: 26 Jan. 1852
   Isaac Roth, James Prince both of Wash. Co. Ms
   Estate of Matthew P. Carter, dec.

p. 168: Adm. Bd. 26 Jan 1852
   Adm. Isaac Roth
   Est. Green B. Whatley, dec. Intestate

p. 169: Adm. Bd. 26 Jan 1852
   Abram F. Smith, Philip A. Cocks of Wash. Co. Ms
   Est. of Thomas W. Endicott, dec.

p. 169: Adm. Bd. 26 Jan 1852
   James Prince, Adm.
   Est. of Joseph B. Penrice, dec.

RECORD OF WILLS - 1   Washington County, Miss.

p. 170: Special Term 6 July 1852
<u>Will of William R. Campbell Written 18 May 1849</u>
Probated 3 July 1852
Names: Wife - Margaret
       Daus. - unnamed
       sons - William & Joseph
       Exec. { Brother: George W. Campbell of New Orleans
              { Richard M. Campbell of Arkansas
              { Joseph Haugh of Ohio
       Atty. to be John J. Guion of Jackson, Ms.
       Wife's mother (unnamed) to be supported comfortably
       Wife's cousin Mary Bateman
Wit: A.K.Smedes, W.L.Robards, David Suggett

p. 173: <u>Adm. Bd.</u> $75,000 24 July 1852
Margaret Campbell, Adm.
<u>Estate of William R. Campbell</u>, dec.

p. 176: Nov. Term 1852
<u>Adm. Bd.</u> $25,000
<u>Est. of John A. Scott</u>, dec.
James S. Guingnard of Richland Dist. SC & W. Hampton
of Wash. Co. Ms. Adms.

p. 176: Dec. Term 1852
<u>Adm. Bd.</u> 27 Dec 1852
Charles L. Robards, Willia L. Robards, James H. Yerger,
all of Wash. Co. Ms
<u>Est. of John B. Everett</u>, dec.

p. 178: <u>Adm & Guardianship Bd.</u> $25,000 25 Apr. 1853
Gabriel. W. Robb (also sp. Rabb), Isaac C. Hill, William
Dodd:
G.W. Robb app. Guard. to Mary MacLin Evans of Wash. Co. Ms
Lewis Fillman, Justice of Peace in Issa. Co. Ms ack.
signature of Wm. Dodds & J.C. Hill: 28 Apr 1853

p. 179: June Sp. Term

RECORDS OF WILLS - 1   Washington Co., Ms.

p. 179: <u>Adm Bd.</u> 20 June 1853 to John H. Likens
        <u>Est. of T.J.Likens</u>, dec. Proof of Will

        <u>Will of T.J. Likens</u>, Washington Co. Ms. Written 19, Mar. 1853
        Names: dau. Kate Knox Likens
               Mother - Mariam Likens
               Nephew - Wm. Richardson Likens - now at West Point
               Niece - Myra Likens - dau. of bro. John Likens of Va.
               Wife - Endora
               Friend - Dr. J.E. Nicholson
               Leaves money to Winchester Presbyterian School
               States he has a plantation of Lake Jackson
               Owns "woodlands" jointly with G.W. Huntingdon,
               J.P. Cunningham, Joseph Cocks
               Has a partnership to buy land in Mexico with Charles
               Fallen
               Exec: Dr. David Blackburn of Carroll Parish, La.
                     Shepherd Brown formerly of Vicksburg
               Wit: A.F.Smith, J.E.Nicholson, W.B. Knox

p. 181: <u>Adm. Bd</u> $130,000 20 June 1853
        John H. Likens of Berkely C. Va. signed Wash. Co. Ms
        Shepherd Brown of Warren Co. Ms signed in New Orleans
        R.P.Shelby of Issa. Co. Ms signed Wash. Co. Ms
        <u>Est. of Thomas J. Likens</u>, dec.

p. 183: <u>Will of Joseph Haugh</u> Written 5 Oct 1852
        Probated 25 June 1853
        Gr. son: Joseph Millikin, son of John M. Millikin &
                 Mary G. Millikin
                 Lydia H. Kelsey now Taylor "Having raised her
                 from infancy" whose husband is dec.
        Only dau. - Mary G. Millikin
        Gr. Children - children of Mary G. and John Millikin;
                 J. Minor Millikin
                 Joseph   "
                 Mary Ella   "
                 Daniel   "

RECORD OF WILLS - 1   Washington Co., Ms.

   Cont. with Will of Joseph Hough:
   States he has propert in Hamilton Co. Ohio, Darke Co.
   and Butler Co. Ohio
   Exec: John M. Millikin and Mary G. Millikin
   Wit: C. Falconer, Josiah Scott, N.C. McFarland, Saml.
        Millikin
   (All 3 witnesses sign Butler Co. Ohio
   Recorded Wash. Co. Ms Sept 1853

p.186: Letters of Adm. to James T. Rucks
   Nov. 1853
   Est. of Daniel P. Marrs, dec.
   Adm. Bd. $20,000 signed by James T. Rucks, Henry Rucks,
   Wm. Yerger all of Wash. Co. Ms.

p.187: Adm Bd $40,000   28 Nov 1853
   Ann L. Robb, Wm. E. Bain of Wash. Co. Ms. signed by E.P.
   Johnson, Attorney in fact
   Est. of John H. Rabb, dec. Intestate

p. 189: Guardianship Bond to S.R. Dunn of Wash. Co. Ms for Betty
   Dunn, John N. Dunn, Thomas W. Dunn, Chapin H (?) Dunn,
   Samuel R. Dunn & Finlay M. Dunn
   Dec. 1853

p. 189: Adm. Bd. issued 22 May 1854 to Mary I. Jackson of Wash.
   Co. Ms.
   Est. of James B. Jackson, dec. Intestate
   Bond $50,000 signed by Mary I Jackson, Eliza Askew, Robt.
   W. Durfey all of Wash. Co. Ms. signed 24 Apr. 1854

p.189: Aug. Term 1854
   Est. of D.Y. Stampley of Wash. Co. Ms., dec. Intest.
   Adm Bd.: Charles L. Robards, Guignard Scott
   31 Aug, 1854

p. 192: Nov Term 1854
   Est. of Theodoric Jeffrey James, dec Intestate

RECORD OF WILLS - 1   Washington Co. Ms

p. 192: **Est of Theodoric J. James**, cont:
    Adm. Bd. signed by James Abell, Thomas V. James, E.C.
    James and Joseph G. James all of Wash. Co. Ms.
    Bond: $150,000

p. 194: **Petition: Est of Theodoric Edward Jackson**, a minor
    between 14 - 21, an orphan without father or mother,
    claims share of grandfather's Theodoric J. James's
    Est. in Wash. Co. Ms. Chooses as Guardian Uncle Joseph
    Gabriel James (Approval granted)
    Guard. Bond signed by: Joseph G. James, E.C.James,
    Theodoric T. James, James Abell all fo Wash. Co. Ms.
    Bond for $25,000.
    Nov. 28, 1854

p. 195: **Est. of Jeremiah S. Ward**, dec. Intestate
    Adm Bd: $12,000   27 Nov 1854
    Signed by W.E.Daniels, and A.W.McAllister of Wash. Co.Ms.

p. 196: **Est of Patrick Gary**, dec Intestate
    Nov. 1854
    A.W.McAllister appointed Adm.

p. 198: Dec. called Term   1854
    Est. of Hugh Barfield - Letters of Adm to Susan Barfield
    Bond: $16,000   11 Dec 1854
    Signed by Susan Barfield and Stephen Barfield of Wash.Co. Ms

p. 200: **Guardianship Bond**: signed by W.H.Lee, James H. Yerger,
    J.W. Percy; William Henry Lee appointed Guard. to Cath
    erine Sarah Lee, Nathaniel Ware Lee, Harry Percy Lee,
    John Monterey Lee of Wash. Co. Ms. 25 Dec. 1854

RECORD OF WILLS - 1   Washington Co. Ms.

p. 201: <u>Est. of James Prince</u>, dec. Intestate of Wash. Co. Ms.
    Letters of Adm. Charles L. Robards
    28 Nov 1854
    Adm. Bd. $18,000 signed by Charles L. Robards, A.F.
    Smith of Wash. Co. Ms.

p. 202: Est. of Eliza James, dec. Intestate
    Adm Bd $1500 22 Jan 1855
    Signed by James Abell and Thomas V. James

p. 203: <u>Will of John Peavie Cunningham</u> of Wash. Co. Ms.
    Written 5 May 1853 at Pass Christian, Harrison Co. Ms.
    Proven Wash. Co. Ms Jan 1855
    Names: "my sister" Mrs Mary Jane Kershaw
        "my bro." Richard M. Cunningham
        Exec: Thomas Kershaw of Harrison Co. Ms &
            Richard Cunningham of Charleston, SC
        Wit: J.P.Harrison, N.S. White, I.F. Roach

p. 204: <u>Est. of John P. Cunningham</u>
    Adm. Bd. $25,000 22 Jan 1855
    Signed by Thomas Kershaw and Richard Cunningham both
    of Wash. Co. Ms.

p. 205: March Term 1855
    <u>Est. of Burrell Fox</u>, dec Intestate
    N.J.Nelson, Adm ad colligendum
    Adm. Bd. signed by Newman J. Nelson, and Wm. Hunt,
    and M. Horwitz all of Wash. Co. Ms.
    Bond: $25,000 26 Mar 1855

p. 206: <u>Guardianship</u> to J.W. Percy of Nathan W. Lee, Harry P.
    Lee, J.M.Lee, minor heirs of Eleanor P. Lee, dec. 3 Apr.
    1855

RECORD OF WILLS - 1   Washington Co., Ms.

p. 207: <u>Guardianship Bond</u>: $50,000 2 Apr 1855
        Signed by J. Walker Percy, Grant A. Bowen, James H.
        Yerger all of Washington Co. Ms.
        J. Walker Percy appointed Guardian to Nathaniel W.
        Lee, Harry P. Lee, John M. Lee

p. 207: <u>Will of Wm. H. Lawson</u> of Wash. Co. Ms,"temporarily
        in city of Louisville, Ky."
        Wife: Frances Ann Lawson
        Children: Samuel, Frances, Wilhelmina
        Owns Plantation with William Hunt in Wash. Co. Ms.
        Exec: William Tompkins of Louisville, Ky.
        Written 19 Sept 1854
        Wit: S.C.Cox, J.A.Miller, T. Joyner

p. 208: <u>Adm. Bd.</u> $15,000 26 Feb 1855
        <u>Est. of William H. Lawson</u> dec.
        John L. Finlay, Wm. Hunt of Wash. Co. Ms to make Inv.

p. 209: <u>Proof of will</u> of Wm. H. Lawson

p. 209: <u>Adm .Bd.</u> $15,000 23 Apr 1855
        <u>Est. of J.R. Fields</u>, dec. Intestate
        Signed by James H. Yerger, James Rucks

p. 210: <u>Guardianship Bond</u>:$50,000 27 Mar 1854
        Signed by James Rucks, Arthur Rucks, Alex Yerger, James
        Yerger.
        James Rucks appointed Guardian to Maria Louisa Rucks,
        Henrietta Rucks, Marion Rucks, Lewis Taylor Rucks all
        of Wash. Co. Ms.

        <u>Petition of Guardianship</u> granted to James Rucks for
        Henrietta Rucks, ~~Marion Rucks~~ Lewis Taylor Rucks minor
        heirs of <u>Louisa Rucks, dec.</u>
        24 Apr 1855

RECORD OF WILLS - 1   Washington Co. Ms.

p. 212: **Will of Turner Joyner** OF Wash. Co. Ms.
      Requested that 3 "disinterested parties" evaluate his
      Plantation: i.e. Col Wade Hampton, Sr. of SC, E.P.
      Johnson, Sr. of Ky. & Isaac Worthington of Ms.
      Partner: Junius Ward
      Request that Junius War set free "my woman" Rachael
      Smith & her 2 sons William Henry and Harrison and
      give them $12,000.
      Names the following brothers and sisters:
            Eli Joyner of Halifax Co. NC
            Mary Whitehead   "   " "
            Amelia King of Ms.
            to children, if any, of bro. John Joyner
      "   "   " "   " SIS. Sally Harris
        "   "   of sister Elizabeth Harris
      Special provisions for Mary Whitehead for "taking
      care of my mother"
      Shot gun to George V. Ward
      Saddle and walking cane to J.W. Coll<u>e</u>ns
      Rifle to Wm. Summers
      An Involead (?) chain to Mrs. Junus Ward
      Exec and Adm: Junius Ward
      Written 6 Feb. 1855
      (No recording date listed)
      Wit: J.W. Coll<u>i</u>ns, Wm Summers, Jno. Butts

p. 213: **Will of John Fulton**
      Dau. Adelia, and Sarah Jane Fulton
      To Andrew Crow (relationship unexplained)
      Wit: SC Cox, Wm (X) Bradford
      No dates given of timewhen written or probated

p. 213: October Term 1855
      <u>Adm. Bd.</u> $200,000   22 Oct 1855
      <u>Est of Isaac Worthington,</u> dec Intestate
      Signed by Ann E. Worthington, adm. & William H. Worthing
      ton, Samuel Worthington, William A. Worthington

RECORD OF WILLS - 1   Washington Co. Ms.

p. 215: <u>Adm. Bd.</u> $120,000   27 Nov 1855
<u>Est. of Alfred G. Carter,</u> dec Intestate
Signed by Robert H. Carter, Elizabeth L. Carter,
Robert M. Carter, Alfred Z. Carter all of Wash. Co. Ms.

p. 216: <u>Petition</u> of E. L. Carter asking that court allow
Robert H. Carter act in her stead in settling estate
of her dec. husband A.G.Carter.

p. 217: <u>Will of Lewis K. Gish</u> of Wash. Co. Ms.
Written 8 Nov 1855
Probated 24 Dec 1855
Names: nephew Christopher Gish, son of bro. William
 "   Lewis Coffman son of sis. Nancy Coffman
sisters Elizabeth Graves, Mary Coffman, Sarah
Neal who had children, Susan Becie (?) Susan
Gish, sister-in-law who has children
Brother-in-laws Jacob Coffman, Henry Graves
Business Partner John L. Penrice
Exec: James Mitchell, Wm. Hunt, Wm. C. Blanton
Wit: John L. Finlay, Jno. S. Penrice, Chas. L. Robard

p. 219: <u>Adm. Bd</u> $20,000 24 Dec. 1855
<u>Est. of Lewis K. Gish</u>
Signed by J. Mitchell, W.C. Blanton, Wm. Hunt

p. 219: <u>Adm. Bd.</u>$25,000   25 Dec. 185<u>4</u> signed by Franklin Valiant and J.W.Percy
Guardianship Bd. for Frank Valiant to be G. to June
C.Valiant, and Leroy B. Valiant orphans of Wash. Co.

p. 220: <u>Est of Denton H. Valiant</u>, dec
24 Dec 185<u>4</u>, Guardianship Bond to Franklin Valiant
for June C. Valiant and Leroy B. Valiant minor heirs
of Denton H. Valiant, dec.

p. 221: <u>Guardianship Bd</u>: $10,000 25 Feb 1856 signed by

RECORD OF WILLS - 1   Washington Co. Ms.

p. 221:(cont.) William A. Percy & J. Walker Percy of Wash. Co.
        Ms. $10,000 25 Feb 1856
        Guardianship Bd of Wm. A. Percy as G. of Thomas G. Percy
        Ellen M. Percy, Josiah Percy, Charles Percy, Henrietta
        Percy, minor heirs of Charles B. Percy, dec.
        Issued 25 Feb 1856

p. 222: Adm. Bd. $2000 25 Feb 1856
        Est. of A.H. Obannion, dec. Intestate
        W.T. Wilson, James H. Yerger.

p. 223: Adm. Bd. 22 Feb 1856
        Est. R.H. Percy, dec. Intestate
        Adm. Wm. A. Percy

p. 225: Will of Isaac Worthington - non cupative - dec.
        Names: brothers Samuel, Elisha, W.W. Worthington
        Wife and eldest son unnamed

p. 225: Will of Andrew Sigourney Barker Written New Orleans
        May 20, 1839: Filed Wash. Co. Ms. 5 Sept 1846
        States he was born City of New York, now a citizen of
        New Orleans, La.; never married; Parents are Jacob
        Barker and Elizabeth Hazard both now of New Orleans
        Signed by E.A. Cannon, Judge in New Orleans, Judge.
        Proof of Will follows for 2 pages

p. 227:-Adm. Bd.: 28 July 1856
        Est. of James Cattin (Cottin) dec. Intestate
        Signed by James C. Yerger & Arthur Rucks

p. 229: Will of Patrick Garry of State of Arkansas
        Names: Father, John Garry
               Eldest Bro., Thomas Garry
               2 bro. Bernard and John
               Exec: Major Thomas D. Carneal of Cincinnati, Ohio
        Written 3 Jan 1852
        Wit: E.A. Meany, W. Nichols, S.H. Lilkins
        Codicil: "When last heard from, father and brothers
                 Thomas and John lived in Parish of Kilbrida
                 County of Meath Ireland and bro. Bernard
                 lived Parish of the Crones, Robinstown in
                 Ireland".
        No filing date

p. 229: Adm Bd $2500 28 July 1856
        Est. of Patrick Garry, dec.
        Signed by Augustus W. McAllister, C.M. Blanton of Wash. Co.

p. 230: Proof of Will of Patrick Gary

RECORD OF WILLS - 1   Washington Co. Ms.

p. 230: **Adm. Bd.** $500,000 28 Apr. 1856
        <u>Est. of Isaac Worthington</u>, dec.
        Signed by Ann E. Worthington, W.H. Worthington,
        Samuel Worthington, W.W. Worthington

p232:   <u>Will of John C. Swan</u>, dec. of Phillips Co. Ark.
        In good health but "about to expose myself to the Miss.
        River" names: "wife and three little children"
                    Wife; Pamelia B. Swan
                        Children; John Raliegh
                                  Mary Jane
                                  Frances Ann
        Adm. Wife
        Written 28 Nov 1843
        Filed Phillips Co. Ark, also Wash. Co. Ms Jan Term 1850
        Wit: Vol Routt, G.W. Rout, Wm. Rout, Thomas Rout, Cynthia
             Rout, James R. Rout, F.B. Collins, Davis Talbott,
             Douglas Saint, John C.O. Smith

p. 235: **Adm Bd.** $2000 22 Dec 1856
        <u>Est. of Jesse Moore</u>, dec. Intestate
        Signed by John L. Finlay & W.E. Daniels of Wash. Co. Ms.

p. 236: **Adm. Bd.** $2400 16 Dec 1856
        Guardianship to James W. Browder for Harris J. Fields,
        Henry C. Fields
        Bond signed by James W. Browder, of Wash. Co. Ms and
        O.C. Rives, and D.D. Jackson

p. 237: Guardianship Bond: 22 Dec 1856
        James W. Browder for Harris J. and Henry C. Fields
        minor heirs of Jesse R. Fields, dec.

p. 238: **Adm. Bd.** $10,000 26 Jan 1857
        <u>Est. of William T. Wilson</u>, dec. Intestate
        Signed by James Yerger, Arthur Rucks, George T. Blackburn

p. 239: Guardianship Bd. $2000 23 Feb 1857
        Signed by James Abell and N.J. Nelson
        Guardianship of Belvidere and Laura James
        (next document reads Bellinda) minor heirs of Eliza
        James, dec. James is appointed G.

p. 240: **Adm. Bd.** $80,000 23 May 1857
        <u>Est. of George G. Gregory</u>, dec. Intestate
        Signed by Pricilla W. Gregory and Samuel R. Dunn of
        Wash. Co. Ms.

p. 241: **Adm Bd**; $15000 25 May 1857
        <u>Est. of John J. Caughey</u>, dec. In testate
        Signed by Mary H. Caughey, John M. Batt, O.M. Blanton

p. 242: **Adm Bd.** $30,000 10 Aug 1857
        <u>Est. of Isaac Roth</u>, dec Intestate
        Signed by Jacob Roth, Charles Roth, Simon Katz

RECORD OF WILLS - 1   Washington Co. Ms.

p. 244: Adm Bd; $40,000 25 May 1857
         Est of J(blank) Jackson
         Guardianship of T.E. Jackson minor heir of J_____
         Jackson awarded to James Abell
         Signed by James Abell, J.V. James, John T. Courtney

p. 244: Adm and Guardianship Bd. $12,000 23 Feb 1857
         Est of John A. Scott, dec.
         Gingnard Scott is G of Calhoun Scott minor heir of
         John A. Scott
         Bond signed by Gingnard Scott, Calhoun Haile and John
         Haile all of Wash. Co. Ms.

p. 246: Adm. Bd : $80,000 23 Nov 1857
         Est of Theodoric J. James, Jr. dec.
         Signed by Thomas V. James, John James, James Abell

p. 247: Will of Joseph B. Botts (Batts)
         Written 26 Feb 1858
         No Probate Date
         Names: Brother Jno. M. Bott
                Sister Lucy J. Fenton
         Wit: Philip A. Schuylor, W.P. Montgomery, Wm. Montgomery

p.247:   Will of John Woodburn Madison, (Jefferson Co.) Ind.
         Names: wife Mary M. Woodburn
                daus: Ellen Shrewsberry, wife of Charles S.
                      Shrewsberry, to get land in Madison, Ind.
                      Mary Louisa Price "   " "   "   "
                      Cornelia Morton, wife of James Morton, gets
                      land in Madison, Ind.
                sons: John Rector Woodburn (has been educated)
                      Isaac Leonard   "   "about 11 yrs old at
                      this writing"
                Mentions land conveyed to him by John M. Price and
                wife but does not identify him as husband of of
                Mary Louisa.
                Mother, Ellen Woodburn at Upper Altore(?), Ill.
         Exec: Rev. Edward R. Ames of Indianapolis, Judge Stephen
               C. Stevens (Stephens) of Madison, Ind. and son
               John Rector Woodburn of Madison, Ind.
         Wit: Stephen C. Stephens, Charles W. Bassnett, John W.G
              Simrall
         Written 17 May 1849   Recorded 28 June 1858

p. 254: Adm Bd. $75,000 28 June 1858
         Est. John Woodburn, dec.
         Signed by John R. Woodburn, John L. Penrice, Wm. P.
         Montgomery all of Wash. Co. Ms.

p. 256: Adm. Bd $6000 28 June 1858
         Est. of James B. Montgomery, dec. Intestate
         Signed by Wm. P. Montgomery, and John L. Penrice

RECORD OF WILLS - 1   Washington Co., Ms.

p. 257: Copy of Will of Robert Woods
Written 1 Jan 1840   Filed 11 Feb 1843
"Robert Woods of Davidson Co., Tenn...engaged in banking, farming, and manufacture of Iron"...
Names: Bother Joseph Woods with whom he owns a large holding, jointly, and without written agreement i.e. Capital Stock in Cumberland Iron Works in Stewart Co., Tenn. Banking Interests in Montgomery and Stewart Co, some town property in Nashville, Tenn, also in Hickman Co. Ky, Trenton, Tenn, and Simpson Co. Ky. Estimates he and Joseph are worth @$854,800 together. Requests that Joseph continue to hold the property together, and wants the proceeds from his ½ to be divided into 8 parts as follows:
  1. wife; Sarah B. Woods
  2. dau. Josephine
  3. son James
  4. dau Jane
  5. son Robert
  6. dau Robena
  7. son Joseph
  8. dau Julia Hannah

Names: Robert W. Walker son of Sister Walker
       Robert Woods son of bro. Andrew Woods
       Robert W. Trabul son of sis Trabue
       Robert W. King son of Joseph King late of Va.
Requests that a "minature of me be taken from the paint- of Jarvis, set in gold and presented to each of the nephews and neices as follows:
    Daus of Andrew Woods, James Woods, Jno. B. West, Eliza Bradford, Hannah Norvell, Maria Price, Sister Walker.
A gold watch to each of the sons of Andrew Woods, dec. and James Woods, Margaret Walker, Patsy Robertson, Jno. B. West, Moses Norvell, Simon Bradford.
States that he is responsible for Guardianship of Jane and John Bell.
Requests that his brother Joseph assume the Guard. of his children.
Exec: Joseph Woods
1st Codicil: Names son-in-law Edward S. Handy of Philedelphia, leaves money to Presbyterian Church and other charities, and requests that burying ground at West Wood be enclosed....Dated 30 Aug. 1842
2nd Codicil: Asks that brothers Joseph and James Wood give neice Samvilla Winchester dau of Mrs. Maria Price, $6000 to be held in trust for Samvilla's dau. Valeria Winchester. Also names neice Catherine Lapsley wife of Robert A. Lapsley to get $2500. Dated 21 Jan 1843
Wit: J.....D. Kelly, Thos. R. Jennings
Probated Davidson Co., Tenn Feb Term 1843

p. 262: Adm Bd. $3000 25 Oct 1853 Est John Finlay, dec.
Signed by John L. Finlay, and George T. Blackburn of Wash. Co., Ms.

RECORDS OF WILLS - 1   Washington Co., Ms.

p. 263: **Adm. Bd. $30,000 19 Jan 1859**
Est. of A.T.Thomas, dec. (Correct sp. is Alfred T.Thompson)
Signed by Marion M. Wallis, James Wallis, E.A.Wallis, all of Wash. Co. Ms.
Marion M. Wallis is appointed Guardian to Mary A. Thomson & Cynthia C. Thomson, minor heirs of A.T.Thomson, dec.

p. 264: **Adm. Bd. $1000 19 Jan 1859**
Est. of James A. Flowers, dec. Intestate
Signed by Wm.S.Nugent, E.A.Wallis, M.M. Willis

p. 265: **Will - Thomas M Smith, dec.**
Written: 18 Jan 1859   Recorded: 24 March 1859
2 brothers: John & Wm Smith
4 sisters: Mary Davis, Elizabeth Lippincott, Harriet Vandyke, Salina Garrett "all of whom reside near Manayunk (?) in Penn."
Nephew: Sidney Smith oldest son of brother John
William Corbett (relationship unexplained)
Asks to be buried in the garden of William P. Montgomery in Washington Co. Ms.
Neice: Mary E. Garrett dau of sister Salina Garrett
Exec: Wm.P.Montgomery
Wit: Wm.L.Nugent, W.P. Montgomery, W.T.Penny, Jno. S. Penrice.

p. 266: **Noncupative Will of Philip A.Schuyler**
Written: 28 Jan 1859 & signed by John McMeeken
Filed: March 1859
Brother: Wm.C.Schuyler, of Albany, N.Y.
Brother - in - law: Dr. John Downs of Catskill, N.Y.
Widowed sister: Mrs. Anna M. Simpson
Requested that he be buried in Natchez on "Mrs. Quitman's Place".
Owned, with Bailey Pinckard, 500 acres near Memphis, Tenn.
States he has another sister that need not be contacted.
Wit: John S. Penrice, W.T.Penny
Adm. Bd. of John McMeekim & John S.Penrice 10 May 1859

p. 269: **Guardianship Bond:** John S. Penrice is app. Guard. of **Kate Knox Likens**, minor heir of **Thomas J. Likens, dec.**
Bond of $8,000 signed by J.S.Penrice, John McMeekem, John R. Woodburn. May 1859

p. 270: **Will of Robert Miller, dec**
Written: 9 Feb 1859 Probated: May Term 1859
Gr. mother - Mary Tringle
Sister: Nancy Jane James
Codicil added same day appaoints friend Joshia M.Powell Exec.
Wit: Thos. V.James, A.J.H.Crow, G.P.Powell

p. 271: **Will of Robert Woods** Recorded 11 Feb 1843 Same as p.257

RECORD OF WILLS - 1   Washington Co. Ms.

p. 276: **Adm. Bd.** $3000 May 1859
       Est. of Robert Miller, dec.
       Signed by Ira M.Powell, Geo. P.Powell, James Abell

p. 277: **Ad. & Guard. Bond:** $50,000 8 May 1859
       Est: of James B.Jackson, dec. (Pkt.#193½ - He decd.1854)
       R.H.Hord, Mary J.Hord of Wash. Co.Ms & J.W.Barnett,
       Robert W.Durfey of Yazoo Co.Ms.
       R.H. & Mary J.Hord guards. to Andrew Jackson, Lizzie A.
       Jackson, minor heirs of James B.Jackson, dec.

p. 279: **Adm. Bd.** $1000 24 Jan 1860
       Est. of Francis Cregan, dec. Intest.
       Signed by Edward P.Byrne, W.A.Percy

p. 280: **Will of Ambrose Knox of Wash. Co.Ms.**
       Written: 10 Dec 1859 Recorded: 23 Jan 1860
       Wife: Elizabeth Knox , who is "incompetent to adm. est.,
       since she is now an inmate of Bloomingdale Lunatic Asylum
       in N.Y."
       Gr.Dau: Marthia Lowry Knox (minor)
       Dau.-in-law: Mary B.Knox
       Relative: Elizabeth Margaret Knox
       Bro.: Thomas Knox
       Exec: friend D.Flournoy Blackburn & brother Thomas
       Knox
       Wit: Thos. S. Redd, Stephen Warren, E.M.Blackburn

p. 283: **Will of John Galatin Paxton**
       Written 16 Sept 1859 Presented for Prob.: 23 Jan 1860
       Exec: Brother Andrew J.Paxton
       Sister: Mrs. Rachel E.M.Buckner & her children
       Wit: W.D.Jones, C(?).G.Greenlee, G.R.Hall, W.T.Penny,
       W.Harrington.

p. 284: **Adm. Bd.** 27 Jan 1860
       Est: Amo Elisee Schwartz, dec. Intest.
       Signed by George T.Blackburn, Sheriff

p. 285: **Adm. of Est. of Arthur P. Bagley**, dec. Intest.
       24 Jan 1860 G.T.Blackburn, Sher.

       Ad.Bd Est of C.L.Alexander, dec. intest.
       25 Jan 1860 G.T.Blackburn, Sher.

p. 286: **Guard. Bd.** 23 Jan 1860
       George P.Powell appoint. Guard. to Frank James, minor
       heir of T.J.James, Jr. Dec.

       Ad. Bd. Est: (blank)   Edgar, dec.
       24 Jan 1860 G.T.Blackburn, Sher.

RECORD OF WILLS - 1   Washington Co. Ms.

p. 287: **Will of Thomas D. Pelham**
         Written 16 July 1859 (no record. date)
         Neice: Helen M. Finlay
         Neice: Ann P. Finlay
         Exec: Dr. John L. Finlay
         Wit: Wm. L. Nugent, A. B. Carson
         Ad. Rd. 25 Feb 1860
         Signed by John L. Finlay, Samuel R. Dunn

p. 288: **Will of Henry G. Vick of** Wash. Co. Ms.
         To: Miss Helen L. Johnstone of Madison Co. Ms.
         To: Mr. Henry C. Pindell, Mrs. James A. Pendell his wife
         both of Louisville, Ky.
         Sister: Mary B. Vick
         Brother: George A. C. Vivk
         Father: Henry W. Vick
         Exec: Friend L. W. Thompson of Madison Co. Ms & Henry C.
         Pindell of Louisville, Ky.
         Written: City of New Orleans, La. 16 May 1859
         Presented for Prob. 4 Feb. 1860
         Wit: L. A. Lockridge, Andrew J. Herron, A. G. Dickerson

         Plea for Examination of Wit: 23 Jan. 1860
         Many depositions followed:
         Andrew S. Herron of E. BATon Rouge, La. 31 Jan 1860
         Henry C. Pindell made his deposition in Wash. Co. Ms
         27 Feb 1860
         Adm. Bd. $160,000 27 Feb 1860
         Signed by Henry Pendell & Thomas C. Redd
         (POA of Henry W. Vick to W. L. Nugent... see p. 294)
         (* Editors' note: Henry Vick, engaged to be married
          to Helen Johnstone, was killed in a duel in New Orleans)

p. 292: **Guard. Bd.** 4th Mon. Feb 1860
         James S. Small is Guard. to Catharine McCaulay, minor
         heir of (blank)

p. 292: **G. B.** 27 Feb 1860
         Nancy I. Powell is Guard. to Franklin James, minor heir
         of T. J. James, dec.
         Signed by Nancy J. Powell, Geo. P. Powell, Jno. James,
         James Abell, all of Wash. Co. Ms.

p. 293: **Adm Bd.** Feb. 1860
         Est: Mary Jane Kirshaw, dec. Intest.
         Signed by Thomas Kershaw

p. 294: **Power of Atty.** to Abram F. Smith, WmL. Nugent by Henry W.
         Vick 7 Mar 1860

p. 295: **Adm. Bd.** $200,000 26 Mar 1860
         Est. Isaac Worthington, dec.
         Signed by Anne E. Worthington, William H. Worthington,
         Wm. Hunt, Aaron Wickliffe, Lycurgus Johnson all of Wash
Co. Ms.

RECORD OF WILLS - 1   Washington Co. Ms.

p. 296:   Inventory Bd: 29 May 1860   Adm. John L.Finlay
<u>Est: John B.Pelham, dec.</u>

p. 297:   <u>Adm. Bd.</u>: $2500   28 May 1860   J.W. Collins, J.L.Finlay
<u>Est: Joseph T. Shindler</u>

p. 298:   <u>Will of Samuel R. Dunn</u>
Written: 9 May 1860
Recorded: 28 May 1860
Wife: Betty Dunn
Children: William, Samuel & Mary "nearly grown" but others smaller, (unnamed)
Son: Wm. Dunn Trustee
Exec: "   "   and wife Betty
Wit: Jno.L.Finlay, R.L.Dixon
Adm. Bd. signed by William Blanton Dunn & Bettie A. Dunn & P.W. Gregory

p.299:   <u>Adm. Bd.</u> $200,000   28 May 1860
<u>Est: Joseph M. Brooks, dec.</u>
Signed by Virginia S.Brooks, W.P.Montgomery, A.B.Montgomery

p. 300:   <u>Adm. Bd.</u> $5,000   27 Aug 1860
<u>Est: Jeremiah W. Collins</u>, dec. Intest.
Signed by Wm.L.Collins, F.G.Turnbull, Jno. Bietts all of Wash. Co. Ms.

p. 302:   <u>Adm. Bd.</u>: $80,000   23 Oct 1860
<u>Est: Thomas J. Likens</u>
John L.Penrice is guardian of Kate Knox Likens, minor heir of Thomas J. Likens: Others who signed were John McMeekem, Jacob Roth.

<u>Will of Isaac Leonard Woodburn of Wash. Co.Ms.</u>
Brother: John Ruter Woodburn
Sister: Ellen Shewsberry (?)
   "   Mary Louisa Price
Friend: William L. Nugent
Sister: Cornelia Morton
Nephew: Leonard W. Morton
Exec: Wm.L. Nugent & bro. John Ruter Woodburn
Written: 3 Nov 1859
Reocrded: 29 Feb 1861
Wit: Wm.L.Nugent, Jno. H. Nelson, John McMeek<u>in</u>

p. 306:   <u>Letters of Adm.</u>: Andrew B.Carson, Sher.   31 Jan 1861
<u>Est: Joseph T. Shindler, Dec.</u>

<u>Lett. of Adm.</u>: Andrew Carson, Sher.   27 Mar 1861
<u>Est: Horace W.Hunter, dec.</u>

RECORD OF WILLS - 1   Washington Co. Ms.

p. 307:   Est: Nimrod T. Lindsay, dec.
          Lett. of Adm. A.B.Carson, Sher.   27 Mar 1861

p. 308:   Est. David FLourney Blackburn, dec.
          Adm. Bd. $5,000 25 Mar 1861
          Signed by Thomas Shelby, Wm. L. Nugent

p. 309:   Est: Robert Marsh, dec.
          Adm. Bd. $45,000 2 May 1861
          John L. Finlay, Thomas V. James

p.310:   Est: Henry W.Vick, dec.
          Guardianship Bd. $100,000 18 July 1861
          Jonathan Pearce of Wash. Co.Ms is appointed Guardian to
          Mary B.Vick, and George N.C.Vick of Wash. Co. Ms, minors
          Bond signed also by Joel H.Willis and C.A.Manlove of
          Warren Co. Ms.

p. 311:   Power of Attorney fro, Joel H.Willis & C.A.Manlove of
          Vicksburg to Jonathan Pearce
          (no date)

p. 313:   Will of W.H.Hammet of Wash. Co. Ms.
          Owned a Plantation called "Lammermoor Place", and asks
          that it be kept intact.
          Wife: E.M.Hammet
          Nephew: William Hammet Martin son of Dr. Joseph & M.J.
          Martin of City of New York to receive $20,000
          Albert Hammet Metcalf son of F.A. & M.P.Metcalfe of
          Wash. Co. Ms. (relationship unexp.)
          Brother: Edward Hammet of Montgomery Co. Va.
          States that wife, E.M. "has an only child"
          Exec: Edward Hammet, James Hammet, Robert C.Hammet all
          of Montgomery Co. Va.
          Written: 23 Apr 1861
          Prob: July Term 1861
          Wit: Geo. V. Ward, Thos. H. Johns, S.Dempsey Goza

p. 315:   Est: James Abell, dec. Intest.
          Lett. of Adm.: to Wm. A.Haycraft 26 Aug 1861 $35,000
          Wm. A.Haycraft, Nannette Abell, John S.Nelson

p. 317:   Will of W.J.Penny
          Written 13 July 1861 Prob: Aug Term 1861
          Brother: B.F.Penny
          Exec: W.L.Nugent
          Wit: Jno. L. Finlay, Stevenson Archer, Wm.L.Nugent

p. 319:   Est: Michael Farrell 28 Oct 1861
          Lett. of Adm: Charles B. Palbutt

p. 320:   Est. T.Edward Jackson, dec.
          Adm. Bd. $20,000 28 Oct 1861
          Thomas V.James, John L. Finlay

RECORD OF WILLS - 1   WAshington Co. Ms.

p. 321: **Will of Harvey Miller**
Oldest Dau: Betty J.Miller
States that he has other younger children but does not name them.
Exec: Edward P.Johnson
Wit: J.W.Johnson, R.J.Ward,Jr., Betty W.Johnson
Written: 4 Jan 1859
Prob: Oct Term 1861

p. 323 **Est of Thos. W.Wilson, dec.**
Adm. Bd. $75,000   25 Nov 1861
Bettie Ann Wilson, A.D.Wilson

p. 324: **Est: Mr. Samuel R.Dunn, dec.**
Adm. Bd. $25,000   25 Nov 1861
W.R.Trigg, W.L.Nugent, A.M.Blanton

p. 325: **Est: Thomas J. James, Jr. dec.**
Guardianship Bd $2500 7 Nov 1861
Nancy J.Powell is app. G. to Franklin James, minor heir
Signed by N.J.Powell, John James, Thos. J. Blackmore

p. 326: **Est: Mrs. E.A.Dunn, dec.**
Adm. Bd. $50,000   4 Oct 1861
Thos. Shelby, Augustus W.McAllister, Jno L.Finlay

p. 327: **Est: Frederick G. Turnbull**
Adm. Bd. $8000 Nov. Term 1861
Mary Turnbull, Wm. Turnbull (all of Wash. Co. Ms.)

p. 328: **Guardianship:** Thomas James is G. to Laura James, minor
Signed by Thomas James, Thomas V.James
27 Jan 1862

p. 329: **Est. Joseph M.Brooks, dec.**
Adm. Bd. $120,000 27 Jan 1862
Signed by Felix H.Boyce, N.J.Nelson, W.L.Nugent
Condition: that Virginia L. Boyce late Brooks and adm. of est of Joseph M.Brooks, dec. make Inventory.

p. 330: **Est: Arthur Rucks, dec.**
Adm. Bd. 27 Jan 1862
Mary M.Rucks, James T.Rucks

p. 332: **Will of James Rucks, dec.** ("of Deer Creek, Wash. Co.")
Son: L.Taylor Rucks, not yet 21, who "has received share of estate of Miss Watts of Va."
Dau: Elizabeth B.Yerger, land deeded from Henry Rucks & wife "to me".
Son: James Rucks
Gr.Son: James R. Yerger
(cont. next page)

RECORD OF WILLS - 1   Washington Co. Ms.

Will of James Rucks, cont.
Dau: Malvina
Son: Arthur Rucks (has children)
Exec: James T. Rucks, Frank Valiant, Henry Rucks, Lewis Taylor Rucks
States that he has a large business deal with Judge Wm. Yerger.
Written: 30 Mar 1862
Presented for Prob: 12 May 1862

p. 334: John Butts, Christopher Hampton, Wade Hampton of Wash. Co. Ms. Adm. Bd. $103,000 26 May 1862
Est: Ambrose Knox, dec.

p. 335: Est: James R. Downs, dec.
Adm. Bd. $80,000 22 Sept 1862
Signed by Lettitia Vick Downs, J.W. Vick, O.C. Rives

p. 336: Est: Eliza G. Mosby, dec
Nov. Term 1862
Gervas S. Mosby presents Will for Probate

Will of Eliza G. Mosby
Written: 24 Jan 1862
States she has husband and children, unnamed
Requests that if she and husband die, Montgomery Mosby and Paulina P. Mosby have charge of the children and pay board of brother, James W. Mosby.
Namesake: Eliza Burks Finlay

p. 338: Est: Peter M. Walker
Adm. Bd. $50,000 5 Aug 1862
Margaret H. Walker, John L. Mears, Walter Lane, Levin Lane

RECORDS SKIPPED 2 YEARS BECAUSE OF THE WAR

p. 339: **Will of John Walker Percy**
Written: 29 July 1864
Adm. to Prob: 23 Jan 1865
Wife: Fanny E. Percy
Dau: Maria Percy
2 brother: Leroy P. & Wm. A. Percy
Wit: J.S. Yerger, L.P. Percy, N.C. Skinner
Exec: wife

p. 340: Est: Evelina M. Hammet
Adm. Bd. 28 Aug 1865
F.A. Metcalf, James T. Rucks

p. 341: Guardianship: awarded to Pricilla W. Grepory & Wm L. Nugent for Thos. K. Dunn, Harriet T. Dunn, Sarah R. Dunn, Orville B. Dunn, minor heirs of Samuel R. Dunn & Elizabeth A. Dunn, dec.

RECORD OF WILLS - 1   Washington Co. Ms.

p.342: Est: Robert B.Smith, dec.
     Adm. Bd. $2,000 23 Oct 1865
     Lucinda Smith, John T.Courtney

p.343: Est: John L.Finlay, dec.
     Adm. Bd. $20,000 30 Aug 1865
     Ann B.Finlay, G.S.Mosby, N.J.Nelson, R.L.Dixon

p.344: Est. Thomas J.James, dec.
     23 Oct 1865
     John S.Nelson, John James

p.345: Est: Isaac R.Moseley
     Handwritten note admitted for Probate:
     "As I am about starting to the war and I amy never get
     back I leave the lines to let you know that I want what
     I have to be equally divided between John H.Moseley &
     Alfred W.Moseley & John E.Denson, March 11, 1862
     Adm. Bd. $3,000 23 Oct 1865
     A.W. Moseley, Jno Bulls (Butts ?), Ira M.Powell

p.346: Will of Henry Johnson
     Plantation of Lake Washington known as "Chatham"
     Wife: Elizabeth J.Johnson
     Son: Henry J. Johnson (has children)
     Dau: Mary Belle Blackburn
     Son: Robert A.Johnson
     (the following were listed without punctuation)
     Charles F.Johnson Benjamin Johnson Matthew F.Johnson Emily
     M Bartley Louisa Elly Mary Belle Blackburn the children of
     "my deceased son Claudius M. Johnson".

     Son-in-law: George T.Blackburn & son Charles F.Johnson to
     act as trustees for Claudius's children.
     Son: Matthew F.Johnson
     Son-in-law: W.T.Bartley
     Dau: Elizabeth J.Johnson
     Dau: Emily M.Bartley
     My sons: Robert A.Johnson & Benjamin Johnson Matthew Charles
     F. Johnson the children of ... dec. son Claudius M.Johnson
     Dau: Louisa Elly & Mary Belle Blackburn
     Gr.Dau: Elizabeth Johnson late Tilford
     Son: Robert A.Johnson has 2 children, Margaret J.Johnson,
     and Robert R.Johnson
     Dau: Margaret A.Dudley
     Exec: wife
     Written: 10 Jan 1862 Prob: Oct Term 1865
     Wit: Thomas S.Redd, WM.R.Campbell, A.S.Fox, John M.McCutcheon
     (the relationship to the writer of the will is listed as
       I have quoted it.)

p.350: Est: Andrew W.Smith, dec
     Adm. Bd. $17,000 23 Oct 1865
     Catherine W.Smith, Thomas H. Hill

RECORD OF WILLS - 1   Washington Co. Ms.

p.351: <u>Guardianship</u> of Laura James awarded to N.J.Nelson. She
       is a minor heir of <u>Eliza James, dec.</u> Signed by Newman
       J.Nelson, Henry H.Morris $1,000 23 Oct 1865

p.352: <u>Est: Colin Floyd</u>, dec.
       James W.Murphy, Henry Morris 23 Oct 1865

p.353: <u>Guard.</u> of John, Katy, Ella Cox, minor <u>heirs of Seth C.
       Cox,</u> dec. awarded to W.L.Nugent 25 Oct 1865

p.354: <u>Est: Edward S.Fraser</u>, dec.
       Adm. Bd. 27 Nov 1865 Alexander G.Fraser, adm.

p.357: <u>Est: Charles Caffal</u>, dec.
       Adm. Bd. $1100 28 Mar 1866
       Louis Caffael & W.P.Montgomery

p.358: <u>Will of Wm. Hunt</u>, dec.
       Written: 1 Feb 1866 Prob: 3 Apr 1866
       Wife: unnamed
       2 sons: George B. & William E.Hunt
       Minor children, unnamed
       Wit: Geo. T.Blackburn, J.B.Gray, W.H.Keene

p.360: <u>Will of Mrs. M.A.Dudley</u>, dec.
       Written: 1865 No Probate date
       Exec: Husband, Wilkins Dudley
       "my" children: Lillie, Emma, Victor, Johnson, Willie,
       Charlie.
       Owns land in Ark. & "Mount Holly" on Lake Washington

p.360: <u>Est: Jonathan Ballard</u>, dec.
       Adm. Bd. 28 Mar 1866
       Geo. B.Hunt, W.P.Montgomery, N.J.Nelson

p.361: <u>Will of James W.Johnson</u> (written in New Orleans)
       Sister: Nannie J.Lonsdale the wife of Fitzwilliam Lonsdale
       of Wash. Co. Ms.
       Niece: Bettie J.Erwin, orphan dau. of Henry C.Erwin and
       Margaret E.Johnson, both dec.
       Brother: Junius S.Johnson (land in Jefferson, Tex)
          "   E.P.Johnson, Jr.
       Niece: Maggie Lonsdale, dau. of Fitzwilliam & Nannie J.
       Lonsdale
       Niece: Henrietta T.Lonsdale
       Exec: Fitzwilliam Lonsdale
       Wit: H.T. Lonsdale, S.P.Scott
       Written: 13 Dec 1864
       Order to interrogate witnesses 17 Mar 1866

RECORD OF WILLS - 1   Washington Co. Ms.

p.364: Will of Samuel Worthington of Wash. Co. Ms. now at
Washington, D.C.
Wife: Amanda
Children: William Mason Worthington, Mary G.Worthington
Amanda Worthington, Fannie Mason Worthington
Plantation named "Willowby", another "Mosswood"
Exec: William M. Worhtington
Written: 23 Oct 1866   Admitted for Prob: 23 Feb 1867
Wit: Ginas Preston, W.J.Minor, L.M.Talbot

p.366: Est: J.H.Yerger
Lett. of Adm. 23 Apr. 1867

p.366: Est. Ann Fulton, dec.
Lett. of Adm. 29 Apr 1867

p.367: Est: H.W.Hunter, dec.
Lett. of Adm. 23 Apr 1867

p.368: Est N.T.Lindsey, dec.
Lett. of Adm. 23 Apr 1867

p.368: Est Seth C.Cox, dec.
Lett. of Adm. 23 Apr 1867

p. 369: Est. Joseph Coffer, dec.
Lett. Adm . 29 May 1867

p.370: Est Daniel Grant, dec.
Lett. of Adm. 23 Apr 1867

p.370: Est Edward P.Johnson, dec.
Lett. Adm. 29 Jan 1867

p.371: Est Edward P.Johnson, dec.
Adm Bd. signed by Edward P.Johnson, Jr., Junius L.Johnson,
Fitzwilliam Lonsdale
29 Jan 1867

p.375: Will of D.G.Olmstead, dec.
Brother: Marcellus Olmstead
To David Freshwater, Mr. John M.Smithhurst"for helping
him when sick"
Asks to be buried in Oddfellows Cemetary in Vicksburg
Written: 28 Oct 1862   Recorded: July 18, 1867
Wit: John M.Smithhurst, David Freshwater

p.376: Est A.W.Smith, dec.
Lett. of Adm. 29 May 1867

p.377: Est R.L._nder, dec.
Lett of Adm. 23 Apr 1867

RECORD OF WILLS - 1   Washington Co. Ms.

p.377: Est: Wm.Satterwhite, dec.
Lett. of Adm.: 29 May 1867

p.378: Est of John F. Warren, dec.
Lett. of Adm. 23 Apr 1867

p.379: Will of Pickens Compton, dec.
Written: 23 Dec 1866 Recorded: 19, July 1867
Mother: Mary Compton
Brother: Jefferson Compton
"   : John Compton
Exec: John Compton
Wit: Stuart White, W.R.Trigg

p. 381: Will of Atkins Gautrey
Written: 18 Aug 1861 Recorded: Mar. 25, 1867
Written at Plum Ridge, Wash. Co. Ms.
Mother: Ann Gautrey living Cothenham, Cambridgeshire, Eng.
Adm.: Robert Davenport

p.383: Est: Henry Rucks, dec.
Adm. Bd. 24 Jan 1868
Sarah. J. Rucks, F.Valliant

p.384: Est: Adam R. Gramling
Adm. Bd. 22 Apr 1867
Jno.L.Gramling, A.D.Gramling, both of Issa. Co. Ms.

p.386: Est of J.M. Bott, dec.
Ad. Bd.: 23 Sept 1867
Elizabeth T.Bott, Geo.T.Worthington

p.387: Est: Sallie Hogan
Guardianship Bd: 23 Sept 1864
George R.Fall, James M.Collier
"   "   " is appointed Guard. to Sallie Isabell Hogan

p.389: Est: Thos. W. Wilson
Adm. Bd.: 25 Aug 1868
D.W.Buckner, L.G.Aldrich, F.H.Boyce

p.390: Will of Alex C.Bullitt, formerly of Louisville, Ky. now
of Wash. Co.Ms.
Written 22Oct 1861 Recorded: 15 June 1868 Jeff. Co.Ky
To "Mrs. Isaac Smith, mother of dec. wife Fanny L. Smith,
Plantations Longwood, Barns (?)
Exec: Wife - Irene Williams
(no wit. listed)

p.392: Guardianship Bd.: of Lydia Mitchell, orphan, bound to
Catherine Ferguson as Lady's maid until Lydia is 18.
Signed by Catherine Ferguson, Saml. W.Ferguson, J.S.McNeely

p.393: Will of Fannie Griffin, asks to be buried beside her children
Husband, unnamed
Written 19 Mar 1870 No recording date given

RECORD OF WILLS -1   Washington Co. Ms.

- p.393: **Will of Wm. Sutton of Carroll Parish, La.**
  Written: 19 May 1872 at Vista Plantation
  No filing date
  2 young daus: Emma Wilsie(?), Sarah Eliza Sutton
  "All my children:" Caroline S.Scott, Virginia S.Williams, Amelia S.Terry, Willie S.Merrill, Stephen T.Sutton, Emma Wilsie Sutton, Sarah Eliza Sutton.
  Exec: William H.Terry, Robert B.Scott
  Wit: John Haring

- p.394: **Will of E.J.Cooper**
  Exec: Husband, R.L.Cooper
  Father: N.Merchant
  Written: 26 Dec 1872   Filed 8 Nov 1873

- p.395: **Will Thomas H.Buckner**
  Written 21 Mar 1866   Rec.: 4 Apr 1872
  Dau: Bettie Aldrich
  Wife ; unnamed, to get Auburn Plantation
  Children; unnamed
  Exec: wife and son Davis M.Buckner
  Wit: W.Mason Worthington, W.W.Worthington, W.E.Ferriday

- p.396: **Will of Soloman (X) Wise**
  Written: 9 Aug 1871   Rec: 7 Feb. 1873
  Wife: Reana Wise
  Son: Isaac Wise
  Exec" Friend, John I. Harris
  Wit: E.Clarence Huggins, John D.Webster, John F.Harris

- p.397: **Will of J.Wilczinski** "being on my way to start home to Europe on a visit"....
  No date when written or recorded
  Brother: Nathan Wilczinski
  Wit: T.Luhring, G.Witkowski, L.Witkowski

- p.397: **Will of Henry (X) Campbell**
  Daus: Lila Campbell, Susan Campbell, Patsey Spearman
  Exec: friend, H.W.Hobbs
  Written: 20 Apr. 1874 at Belzoni, Yazoo River (Miss.)
  No rec. date
  Wit: Jeff W.Moore, W.W.Lomax

- p.398: **Will of Irene Smith**, State of Ky., Jefferson Co.
  Written: Louisville, Ky 17 Aug 1869
  Adm. to Prob. in Ky. 6 Oct 1873
  To Mrs. Irene S.Bullitt wife of A.C.Bullitt, dec., "all of my estate in La., Ms., & City of Louisville, also Mo.

- p.399: **Will of W.H.Douglass**   Hollywood, May 27, 1862
  Wife: Kate R.Douglass
  Sister: Kate N.Douglass
  Brother: Robert F.Douglass
  No Wit. or Probate dates

RECORD OF WILLS - 1   Washington Co.Ms

p.400: <u>Will of Chas. W.Wolfe</u>
       Written: 26 Aug 1875   Rec: 29 Sept. 1875
       Friend: Joe Wilcyinski
       Exec: Leopold "
       Wit: W.D.Hill, John Davidson, Trim L.Skinner

p.401: <u>Will of Julia (X) A.Sanford</u> of Greenville, Wash. Co.Ms.
       Children: Sarah Elizabeth Sandford, William Peter Sandford.
       Written: no date   Rec: 3 Nov 1875
       Wit: J.L.Griffin, Wm.J.Molowy, N.B.Johnson

p.402: <u>Will of M.L.Peters</u>, dec.
       Written: 1 Dec 1875
       Matthew L. Peters asks to be buried on Avon Plantation
       in garden adjoining his residence. States he has land
       in Ky. as well as Plantations in Wash. Co.Ms called
       London & Ashland.
       Wife: Harriet H.Peters*to be Exec:
       Children: Julia H.Peters, Mollie G.Peters, Bettie T.
       Peters, Minnie Peters
       Wit: J.H.Buckner, J.H.Robb, W.W.Mangum
       1st Codicil: 1875 asks that family keep Avon Plantation
       and give Col E.Richardson, whom he had business with,
       Granicus Plantation.
       *Someone has written in in pencil Harriet Hooe Peters

p.403: <u>Will of W.H.Douglass</u> Copy of Will on Page 399 of this
       Will Bk. 1.
       Wit: not listed in previous document, F.H.Boyce, D.
       Hensicker
       Pro: Nov Term 1865 (the one on page 399 not dated)

p.404: <u>Will of Flora Ann Dyer</u> of Wash. Co.Ms. formerly of
       Unionville, Conn.
       Son: Wm.H.Griswold of Unionville
        "   Edwin   "   " New York City
       Dau: Jenne E."   wife of H.W.Barnes of Wash. Co.Ms
       Adm.: son-in-law H.M.Barnes (Bains?)
       Written: 26 June 1877 at Argyle Landing, Wash. Co.Ms
       No Probate date
       Wit: J.M.Sutton, Aug. J.Nelson, E.Clarence Huggins

p.405: <u>Application for liscense for</u> Public Ferry across Atchafaloya
       Bayou on road leading from Yazoo Co.Line to J.M. Carr's
       sawmill at North end of Lake Wash.
       W.W.Lomax, John Burton, W.W.McMurtrey
       29 Mar 1876

       <u>Est. of Sterling Neblett</u>, dec.
       Adm.Bd. $50,000 17 May 1876
       Wm.J.Neblett, Ann S.Neblett of Lunnenburg Co. Va.

RECORDS OF WILLS - 1

P.409: Will of Sarah (X) Black: Parish of Point Couper, La.
Names: son-in-law Charles D.Stewart
       gr.son. John Black Stewart
Wit: (very hard to read)
Written: 4 Feb.1876 - Lakeside Plantation
Probated: 17 Nov.1876

P.410: Will Laura Sutton, wife of Junus M.Sutton (James) of Washington Co.Ms.
Written: 27 Feb.1872
Probated: 27 Dec.1878
Names: Children of my "said husband" - Mary W.Vanonum
      (Van Norman ?); Benjamin H.Sutton; Emeline T.
      Mulcher (Melchoir); Thomas J.Sutton.
Wit: Norris Selig, Jacob Alexander, N.Jackson.

Will Book #1 to be cont. in Vol.II

RANDOM LISTING FOR SOME OF THE NAMES IN GREENFIELD CEMETARY
Located outside of Glen Allan, Ms. Wash. Co.
Incomplete list

R.T. CARTER
1879 - 1913

SUSAN BANKS ALLEN
July 5, 1857
Feb. 2, 1953

RICHARD B. PHIPPS
1848 - 1912

WM. GEORGE ALLEN, MD.
Apr 12, 1846
Jan 12, 1922

N.B.
son of J.J. & M.M. Morris
Oct. 17, 1854 - Nov 18, 1903

JOHN WILLIAM BOYD
1868 - 1912
(See Issa. Co. Will Bk. C
   p. 259)

MARSHALL WAKEFIELD
Died
Nov 1, 1873
aged 43 yrs.

Sacred to the memory of
CHAS. FREDERICK TURNBULL
died
July 27th 1870
aged
29 years 11 months 9 days
This tablet erected by his
bereaved Mother

ANDREW TURNBULL
Who went to his rest
on this 20 day of March
    1870
aged 69 yrs. 1 Month 20 days
a wife's tribute

(Ed: See Issa. Co. Ms.
    Will Bk. B, p.107)

MARY E. DINKINS
wife of
R.T. Dinkins
  born
Aug 8, 1854
  died
Oct 20, 1891

ADA LOGAN GILKEY
wife of A.J. Gilkey
b Jan 11, 1838
d May 29, 1879

ANDREW J. GILKEY
Sept 28, 1827
June 13, 1910

MARY E. wife of
A.J. Gilkey
June 8, 1890
Nov. 1, 1910

(Ed: Will of Ada Logan Gilkey; Issa. Co. Will Bk. C, p133
    Will of Mary E. Gilkey; Issa. Co. Will Bk. C, p 207)

CENSUS 1870   Washington Co., Ms.
Random Listing

1-1 Percy, William A.   86   Lawyer   bAla.
      " , Annie   34   Ark.
      " , Fannie   11   "
      " , Leroy   9   Ms.
      " , William A.   7   "
      " , J.Walker   5   "
      " , Ladie   3   "
     Gains, Julia   39 (b) domestic bMs
     Johnson, Clarissa   15 (b)   "   "

25-25 Lingefield, Julias 28m retail merchant b Mo.
       "   , Augustus f keeping house b Nassua
       "   , Julius   1
      Broomfield, John   61 clerk in store bPrussia
      (also 2 blacks)

31-31 Alexander, Jacob   36 Merchant bPrussia
       "   , Clara   28   "
       "   , Rachel   2   Tenn.
       "   , Hester   1   Ms.
      (Also 2 blacks)

32-32 Readjeski, Joseph   39 merchant bPrussia
       "   , Arabia   38   "
       "   , Jacob   15   "
       "   , Lemon   15   "
       '   , Lewis   10   Ms.
       "   , Racheal   2   "
       "   , Ella   3/12   "
      Black, Henry   20 clerk in store bMo.
      White, Charlie   35 bookkeeper   bPrussia
       ", Laura   23   bMo.
      (also 2 blacks)
      Levy, Hulda   17   bPrussia

35-35 Picard, Samuel   28 Merchant bFrance
       "   , Amelia   24   La.
       "   , Hattie   3   "
       "   , Belle   1   "
       "   , Aron   2/12   "
      Selig, Ferdinand   21 clerk   bHessin Davinslo
      Steward, Jennie   28 (black)   Ms
      Paterfield, Allie   24   "   "

36-37 Longsfield, Julus   44 Merchant bBavaria
       "   , Elizabeth 42   Tenn
       "   , Ignacion Y. 23   La.
       "   , Henry E.   13   Minn.
       "   , Lizzie   9   Ms.
       "   , Laura   6   "
      Pelway, Thomas   20 clerk   "
      (also 2 blacks)

CENSUS 1870　　　　　　　　　Washington Co. Ms
Random Listing

38-39	Wilzinsky, Leopold	24 merchant	bPrussia
	", Joseph	20 clerk	"
	Wilkoski, Lewis	32 "	"
	", Annie	24	Ohio
	", Julius	6	"
	", Francis	3	"
	Feltenbera, Henry	27 clerk	Prussia
	Cohn, Phillip	40 Peddler	France
	Fall, Caledonia	20 (B)	Ms.
44-45	Ginsberger, Mark	34 merchant	bFrance
	", Julua	20	"
	", Sarah	2	Ms.
79-86	Geoghegan, C.F.	29 merchant	Ky.
91-99	Penny, Benj. F.	34 Physcian	La
	", Amelia	29	R.I.
	", Carrie	3	Ms.
	Sommers, Charles	21	Prussia
	Bowling, Barton	15 (B)	Ms.
92-100	Nelson, Newman	60 Farmer	Tenn
	", Mary	40	Va.
	Clark, Mary	18	Ms
	McCrae, Carroll	12m	La.
	Bland, Doff	55 Laborer	Ky.
	Byas, Clark	13 (B)	Ms
	Johnson, Boston	12 (B)	"
	Nelson, Laura	6	"
93-101	Hunter, William	30 Retail Merchant	"
	", Belle	22	"
94-102	Nelson, John	33 Ret. Mer.	" (RE 8000/PE 10,000)
	", Martha	30	" (PE 2000)
104-113	Valliant, Frank	37 Lawyer	Ala (RE 10,000/PE 500)
	", Marian	30	Ms
	", Fannie	7	"
	", Henry	3	"
	", Mary	8/12	"
	(Also 5 blacks)		
105-114*	Valliant, Leroy	31 Lawyer	Ala (RE 10000/PE1500)
106-<u>114</u>*	", Janis	28	Ky (" " /" 500)
	", Frank	6	Ms
107-<u>115</u>*	", John	1	"
	(Also 4 Blacks)		

* (The underlined numbers are copied as they appeared on the Census)

CENSUS 1870   Washington Co., Ms.
Random listing:

109-117 McNeeley, John S.   27   bMs
         Miller, Feldon   17   "
         "   , Albert   19   La
         Mercer, Corbin W.   24   Va.
         "   , John   22   Va
         Finlay, Nora (Nina?)B. 42 "   (RE 5000/PE 1000)
         "   , Helen M.   23   Ms (RE 1600)
         "   , John   21   " (RE   ")
         "   , Betty D.   19   (RE   ")
         "   , Sam D.   18   " (RE   ")
         "   , Eliza R.   16   " (RE   ")
         "   , Mary N.   14   " (RE   ")
         "   , Pricilla W. 12   " (RE   ")
         "   , Tomas R.   12(f)   " (RE   ")
         Shelby, Ann   34(B)   "
         "   , "   10(B)   "
         "   , Chupin   22   " School Teacher
         Trigg, Abraham   34   Va Merchant (RE8500/PE6500)
         "   , Susan Q.   30   "
         Elliot, Samuel   54   Ind. Hardware dealer
         Wetherbee, Hiram E. 28   "   Farmer
         Luthan, John   60(B)   "
         Thomas, Mary   31(B)   Ky
         Brown, Margaret   21(B)   Tenn
         Lee, Nellie   4   Ms
         Sanders, Martin R.   32   Ky Stabler
         "   , Elizabeth   25   NC
         "   , Elly   1   Ms
         "   , Vincino   20   " Stabler
         Holmes, Edwin   18   England Hostler
         (All of the above were in the same household)

145-144 Haycraft, William   39   Ky Real Est (RE 5000/PE 9500)
                                         Broker

148-147 Yerger, Mary H.   50   Tenn (RE 15000/PE 250)
         "   , Campbell   14   Ms
         Drinkard, George   25(B)   Ga
         "   , Frances   30(B)   Ms
         Ellis, Catherine   14(M)   "

158-157 Yerger, William   29 Lawyer Ms (RE6000/PE5600)
         "   , Jennie   27   "
         "   , William A.   8/12   "

201-212 Blanton, Martha   42   Ms (RE 75000/PE 5000)
         "   , Oville M.   41   " Physcian
         "   , Lolla   16   "
         "   , Oville   12(f)   Ms
201-213(?)"   , Georgia   35(f)   " (PE 5000)
         "   , Willie   14   " (RE 15000)
         "   , George L.   9   " ("   ")
         "   , Idea H.   10   " ("   ")
         Smith, George   72   Va Physcian
         "   , Jane F.   27   Ms

CENSUS 1870   Washington Co. Ms

Random Listing

201-213 (cont)
         Smith, Henry   21   Ms Dep. Shef.
           " , Fannie   19   "
         Bolton, William   38   Ireland Planter

285-296 Teidman, Rebecca 78   Pa.
         Campbell, Margaret 54" (RE 50000/ PE 3000)
         Hanaway, Elleta   23   Ms
           " , John   2   "
           " , Maggie   18   "
         McIloam, Roger   27   Ky (RE 30000/PE 3000)
           " , Mattie   23   Ms
           " , Margaret   2   "

300-310 Worthington, George 44 Ky (PE 600)
           "   , Pose 27 Ms (RE 27000/PE 2500)
           "   , Mary   6 Tex.
           "   , Carrie 4 Ms
           "   , Fannie 2 "
         Botts, Elizabeth   47 Va (RE15000/PE 1500)

430-433 Carter, Elizabeth 63 Va (RE 60000/PE 2300)
           " , Robert H.   35 Ky
           " , Ellinor   26   "
           " , William G. 24   "
         Wilson, Lea   38 (B) Va

480-487 Barnard, Thomas   29 Ms Planter (RE15000/PE 200)
           " , Corinne   31   "   (10000/PE 500)
         Chartard, Mary   35   "   ("   ")
           " , Charley   6   "

777-786 Mecalf (Metcalf), Frederick 39 Ms (RE1200/ PE4350)
           " , Martha   34   " (PE 4275)
           " , Albert   15   "
           " , Drusilla   13   "
           " , Sally   12   "
           " , Frederick   11   "
           " , John A.   9   "
           " , Cleve   7   "
           " , Harley   5   "
           " , George   9/12 "
         Rupp, John   45 Switzerland (Sch. Tea.)
         Borsurer, Michael C. 55 Prussia farm hand

791-807 Shall, Susan   73 Md.
817-828 Courtney, John   52 Ky (RE 100000/PE 25000)
           " , Jane E.   55 Va
         Gay, Caroline   51   "
         Parker, Howard   12 La.
           " , William   40 Va
         Boyd, John   75 Tenn stock-minder

CENSUS 1870   Washington Co. Ms

Random Listing

944-954 Rucks, Sarah   35   RE8000   PE1000   bTenn
     " , Arthur   12   Ms
     " , Benjamin   9   "
     " , Samuel   7   "

982-992 Rucks, Mary   36   10000   1000   Tenn
     " , Amanda   18   Ms
     " , Grant   14   "
     " , Sallie   12   "

983-993 Yerger, William   23   3000   300   "

984-994 Yerger, Alexander 47   Planter   Tenn
     " , Elizabeth   42   2000   2500   Ky
     " , Maria   15   Ms
     " , Edwin   12   "
     " , James   10   "

1000-1011 Burdette, Richard 29 5000   3000   Va
       " , Manuarve   24f   Ark
       " , Fanny   9   Ms
       " , Emma   5   "
       " , Willie   3   "
       " , Nannie   4/12   "
       (Also 2 blacks, 1 mulatto)

1212-1222 Paxton, Andrew 54 Planter 30000 7000 Va
       " , Hannah   40   Tenn
       " , Lucy   15   Ms
       " , Andrew   13   "
       " , Alexander   12   "
       " , William   10   "
       " , Hannah M.   4   "
       " , Nannie   2   "
       " , Cornelia   8/12   "
       Beasley, Louisa   25   "
       Buckman, Colin   19   Va.
          " , Willie   13   "
       McLellann, Annie   21   Ms
          " , Emma   19   "

1281-1291 Hill, Thomas H. 44   PE2000   Va
       " , Mary   33   "
       " , Charlee   17   Ms.
       " , Thedona   14   "
       " , Thomas   13   "
       " , Mary M.   1   "

CENSUS 1870   Washington Co., Ms.

Random Listing

1292-1302	Walcott, Theodore	34	Planter	bMs
"	, James E.	15		"
"	, Robert H.	11		"
"	, Theodore G.	8		"
"	, Charley	6		"
	Dunn, Byron	20		"

1414-1424	Phelps, Alonzo	35	Phy 120000 27000	bOhio
"	, Mary B.	27		Ms
"	, Nannie W.	4		Ky
"	, Henry V.	1		Ms
	McCabe, Jane	35	white nurse	Ireland
	Phelps, William G.	33	Lawyer 3000 50000	Ohio
"	, James H.	26	Planter 2000 3000	"
	Day, Samuel	40	Farm hand	"

1574-1584	Chew, Augustine	52	Planter 8000 5000	Ms
"	, Margaret E.	30	500	NC

1683-1693	Aldridge, Alfred	30	ret. mer.	Ms
"	, Fanny	27		"
1684-1694(?) "	, Annie	9		"
"	, MAry	5		"
"	, Hall	3		"
"	, William	8/12		"
"	, Thomas	24	Planter	"
1685-1695(?) "	, Frank	22	Merchant	"

(Number sequence copied from census record, no explanation for the new no. within a household!)

1763-1776	Worthington, William	69	Phy			Ky
	, Elizabeth	51	10000	700	"
"	, Edward T.	30	"	"	"
"	, Thos.	27	"	"	"
"	, Sallie	22	"	"	"
"	, Mary	20	"	"	"

1768-1779	Worthington, Amanda	64	9000 500	Ky
"	, Wm. M.	34	Farmer 5000,2000	"
"	, Samuel	21	" " "	Ms
	Stone, James	32	Planter 20000 3000	bKy
"	, Mary W.	28	500	"

1985-2000	Yerger, Harry	27	Planter 12000 2500	Ms
"	, Sallie	21		Ky.
"	, Jacob S.	1		Ms.
"	, Harvey	3/12		"
	Miller, Maggie J.	18		Ky
"	, Malvina	17		"
	Emmons, Eliza	69		NC
	Miller, Harvey	11		Ky
	Levrett, Joan	18		Prus

CENSUS 1870   Washington Co., Ms.

Random Listing

1988-2003 Humphrey, Hugh   35   bOhio
           "   , Edward   29   "

Skipworth Landing
2431- 2490 Shelby, Evan   53 Merchandizing bTenn
           "   , Margaret   35   NC
           "   , Flournoy   12   La
           "   , Robert   7   Tex
           "   , Katy   5   "
           "   , Mary   2   Ms
           "   , Evan, Jr. 6/12   "

Leota Landing
           Worthington, Ann 53   Ky
           "   , William   38   "
           "   , Isaac   22   Ms
           "   , Thomas   15   "

2977-2897 Aldridge, Limon G. 37 Planter 55000 7000 bMs
           "   , Bettie A.   35   Va.
           "   , Lyman   2   Ms
           Wilson, Mary Wells 13   Ky
           "   , Betty B.   10   Ms
           "   , Anna   8   "

2945-3006 Buckner, Davis   29 Lawyer   bMs
           "   , Amanda   24   "
           "   , William   1   "

2946-3107 Montgomery, Pinkey 70   bSC
           "   , Emeline   45   Ms
           "   , Samuel   21   "
           "   , Hellon   26   "

2947-3108 McCalister, Augustus 70   bGa
           "   , Caroline   54   Va
           "   , Louisa   20   Ms
           "   , Charles   18   "
           "   , Gervas   16(B)   "

2988-3149 McGrath, Caldwell   34   b Ky
           "   , Alice   31   Ms
           "   , Julia   10   "
           "   , Mary   8   "
           "   , Billy   6   "
           Penrice, John S.   59   bTenn
           "   , Amelia   45   Mo.
           Hines, Thomas   34   Ms.

INDEX: WILL BKS.A,B,C: Issa.Co.Ms.

Book A Feb.1846 - Dec.1853 (Microfilmed)

Barrow,A.H.	W. p.5
" "	L.A.-7
" "	P.7
" "	A.E. 17
Barnet,J.W.	A.E. of Hiram Hagan (W) p.21
" "	Letters p.23
" "	Adm. of Hiram Hagan Est. p.42
Barnard,W.L.(T)	Guard.,et al p.129

(12May 1857 - Wm.T.Barnard appt. Guard. of Sarah Louisa, Mary Jane,Wm.Bailey Barnard, infant children of Wm.T. Barnard by Sarah E.Barnard,decd.)

Briscoe,Wm.P.	Adm.Est.of James M.Briscoe PP.183-187
Barnard,Wm.T.	Exec.S.H.Chaney, annual settl. pp.187-189
" "	Exec.H.C.Barnard;Final settl.pp. 190,191

(1852 - Witness states: Henry C.Barnard is minor brother of Wm.T.Barnard, now reached majority.)

Briscoe,Wm.P.		Let. of Adm. p.225
" "		Decree of Sale of Est. p.226
Barnard,Wm.T.		Exec.,Adm.S.Chaney and a/c p.236
" "		Lett. of Est. of R.P.Shelby p.250
"	J.S.	Apprais.of Est. p.254
"	Wm.T.	Letter de bonis non;Est.J.F.Chaney p.258
"	"	Est. of Sarah Foster (of Adams Co.Ms decd.Testate 1853)

Book B (badly water marked, parts illegible) Nov.1853 to Feb.1861

Barnard,J.L.   W
(Jos.S.(L?) Barnard names wife Rebecca F.;2 ch.Henry & Jos; his bro.Wm.T.Barnard exec. without bond;Wit:Saml. M.Wells,E.Jones Harvey,D.D.Jackson - 16 July 1853 - Probated - Aug.1853)

Barnard,J.L.	Let.Test. Est. p.6
Bass,Jno.M.	" " ". p.18
Blackburn,D.(David)	F. Guard. p.36
Barnard,Wm.T.	Final Settl. p.46
Blackburn,D.F.	Est. R.P.Shelby p.47
Belcher,C.(Est.)	Let. of Adm. p.64
Bradford,M.	" Guard. p.66
Belcher,C.(Est.)	Appraisment p.77
Butts,J.	Lett. of Exec. p.94

Key:L.A.Letters of Adminstration; W - Will;P - Petition; A.E. - Appraisment of Estate;Ad.ofEs. - Adm. of Estate. A. - Adminstrator.

Issa.Co.,Ms.

INDEX TO WILL BOOK "B": cont.(1853 - 1861)

Blackburn,D.F.	Guard.(I)	p.145
	" 1st.Annual a/c	147
Bolton,M.	" Transf.to M.E.Pharr	155
Brittle,J.W.	W.Est. of-T.B.Green,Adm	195
Briscoe,J.M.	D.Harrison,Wiley Stewart,Exec.	196,200

(Badly water-marked - document states David(?) Harrison & Wiley B.Stewart,exec.of Will of Wm.P.Briscoe,decd. and Adm. of Est. of James M.Briscoe,decd., give a/c of sizeable Est.;P.198 - Mary Briscoe,Ann Briscoe,Wm. Briscoe,Mason Briscoe are minor heirs of James M.Briscoe,decd.,residing in the state of Texas - 2 July 1855)

Butts,M(ary),et al	I.by J.M.Butts(badly blurred)	220

(Eva Butts,minor heir of Mary and ----- Butts,signed by Jno.Butts,dated,possibly 1859)

Brittle,J.W.(Est.)	Warrant Apprais.	229
" , "	I.of money & debts	230
Blackburn,D.T.	Guard.of M.B.Creath	248
	Final a/c	248
	Guard.of Shanline Creath & Alberta Creath	253
Butler,L.(Est.)	I.	319
	Annual a/c 1858	359
Barnard,Wm.T.	Pet/Guard.	391

(Alberta Creath,now over 14 yrs.chooses Wm.T.Barnard as her Guard.She is an heir of Mary B.Creath,decd; Est.consists of @$3,000 from Mary B.Creath,decd.undiv. share as legatee of Robt.P.Shelby,decd. - 5 Apr.1858- Robt.Prince Shelby's Will(Not listed in Index) is in Will Bk."B",P.39:names - Thos.J.Likens,Wash.Co.,Ms;Wm. B.Prince,Carroll Co.,Ms.;David Flemoy Blackburn,Carroll Parish La. - all friends;Names neice Mary B.Creath,Endora J.Creath,now Endora J.Likens;D.H.Creath;Mary B. Creath;Shallina Y.Creath;Alberta Creath - all children of Albert G.and Mary B.Creath.Also the ch. of Thos.J. Shelby - namely - Evan Shelby,Creath Shelby,Thos.Shelby; Also John S.Joor,child of Geo.Joor and Catherine P.Shelby. Written 15 Apr.1853.Codicile states Thos.J. Likens has decd.the other 2 exec.to cont. Names bro. Thos.J.Shelby.Codicile written Pass Christian,Ms. -Aug. 1853)

WILL BOOK "A":(Feb.1846 - Dec.1853)

Coalter,G.(Est.)	L/Adm.	78
Crouch,P.(Est.	----	---
Coalter,G.	I.	121
Chaney,Susan H.	W	130
Coalter,John	Pet for Sale of Prop.	149
Chaney,Mrs.Ann S.	W.	155

Issa.Co.,Ms.

WILL BOOK "A": Cont.(1846 - 1853)

Chaney,John F.	Apprais./Est.	p.157
" , Margaret A.	Pet.	158
Coalter,John	Adm./Geo.Coalter,decd.	
	Annual settl.	200
Chaney,Ann S.(Est.)	Writ of Apprais.	219
	I.	219,220
Chaney,Marg.A.	Pet/Guard.	222
" ,Ann S.	Pet./Part.	235
" ,J.T.(Est.)	2nd annual a/c	239

WILL BOOK "B":Cont. (1853 - 1861) Badly damaged)

Chaney,J.F.	I	8
Commack,R.B.& wife	Guard.Let.	74
Coffield,H.D.	" "	83
Chaney,A.T.	Final a/c	160
Cobb,Henry (Est.)	J.E.Mayfield,Adm.	218
Chaney,J.F.	2nd Annual a/c by W.T. Barnard	221
Council,W.S.	(His name's Washington,) I& Apprais.- Allowance to widow & ch.	
	I.of money & debts	388
Creath,A.	Pet.to choose Guard.	390
Chaney,I.F.(minor)	Pet.for Let. of Adm.	415
	Pet.for Let.Division	415

WILL BOOK "A": (1846 - 1853)

DeLoach,M.P.decd.	W	27

(Mathison (Madison?)P.DeLoach's Will requests burial in Baptist Church Graveyard in Vicksburg,Ms;gives Chas.J.Fore & Lorenzo B.Anderson of Issa.Co.,Ms. everything.Written 26 July 1848...Prob.Sept.1848.)

DeLoach,M.P.	I.	26
Dodds,Wm.& N(ancy) Y.	Adm.of Est.of Saml.N. Sullivan,decd.	106
	Copy of final a/c	106
Dodds,Wm.	Guard.;Final a/c	111
DeLoch,M.P.(ESt.)	1st annual a/c;C.J.Fore	131,132
Dodds,Wm.	Guard.Annual Settl.	138
	Annual Settl.	203,204
	4th Annual Settl.	246
Duval,A.D.,Decd.	W	260

(Alexander D.Duval - Will written 23 July 1850;names wife - Margaret,3 "younger children Claiborne Alex. daus.Matilda N.Duval,Gwinnet S.Duval.Other Ch.Caroline Cook,Mary C.Duval,Elizabeth P.McNairy.Exec.- wife. Probated:Dec.1853)

WILL BOOK "B":(1853 - 1861)

Duval,A.D.(Est.)	I.	61
Dodds,Wm.	Guard.and a/c	73

Issa. Co. Ms

WILL BOOK A (1846 - 1853)

Farr, Mary A.	L.A. (Est of John F. Farr, dec)	p 20
Fore, C.J.	Exec. of est of M.P. Deloch; LT,I	25,26
Farr, J.H.	I	48
Hill, Isaac C. (obviously out of place) Guard. of E.W. Sellers		61
Farr, J.H. (Est)	Guard. of J.W. Sellers	61
	1st a/c	67
	Inv. a/c	71
	Report of sale	72
		74, 86
Fore, C.J. exec;	Final a/c	216

WILL BOOK B (1853 - 1861)

Foster, Sarah	I	1
	Div. of Property	10
Farr, W.B.	Guard. ad litem	152

WILL BOOK A (1846 - 1853)

Gray, L.	I	92
Gray S. (Est)	Final a/c	243

WILL BOOK B (1853 - 1861)

Gregory, G.G. (est)	(Pricilla W. Gregory, LA, est. of G.G. Gregory, decd. died intestate - doc. signed by W.B. Farr, clerk, 2nd Mon. Mar. 1854)	21
Gregory, P.W.	Letters of Guard. (Of Peter and Mary Dunn Gregory, inf. ch. of Geo. G. Gregory)	37
Gregory, G.G.	I & Apprais.	52
Gray, J.M.	W (John M. Gray Names wife Nancy T.; ch. Mary Leah, Sarah Ann, Samuel Baily, John M. Gray. Written 1 June 1854, Prob. same day)	55
Gray, J.W.	Codicile	56
	Wit. to last codicile	57
	Letters of Exec.	
	Warrant of apprais.	86
Gregory, G.G. (Est)	P.W. Gregory 1st a/c	276
	" " 2nd a/c	283
Gray, J.M. (Est)	N.V. Gray - sale	293
Green, T.B.	Guard. - S.T. & M.C. Williams, Pet. of rel.	317

Key: LA - Letters of Administration
I - Inventory
W - Will
Guard. - Guardianship
Exec. - Executor of Estate
LT - Letters of Testimony

Issa.Co.Ms.

(From this point, Est. Packet numbers appear on the left margin of some of the estates.)

WILL BOOK "A": (1846 - 1853)

9	Howard,S.D.	A.E.	P.8
6	Hill,T.W.	"	15
9	Howard,S.D.(Est.)	L.A,to Wm.Myers	17
16	Hagan,Hiram	W	21

(Names: wife-Martha;bro.-Henry Hagan Execs; states he has ch.but does not name them;Will written 17 Feb.1847;Prob.13 Nov.1848;Wit;T.W.Barnete,E.Lowe,David Hagan)

16	Hagan,Est.	Let. to Exec.J.W.BArnete	23
9	Howard,S.D.Est.	Report of sale	37
	Hagan,Hiram Est.	Apprais.	42
6	Hill,T.W.	" Sale	44
9	Howard,S.D.Est.	" of Negroes;1st a/c	54,56,
6	Hill,T.W.Est.	Final A/c;surrender	59

(John A.Hill,W.R.Hill Adms.)

Hill, Ann   Adm.Est.of Isaac Sellers,Let.   58
"   "   Apprais.   "   "   62
Hill,I.C.   Guard.E.Sellers (Edwin   61
   Ruthman Sellers is a minor)
Hill,I.C.   Guard.of T.W.Sellers (Thos.   61
   W.Sellers is a minor)
Hester,John Est.   Let.& Coll.   95
Hill,I.C.   Adm.Bd.   142
"   "   L.A.   143
Hill, Mrs. Ann   Pet.   144,145
"   "   "   Adm.Bd.   145,146
"   "   "   L.A.   146
"   "   "   Pet. for sale of Prop. of B.C.153
   Sellers, decd.
Hill,I.C.   Pet. for sale of prop. of   154
                   John McLauren,decd.
"   "   "   Guard.of T.M.Sellers   204
"   "   "   " E.R.   "   205
Hill, Mrs. Ann   Adm.of Isaac Sellers,decd.A/c 208
Hodgden,M.   "   Final A/c   217
   (Hodgen, Morrel, Adm. of Est. of Jos.Steiff)
Hill,Mrs. Ann   3rd A/cEst. of Isaac Sellers   247
Hill,I.C.   Guard.of T.W.Sellers,2nd A/c   248
"   "   "   " E.R.   "   "   249
"   "   Adm.Est.of J.McLaurin,1st a/c 252
Hill, Mrs.Ann   " a/c B.M.Sellers 1st a/c   253

WILL BOOK "B": (1853 - 1861)

Hill,H.R.W.   Will (Sec.Dist.Court,New
   Orleans,La. Will of Henry R.W.Hill - names;
   To Jane Knox McAllister,neice of my late wife
   1000 acr.in Shelby Co.Tenn,"Igot from Willard's
   Est." : Also money to cover legacies James Dick
   left her: To P.Homer Leslie: To Violet Miller -
   nurse for my late wife:To Wm.-----McAllister of
   Nashville:"my own dear son James Dick Hill - the
   rest of the Est." (over a million $) lands in
   Texas,Tenn.Ark.+ the Deer Creek Est. in Wash.Co.
   Ms.(now Sharkey) 2 houses on Canal St.N.O._cont.

Issa. Co. Ms

WILL BOOK B, cont.

loving friends Charles J.Tore special exec. of
Deer Creek est; John Armfield of Sumner Co. Tenn.
and John M.Bass of Nashville exec. of will. Request to be
buried beside his wife and children. 19 Sept 1853   p.14

Hill, H.R.W. Est	I & Apprais	136
HILL,J.C.	3rd a/c	137
	" "	
	Guard. of T.W.Sellers	189
	" " E.P.Sellers	190
Hampton, W. Sr.	Pet. L.A.	376

BOOK A (1846 - 1853)

Joor, Geo. Est	Lett. of E.W.Shelby	31
Johnston, G.P.	Sher. Adm. Wm.Taylor letter	32
	" " W.H.Shallis "	31
Joor, Geo.	I	35,53
	I	63
Jones, G.P.	Report of sales of est.	147
	Pet. for value of hire for slaves	147,148
	1st a/c	148
	Final Settl.	237,238

No J's listed in Book B:

Book A.(1846 - 1853)

5 Ledbetter, H(omer) V. Will (Will states that Violet   4
   and her 3 ch. Daniel Leon, Elizabeth, Laura be
   const. legal heirs; Request that exec. Wm.Deeson
   take Violet and her 3 ch. to some free state, a
   home purchased for them and their ch. Wit; R.W.
   Pettway, John T.Fortson, H.G.Martin. Written 5Apr
   1846-Prob. 24 Aug 1846)

5 Ledbetter, H.V.	Apprais. of hiring negroes	9
	I	10
	R.W.Pettway, Adm. ad colligendum	11
	Sale of perishable prop.	14
14 Lowry, Wm.	Letters (Wm.Lowry, decd, late of	24
	Madison Co.Ms - Wm.T.Lowry, exec.) Will of----	28

(Will of M. Lowry, orig. from Fairfield Dist. S.C.
now of Sharan, Madison Co.Ms. 3 May 1841; Names
dau. Agnes Eugenia, son Wm.Thos, dau. Elizabeth Caro-
line, dau Lucia Cornelia, dau Susanna Cusehia (?); b̸ẙ
A̸p̸p̸t̸. J̸.C̸o̸l̸l̸i̸n̸s̸/ m̸y̸ s̸o̸n̸-i̸n̸-l̸a̸w̸ (struck out)& my dau
Agnes Eugenia (his consort) app. Guard. of minor ch.
App. son Wm.T. Lowry exec. w̸i̸t̸h̸ R̸o̸b̸t̸. J̸.C̸o̸l̸l̸i̸n̸s̸/. Wit;
Rich.Beard,Alexander Campbell, M,J.Austin. Note by
Clerk - Words seem to have been scratched out, with
a knife, or nearly so. Prob. Apr. Term 1843)

Omitted from above; Book A

Johnston,G.P.	A Wm.Taylor sale	67
Joor, Geo	1st a/c	79
	2nd a/c	120

Issaquena Co.

Will Book A, cont.

5 Ledbetter, H.V.M.	2nd a/c, final a/c	p.46
Lowry, W. Est.	a/c	94
" , Wm.T.	Reling. of Heirs	163,164

(signed by James H. Hughes, Lucia C.Hughs, Agnes E.Collins, dated 12 Apr. 1852)

Leigh,T.J. Est.	I	244

Book A: (1846 - 1853)

2 Mayfield,M.A. Est	A.E.	2
3 McQuillian, J.& C.A.	Apprais.	2

(Jos. & Cynthia A.McQuillian,decd.Est. signed by N.H.Vick, Wm.Rushing, Wm.Myers. 3 Mar 1846 - Wm.B. MacQuillian, G. of the heirs.)

McQuillian, Wm.B.	Ad. Minor ad Coll. of Est. of Peter Crouch, decd.; Letters	60
McQuillian, J.&.C. Est.	1st a/c	91
	I of negroes (1846,1847, 1848,1849,1850)	135
McCOYIM (?) W. Decd.	L.A. of J.Leigh	136

(Spelling varies: Walter Coyin, McCowyan)

	I	139
McQuillian, Wm.B.		141,142
McLauren,Sarah G.	Pet.	141
McQuillian,	G. Bond	143,144
McLauren, John	Warrant of App.; Ret. of Adm.	149,150
Mott, R.	by Atty. Haskins, bond... Jno.McLauren report of sale	137,168

(on P. 137 - pet. of admin. of Thos.J.Leigh for Est. of Walter McCoying, decd.; on p. 167,168 Report of sales of Est of John McLauren,decd. 10 Apr 1852 by J.(I?)C. Hill, Auctioneer E.W.Shelby)

More, Mrs. R.	Adm. Est of S.L.More,decd.	209,210
	Report sales; a/c	211 to 216

Book B.(1853 - 1861)

Myers,Wm.	Let. of G.	9
Magee, Wm.Est	L.A.	67
McLauren, J.	Final Settl.	96
Magee, W.Est	I	375

Book A (1846-1853)

Nelson, M.L.S. Est.	Let. of G.	96

(Samuel Nelson, Guard. of M.L.L.Nelson, minor heir of T.C.Nelson, decd., Mary L.S. Nelson, infant child of Thos. C.Nelson, decd.)

Nelson, N.T. & J.W.	P	159

(Nathan T.& John W.Nelson, let. of Guard... being of age to choose a Guard., choose their father Samuel Nelson to act in their behalf as heirs to grandfather Thos. Nelson who died Rutherford Co. Tenn May 1851. This document dated 12 Apr. 1852: A copy of Thos. Nelson's Will followed: leaves to gr.children; son Thomas Nelson, dau. Mary Louisa, gr.grandch.; dau or son of Wm.S.Watkins,

Issaquena Co.

Will Book A, cont.

son John Nelson's children; son Samuel Nelson's ch.; dau. Sarah Crechlours. Exec. wife, (living) son John Nelson & Arthur M.Edwards; written 19 Feb. 1850 - Recorded 14 Apr. 1852

Nelson, Thomas	Copy of Will (see above)	159,160
Nelson, Samuel	P of G	160
	Lett. of G.	162
	Fianl Settl. & decree of Ct.	223,224
Pharr, Elias	G. et al	127,128

(Apr. 1851,Elias Pharr, Guard. of Margaret B. Pharr, Jane M.Pharr, Henry N (?) Pharr, Saml. A.Pharr, Walter N.Pharr, Theresa J.Pharr - legal heirs of Robt. Pharr, decd; Also Margaret Allen, Mary Allen, Henry Allen - heirs of Sarah C.Allen,decd.; also Mary,Sarah, Henry, Hester Pharr - heirs of Jas. Pharr, decd.; also Henry,John,Wm.Beavers - heirs of Margaret M.Beavers, decd.)

Powell, Mordica	L.G.	156
	L.A.	162
	I	221,222
	Lett. Apprais Est Margaret Chaney	221
Powell, M. Guard.	Report of Prop. of Marg. Chaney	222
Powell, M. Exec.	Report of prop. of Mrs. Ann S.Chaney	220
Pharr, E. decd. Est	L.A. (10Jan1853, R.M.Smith Adm.)	228
Pharr,M.E. (infant)	L.G.	229

(Ursilla M.Pharr, Guard. to Mary Eunice Pharr, 2 Apr 1853, infant ch. of Elias Pharr, decd)

Pharr, Elias Est.	I	232

Will Book B (1853-1861)

Pharr, Est.	1st a/c	20
	Report of sales	32
	" " " of Real est.	68
Parks, G.N.	Proof of Will	80,81

(Will of Geo. N.Parks - 3 May 1852: wife Susan E.Parks; dau. Amanda Parks wife of Horatio D. Coffield; son Geo.N.Parks, Jr.; dau. Margaret E.Parks. States that son Geo. is a minor and crippled; exec. son-in-law Horatio D.Coffield and bro. Thos.Parks; had will written by WmBryant, esq. of Providence, La; Wit. Washington B.Farr, Jones S.Mayfield, Robt. B.Commack)

Parks, S.A & H.D.Coffield	L.G.	84
Parks, G.N. Est.	Lett. Test. (huge Est)	85
Parks, S.G.	G. Let.	95

(S.G.Parks, Guard. of minor heirs of J.J. Sullivan,decd; Saml. G.Parks Guard. of Mary Eliz., Emily Ann & Martha Kate Sullivan, inf. ch. of J.J.Sullivan, decd)

Parks,G.N.	War. of App.;I (t.$391,203)	97 to 105
Pharr, H.M.	G final a/c	150
Powell, M.	" " "	161
Pharr, E. Est.	" "	162

WILL BOOK B, Cont.

Pharr, E.A. minor	R.M.Smith, G 1st a/c	203
Pharr, S.E. "	" " " " " "	207
(Elizabeth)		
Parks, G.N.	H.D.Coffield &T.Parks 2nd a/c	232
" "	" " ,Exec. " "	236
" " Minor	" " , G. 1st a/c	239
" "	" " , "	183
" "	" " ,&T.Parks	186
Parks, S.G.	G/Louisa 1st a/c	267
" "	G/Ann " "	269
" "	G/Martha Kate " "	271

(Pages 267, 269, 271, 274 are badly damaged)

Parks, G.N. Est.	Coffield reports land sale	299
Parks, G.N. Minor	" G. Final a/c	383
Pharr, E.A. Minor	G/Smith 3rd a/c	386
Parks, M.E.	G/Coffield a/c	389
Parks, G.N. Est.	P Coffield & Parks	412
" "	" " "	413

Will Book A.: (1846-1853)

Robertson, J.W. Est.	Proof of Will	315
Sullivan, S.N. Est.	Appraisal	3
Shelby, E.W.	G/ of J.S.Joor	21
" "	A " "	31
" "	LA "	31
Shallis, M.H. Est.	Adm. G.P.Johnson	31
Shelby, E.W.	A.&G. & I.	35, 53
Sellers, Isaac Est.	L	58
" " "	Appr.	62
Swanson, James, Est.	L ad col.	77
" " "	I.	80
Sullivan, S.A. Est.	(blank) 1st a/c	81
Swanson, James Est.	L A	92
Sellers, W.B. Est.	I.	93
Scott, John Est.	L A	135
Sellers, E.M.	Comm. of Appr.	151, 152,
Shelby, E.W.	Adm. S.Grey a/c	168
" "	Adm. Est. Barton Millsaps	169
Swanson, J. Decd.	2nd a/c	192
Shelby, E.W.	Adm. of P.W.Crouch, decd, sales	206
Swanson, J.	Adm. 3rd a/c	230
Smith, Minerva G.	Report Comm. to allot. dower	234

(Minerva G. Smith, widow of James Swanson, decd...
Document dated 14 Dec. 1853)

Shelby, E.W.	Adm. P.Crouch	249
" "	" E.Tidwell	252

(E.W.Shelby was Sheriff of Issa. Co. in 1852)

Shelby, E.W.	L G	158
Scott, John	A E	164
Sellers, E.M.	Report of Sales	166,

Issaquena Co.

WILL BOOK B; (1853-1861)

Shelby, R.P.	W; Let. Test.; I;	39,47,49
Sullivan, J.J. Est.	L.A.	65
Shelby, E.W.	G.	72
Sullivan, J.J. Est. War. Appr.		75
Smith, R.M.	G.	92

(Guard. of Sarah E. Pharr, infant of Elias Pharr)

Smith, R.M.	G.	93

(Guard. of (blank) Pharr, infant of E. Pharr)

Sullivan, J.J.	Report of sale	124
Swanson, J.	Final a/c	128
Sellers, J.(I?)	4th a/c	134
Sellers, B.M.	Final a/c	135
Shelby, R.P.	Statement	144
Swanson, J.	Report of Comm.	153
Sellers, J.(I)	Ann Hill, adm. 5th a/c	211
Shoaf, J. Est.	P.L.A. by H. Shoaf	231
Smith, R.M.	G. - E. Pharr 2nd a/c	257
Sullivan, J.J. Est	S.G. Parks Adm. 1st a/c	260
Shoaf, J(acob) Est.	P: I: A:	351,314
	Annual a/c 1868	365
	I money	371

Will Book A; (1846-1853)

18	Taylor, Wm. Est.		no p. no.
	Johnston, G.P.	Sheriff A. (out of alph ord)	32
18	Taylor, Est.	Appr.	55
	Taylor, W. Est	Final a/c	123
	Tudwell, E. decd.	I	140

Will Book B; (1853-1861)

Thanly, J.E. Est	L.A.	63
Turnbull, R.J.	W	107

(Will of R.J. Turnbull, decd.: Westchester County, Surrogates Court (New York): To Lewis C. Platt, Surrogate of the county of West Chester, petition of Gouverneur M. Wilkins of Westchester states that R.J. Turnbull, late of the town of Westchester, died at Cincinnatti on the day of (blank) 1854, to admit the following will as valid & names: Turnbull's widow - Cornelia Turnbull; Robt. Turnbull, Lewis Turnbull, Sinclair Turnbull, Ann Turnbull, Matthena Turnbull, Catherine Turnbull...all residing in Westchester except Robt. and Lewis who are in school. All issue minors of whom Andrew Turnbull and Gouverneur M. Wilkins are Guard. ; dated 28 June 1854

28 June 1854 - John P. Jenkins of White Plains, Atty. at law, app by Surrogate to become Guard. of Robt.J. Turnbull's 6 minor ch.; Wit; Benj. S. Dick   109

New York - G.M. Wilkins files document dated 17 Nov. 1847, purported to be the last will and testament of Robert J. Turnbull.   110

Will Book B, cont.

Turnbull, R.J., cont.(Will accepted as legal 11 July 1864 was as follows: Wife - Cornelia; Sons - Robert,Lewis,Sinclair; Brother - Andrew Turnbull;Brother-in-law - Gouverneur M. Wilkins, Exec. and Guardian of infant children...States that he has sons and daus. Wit: Wm.C.Brinkerhoff, #17 Warren St. City of New York; Wm.R.Stafford, 164 Ludlow St.,N.Y. Written 7 Nov. 1847...Thos.L.Wells also a wit. Will filed Issa. Co.Ms 3 Jan 1855: Will Bk. B from P.107 - 111 to 122. signed W.B.Farr, clerk. Page 123 Andrew Trunbull 123 accepts as Exec.

Tidwell, E.	Comm. rep.	149
Thorney, J.E.	Rep. of Sale	151
Travis, E.R.	Pet. for G.	242

Will Book A: (1846-1853)

Varner, Samuel   W & papers pertaining to   170 to 183
(P.170 - Will of Samuel Varner of County of Oktetluka ((Oktibbeha?))Ms.: 2 Daus. Sarah Bevel, formerly Sarah Varner and Martha Lasater, formerly Martha Varner; Sons Joseph Varner, James Varner, John Varner; Daus. Mahaly Varner, Minerva Jane Whitely, formerly Minerva Jane Varner...States that Joseph Varner, James Varner,& Mahaly Varner "are unfortunately being deef and dumb"... Son-in-law Decature (?) Whitely and son John Exec. & Guard. of the 3 afflicted ch...Wife survives him, but is not named: Signed - Samuel X Varner, 18 July 1846. Wit. are scattered about...J.H.Willingham testified in Chickasaw Co.Ms.: Will filed in Marengo Co.Ala, also Issa. Co.Ms. Pages of litigation over the authenticity of this will follows: Wm.E.Bevel and his wife Sarah, James R.Lasseter and his wife Martha have depositions; Wit. to this document - J.H.Willingham,Wm.Champion, Catherine Gibson.)

10-1: White, Wm.,decd.	I.&A. of Henrietta E.White 28Feb.1846	
Williams, R.Est.	Adm. G.P.Johnson	19
1:White, H.E.,Adm.	Est. of Wm.White 1st a/c	40,41
Wells, Saml. W.	G/inf.ch. of J.F.Chaney,decd.	128
" " "	Adm. of J.F.Chaney, decd.Est.a/c	199
White, Wm. Est.	Final a/c	240
Williams, R.Est.	" "	243
Wells, M.A.&E.J.Harvey	L.of A.	256

Will Book B: (1853-1861)

Wells, S.W.	I	2
" "	Adm. Acc.	79
" "	Warrant Appr.	89
" "	Adm.	139
" "	Report Sales of Pers. Prop.	139

Will Book B, cont.

Wells, S.W.	Bond Rec.	143
" "	I	158
" "	Est. & a/c by W.T.Barnard, Adm.	214
12:Williams, D.T. Est.	Adm. Wm.Gibbons	217
" " "	I, money & Debts	228
" " "	I	225
Williams, S.J.	Pet. for G.	243
Williams, M.C.	" " "	245
Whitehead, S.Y.	I & Appr.	354
Williams, D.T. Est.	Division of Prop.	317

(BadlyBlurred...Daniel T.Williams Est.; Wm.Gibbons Adm. Petitions for wives by John R.Pettway for his wife Mary Caroline, and Lewis S.Jones for his wife Sarah Jane...wives an heirs-at-law of Est. of D.T. Williams; 5 Jan 1858 - Doc. states D.T.Williams left 2 children, the mentioned heirs.)

Whitehead, S.Y. Est.	Pet. for Sale of Prop.	380
" " "	Rep. of Sale	382

Will Book C: (1859-1926)

Anderson, Mrs. C.C.	W	297
Asbey, Saml.	W (filed 24 Oct.1881)	134
Brown, W.D.	Pet.	3
" "	L	4
" "	Pet. for L of Adm.	5
" "	L of Adm.	6
Barnard, W.T.	Pet. for G.	7
Barnard, R.F.	G	8
Barnard, W.T.	L of G Granted	8
Brown, W.D.	Sec. Bd.	6
Barnard, W.T.	G - Pet. for Division	26
Burm, William H.	P Adm.	31
Burm, Burwell Est.	P Adm	31

(William Bunn; Bro. of Burwell Bunn, Dec. who leaves no issue...5 other Bros. 2 Sisters.)

Bonham, Mary T.	Pet. for L of Adm.	56
" " "	L of Adm.	57
Boyd, James L.	P for L of Adm.	90

(Est. of Alexander P.Boyd - his Brother James L.Boyd, Adm.; other heirs - Martha E.Boddy, E.Beard, WM.W.Boyd, J.Miller, Mary A.Boyd; 7 Jan 1868)

Boyd, J.L.	L of Adm.	91
Boylan, Jno.H.	W	155

(John H.Boylan, decd. of Chatham Co.NC, names"reputed" dau. Adlaide, nephew William Boylan - son of Bro. Wm. W.Boylan, James Boylan (unidentified): Written 20 Mar 1869. Wit; W.E.Anderson, John G.Williams; Wit. and acknowledged - 7 Apr. 1870:
In Wake Co. N.C., another Will turns up, dated 12 Dec 1870, with same witnesses. No copy of this will here.)

Issa. Co.

Will Book C, cont. (1859 - 1926)

Baker, Joe	W (names w Lucy Baker)	170
Bronner, Flue	W	246
(Of Tallula, La.; 42 yrs. old in 1907, names wife - Triffie Bronner)		
Boyd, John William	W	259
Blair, Meta Lach	W (1915, Parish of Orleans, La.)	281
Brown, Charles	W	265
Bland, Elizabeth	W	299
Baskins, Frank	W	320
Birdsong, Frank, Decd.	W	373
Benton, Thomas H.	W	375
Benton, Dr. J.B., Decd.	W	393
Bridges, Corriner	blank	400
Chaney, Thomas Y.	W (Filed 2 Apr 1861)	47
" " "	Proof of W	47
Coffield, Mrs. Amanda E.	(blank)	132
Christmas, H.H.	W	128
Curd, David	W	153
Curd, Elizabeth	(blank)	157
Chilton, Alice P.	W	176
Cowan, T.B.	W	164
Coleman, Nancy	W	182
Cunningham, John	W	221
Chilton, St. John	W	294
Cook, Mary Jane	W (Packet #345)	325
Chisholm, Anthony	W (Packet #399)	371
Chism, Mattie	W (Packet #382)	382
Cooper, Jacob	W	364
Davis, Fielding	W	18
" "	Proof of W	19
Davis, Lucinda	Pet. for L of Adm.	20
" "	L test. to	21
Duval, Margaret, Est.	L of Adm to Eaton	82
Duncan, Stephen	Wb	208
Duncan, Henry P.	W	224
Duncan, Stephen	W	225
" "	Certified copy of Will	230
Davis, S.M.	W	239
Duncan, Sam P.	W	242
Duncan, Stephen B.	W	267
Diggs, A.R.	W	276
Diggs, Cornelius Washington	(blank)	287
Dreyfus, Albert, Decd.	W	333
Dean, James, decd.	W (Packet #356)	342
Dean, Ann, Decd.	W (Packet #356)	342

Issa.Co.Ms.

Will Book C, cont. (1859-1926)

Eustis, Horatio G.	W (Probated 1859)	13
Eustis, C.C.	Pet. for L Test.	14
" "	L of T	15
Ford, Manley, Decd.	W	45
" "	Proof of Will	45
Fore, C.J., Est.	Pet. for L of Adm.	80
" "	L Ad col.	81
" "	" " "	66
Farr, W.B. Decd	W & a/c	84
Foster, John Tilman	W & a/c	97
Farish, W.S.	Exec. Jno. Irwin (Sp. Irving, Irvin)	139
Fowler, Sarah	(blank)	167
Fayssous, Callender	(blank)	254
" "		256
Freshwater, Peter	"	264
Garrett, Lizzie	Pet. for L. of Adm.	71
" "	G	76
Given, A.M, Est.	Pet. for Dower	119
Gilkey, Mrs. Ada L.	W	133
Green, Francis	W	168
Grant, Taylor	(blank)	184
Gilkey, Mary E.	W (dated 1910)	207
Guy, John H.	W	219
Gravais, George	W	300
Grant, James	W	329
Graveas, George	W	353
Grisham, Leon M.	W	395
Griffin, Hines	W	397
Grisham, W.D.	W	401
Hill, Ann	Adm. Bond	9
" "	" "	11
Halloran, Pat	Pet.	23
Halloran, James	Est.	24
Harris, James. R., Est.	Pet. for Probating Will	34
" "	Will (Proven - 1860)	35
" "	Proof of Will	37
" "	L of Test.	39
" "	" "	40
Hughs, T.	Adm. & G.	63
Hill, Emily C.	Pet. for L of Adm.	70
" "	G	78

Issa.Co.Ms.

WILL BOOK "C: Cont..(1859 - 1926)

Hill, Eleanora, et al	L. of Guard.	79
Hill, Emily C.	Pet. for Dower	104
" "	Writ of Dower	105
" "	Report of Comm.	106
" "	Plat. of final Decree	107
" "	Pet. for Exempt.	109
" "	Report of Comm.	110
" "	Final Decree	111
Harwood, Agnes E.	W	130
Hines, George	(blank)	166
Heath, John W.	W	185
Hennessy, Margaret A.	W	248
Hennessy, Dennis M.		288
Human, Louis	W	290
Heath, John W. Est.		420

Irvin, John (sp. Irwin, Irving)	W	139

Johnson, A.G.		192
Jeffords, Mrs. Nancy P.		205
Jones, L.J.	W. (Dated 1906)	206
Jackson, Matthew	W	252
Jennifer, B.J.	W	360
Jeffords, Chas. S. Est.	W	358
Jones, Peter Stokes	W	383

Keep, H.V.	Pet. for Guard.	65
" "	W	137
Killiam, Max	W	161
Killiam, V.A.	W	291
Keep, Miss Sallie B.		301
Keep, Oliver H., decd.		366

Leatherman, Saml. decd.	Pet. for Let. of Adm.	86
Lachs, Meta Blair	W	281
Lindsey, Mrs. Ida B.		311
Luhm, Mary F.	W	327

   (Husband - Robert J. Luhm; Children - Katie Luhm
       Jones, Emma L. Sturgis, Otto A. Luhm, Robert H. Luhms,
       Eada Luhm Royce, Anna Luhm Davidson, and gr. son
   Joseph Tonnar - only child of dau. Julia Luhm Tonnar*)

Logan, Mary		343
Levy, Charles		404

---

* The writing of the Luhm Will very difficult to read.
  It was thought that Julia Luhm Tonnar and son Joseph's
  last name was Gorman, Norman. It definitely is <u>Tonnar</u>.

Will Book C; Cont. (1859-1926)

Mayfield, J.L. Adm.	Est. of J. Halloran	24
Morton, Washington, Est.		25
Marsh, Robert	Pet. for L of Adm.	25
Miller, Lewis, Decd.	W & Proof	28
MacQuillen, M.A.	W	49
MacQuillen, R. Decd.	W	53
Messinger, G.W.B.	W	58
Mosely, A.W.	Pet. for L of Adm.	74
" "	G of Eugenia Burwell, Lucy Mosely	77
Minor, Robert	W	138
Morris, W.J.	W	187
Maitland, Robert L.	W	194
Mason, C.L.	W	203
Marshall, Henry	W	204
Moore, Alex.	W	218
Moore, Wm.W.	W	271
Mayer, Henry L.	W	293
Miller, Elizabeth	W	368
Mayer, Emil	W	369
Mitchell, Amanda	W	399
Nelson, Saml.	Pet. for L of Adm.	16
" "	L. Adm.	17
" "	Adm. Pet for sale	30
Nicholson, J.E.	Pet. for L of Adm.	57
" "	Rachel Moore, Est. Adm.	58
" " , & wife	Adopt. of Laura May	61
" "	Pet. for Homestead & Proc.	92
Nutt, Mary D.	W	284
		285
Prescott, J.W.	G	2
Pettway, R.W., Est.		16
Pettway, Julia J.	Pet. for App. S. Nelson Adm.	17
Pettway, R.W., EST.	Pet. for final sale	30
Preston, Zenas	W	142
Pinckney, Ned.	W	322
Pittman, H.P., Decd.	W	380, 381
Paepcke, Elizabeth Julia		408
Paepcke, Herman		415
Robertson, Leanah	W & a/c	1
" "	Wit.	1
" "	Minors, Rep. G.	2
" "	Pet. L of Exec.	3
" "	Pet for l of Adm.	4
Robertson, Jos.W., Est.	Pet. for L of Adm. & Letters	5
Robertson, Leanah	Appraisers app.	4
Robertson, Jos.W.	Adm. Ed.	6
Rushing, Wm., Est.	W & a/c	41

Issa. Co. Ms.
P. 122

Will Book C, cont. (1859-1926)

Rushing, Wm., Est.	W	42
" "	Proof of Will, & L Test.	43
Robirds, W.D., Decd.	W	345
Robertshaw, W.D.		419
Ritter, Ida Pitt		280
Sellers, Joana, Est.	Pet. for sale of land	9
" " "	Citation Minor a/c - Publ. Proof	10
" " "	Bond Pet.	11
" " "	Decree of Sale	13
Skinner, Kate B.	Pet. of Letters	22
" "	Lett. of G.	22
Shelby, Thos. J.	Pet. of G.	22
Sweet, Sophia	W	175
Scott, H.P.	W	162
Sessions, R.	W & Probate	293
Spencer, Selden		296
Simpson, O.P.	W	326
Taylor, Wm. Decd.	W	362
Stanton, Amos O., Decd.	W	377
Sias, Oliver Sr., Decd.	Adm Hy Sias	379
Spiars, Marshall M., Decd.		402
Thompson, J.M.	Pet. for L of Adm.	32
Thomley, J.E., Est.	" " " "	32
Tillman, Louis	" " " " G.	33
Taylor, E.A. (widow)	Pet. for L. of Adm.	67
Tillman, A.M.	" " " " G., Let. of G.	89
Turnbull, R.J.	W	134

(Will of Robert J. Turnbull of Issa. Co. Ms: to Mother 171 of "my" decd. wife Heonard Elizabeth, Mrs. Mahala P.H. 172 Roach. App. kinsman Robert J. Turnbull Exec.)

Turnbull, R.J.	W	188
" "	"	193
Temple, Archie	----	353
Taylor, Wm., Decd.	W	362
Taylor, Diana	W	390
Taylor, Mrs. J.S., Decd.	W	392

P. 123
Issa. Co.Ms.

Will Book C, cont. (1859-1926)

Woolfolk, J.E. & L.T., Minor	G	64
Wright, C.E.	Pet. L. of Adm.	73
Wright, R.I.	L	73
Williams, Jacob	W	130
Williams, Teda	W	135
Williams, John		183
Williams, Charles	W	220
Williams, James	W	279
Walker, F.W., Decd.		298
Watson, Harriet, Decd.		321
Williams, James	W	286

Ed. Note #1:
Abstract of the Will of Absolom H. Barrow (Will Bk. A; P.5)
Names: Sister - Frances A. Peace; Neice - Marinda L. Peace;
Brother - Joseph J. Barrow; To Dr. Richard W. Pettway (relationship unexpl.) Brother - Wm. J. Barrow; Sister - Sarah J.
Connelly; Sister- Eliza G. Cole; Brother-in-law - Willis
Peace; a negro woman - Sarah Smith; a son of Willis Peace
gets his watch.
Written 7 Oct. 1846 - Probated 15 Feb. 1847

Note #2:

In the Index to Estate Packets are the following:
Turnbull, Dr. Robert J.   #93
Turnbull, Chas. F.   #7
Turnbull, Lewis & Mary Rubin (Minors) #8
Turnbull, Robert J.   #187

ADDITIONAL ABSTRACTS OF WILLS, ISSA. CO. MS.

WILL BOOK B : (1853 - 1861)

Will of R.P. Shelby, p. 39

Robert Prince Shelby to Neice Mary B. Creath; other heirs... Eudora J. Creath (now Endora J. Likens), D.H. Creath, Mary B. Creath, Shallina Y. Creath, Alberta Creath, all children of Albert G. and Mary B. Creath, the children of Thomas J. Shelby -namely Evan Shelby, Creath, Thomas, and also John S. Joor, child of George Joor & Catherine P. Shelby.

WILL BOOK C : (1859 - 1926)

Will of R. J. Turnbull, p. 188

Robert J. Turnbull of Duncansby, County of Issa. Co. 1st to release Mrs. Grace M. Walton from all claims of moneys; 2nd (names) wife Catherine Van Rensselaer Turnbull, son, Robert J. Turnbull, Jr. and <u>other</u> children;
6th Nov. 1901
Witnesses sworn on 1903 in N.Y.: Elizabeth K.S. Lorillard, New Rochelle, N.Y.; Ernest E. Lorillard, New Rochelle, N.Y.; George Waddington, N.Y.
Refiled & Rerecorded 22 Oct 1909

Will Book C p. 193 (1859 - 1926)

Will of Robert J. Trunbull:"Not knowing when he will have cause to give his life for South Carolina:... Names: sons -- Andrew, Robert; Daus. Mary, Gracia; wife Anna; gr. son Robert (son of Andrew) gets est. ans S.C. estate; son-in-law Robert M. Allen; Exec. Gracia Turnbull and Robert M. Allen
Written 4 Feb 1833, Proven 22 July 1833
Wit: N.R. Middleton, F.M. Beusemen, John Wilkes
Exec. qualified---R.M. Allen, Andrew Turnbull
16 Nov. 1833--Ex. Qualified--Robert J. Turnbull
State of South Carolina, Charleston County
All of the above filed for record in Issaqueena Co. Ms., 22 April 1910

WILL BOOK C : (1859-1926)

   Will of John Tilman Foster: p. 97
Written Henry County, Va. 31 Aug 1863: States he has a
wife and 2 children; 1st dau Leila, a son Till_man_;
wife Anna M. executor: Codicil marked Franklin Co., Va.
3rd Aug 1868

   Will of Evan B. Shelby, et al by Thomas J. Shelby Pet.
Thomas J. says he is the father of Evan B., Albert, Creath,
Thomas J. & Mollie Kate Shelby, all minors: States that
all 4 are legatees of estate of R.P. Shelby, dec.
Signed 30 Oct 1866

PACKET #93: Dr. Robert J. Turnbull:
   Robert J. Turnbull, exec. of Dr. R.J. Turnbull, dec.
dated 13 April 1887
Inventory: 1882
Will filed for Probate 3 Jan 18_55_(or 1854) of Robert
J. Turnbull of Westchester, N.Y.
Son, Robert J. Turnbull (minor) to take over estate at
age 25 from Uncles Andrew Turnbull & G.M. Wilki_ns_
1882: Robert J. Trunbull petitions for Probate of Dr.
R.J. Turnbull's estate
1887: Insurance files 1887
16 Feb. 1882: Bill from J.O. Arnols, City sexton & Gen.
Undertaker at Vicksburg, Miss., Corner of Grove & Monroe
Streets...$43 to Mrs. James Roach, pd by R.J. Turnbull, adm
8 Jan. 1885: Mrs. M.P.H. Roach received from R.J. Turnbull
exec. $200, New Orleans
1891: Mahala (Mahala Roach) dissolves R.J. Turnbull from
any further duties

CENSUS 1850 ISSAQUENA COUNTY, MISSISSIPPI

1 - 1	Alexander M. Gwin	33	Planter	7,600 ac.	b	Tenn.
	Elizabeth C. "	24				S.C.
	Ida H.	6				Ms.
	Robert C. Dameron	30	Physcian			"
2 - 2	George N. Parks	42	Planter	13,750		"
	Susan E.	38				La.
	Margaret E.	6				Ms.
	Geo. N., Jr.	13				"
3 - 3	Elias Pharr	51	Planter			N.C.
	Ursilla M.	28				Tenn.
	Hampton (male)	16	Mail Carrier			N.C.
	Elizabeth	14				Tenn.
	Albertus	12 (male)				"
4 - 4	Washington B. Farr	34	Overseer			Ms.
5 - 5	William A. Bovard	32	"	3,000		"
	Ellen E.	18				La.
	Laura R.	2				Ms.
6 - 6	Jonathan G. Cox	33	Overseer			Tenn.
7 - 7	James Glenn	30	"			S.C.
	Mary	17				N.C.
8 - 8	William D. Huggins	30	"			"
9 - 9	Robert E. Cox	32	"			Ala
	Musadoia "	28				Tenn.
10-10	William Ryan	30	"			Ireland
11-11	Robert Glasscock	33	"			Ms.
12-12	John Fitzgerald	27	"			S.C.
13-13	James Wiley	35	Labourer			Ohio
14-14	Joseph T. Rollison	24	Overseer			Ms
	Sarah A.	23				"
15-15	William Dodds	34	Planter	20,000		Tenn.
	Nancy Y.	35				Ala.
	Mary A.	15				Ill.
	Cornelia	6				Ms.
	Elizabeth T.	3				"
	Cecil E. (female)	2				"
	Susan A. Sullivan	12				
16-16	James Bain	32	Overseer			Ill.
	Mary	23				Ms.
	Robert J.	10/12				"
17-17	William S. Brown	38	Overseer			Ky.
	Elizabeth M.	36				"
	James	1				Ms.
18-18	Isaac C. Hill	32	Planter	7000		"
	Ann	55				Tenn.
	Emily C.	19				La.
	Glenara A. (female)	1				Ms.
	Thomas W. Seller	17	none			"
	Edwin R. Seller	10				"
	Benjamin M. "	50	Overseer			Tenn.
19-19	H. Clinton Sellers	18	none			Ms.
	James T.	16	"			"
	Isaac F.	12				"
	Elbert A.	10				"

, Issaquena Co. Ms.

Census 1850, cont.

	Edward B. Sellers	8			Ms.
	Amelia A.	7			"
	Alice G.	2			"
20-20	Edmund Tidwell	43	Overseer		S.C.
21-21	Abram Owens	54	"		Va.
	Emily A.	20			"
	Elvira H.	16			"
	Henry T. Hollis	25	Labourer		Tenn.
22-22	Alexander B. Weeks	38	Overseer		"
23-23	Clinton Smith	37	Labourer		KY.
	Mary	26			Tenn.
	Elizabeth A.	14			Ky.
	Thomas	12			Ms.
	Tobias	5			Ms.
	Sam B.	3			Tenn.
24-24	Thomas Smith	35	"		"
	Margaret	30			"
	Clinton	10			"
	Jane	8			"
	Aleck	6			"
25-25	Elijah McRoberts	35	Labourer		"
	Martha Booth	55			"
	Dempsey Peel	30	"		"
26-26	Jeremiah Osborne	30	"		Ms.
	William	32			"
	Susan	24			"
	Ann	26			"
27-27	Robert J. Fitz	40	Planter	5,370	La.
	Martha E.	28			Ms.
	John W.	4		800	"
	Henry Smith	35	Overseer		N.C.
28-28	Emeticus Murphey	44	"		"
29-29	Patrick Hamel	35	"		Ireland
	Lavinia	23			S.C.
	James H.	3			Ms.
	Mary E.	1			"
30-30	Nathan A. Heard	27	"		Ga.
	Minerva L.	22			Ala.
	Minerva A.	6			"
	Joseph C.	4			Ark.
	Julia W.	2			Ms.
31-31	David F. Castleman	35	"		Va.
	Mary M.	27			Ala.
	Louisa F.	8			La.
	Charles F.	6			Ms.
	Margaret J.	3			"
	Hannah E.	1			La.
32-32	Lewis Tillman	34	"	500	Va.
	Ann M.	22			Ala.
33-33	Thomas W. Deman(?)	23	"		La.

Issaquena Co. Ms

Census 1850 cont.

34-34	Walter C. Lofton	42	Planter	15000	Va.
	Mary A.	28			Tenn.
	William B.	10			Ms.
	Eldridge	6			"
	Evan S.	5			"
	Lucinda	2			Tenn.
	Barton H. Millsaps	34	Overseer		"
35-35	Robert P. Shelby	45	Planter	14000	"
	Aaron H. Sanders	35	Overseer		N.C.
36-36	Henry M. Moss	27	"		Tenn.
37-37	J(blurred) N. Collier	26	"		Md.
38-38	Joseph W. Robertson	42	Planter	10000	Tenn.
	Leanah "	30			Ms.
	Olive V. "	8			"
	Joseph H. "	3			"
	Alta California "	1			"
	Evan J. Harvey	23	none		"
39-39	James R. Harvey	18	Planter		"
	Eleanora W.	17			Mo.
40-40	Joseph J. Sullivan	42	Planter	1600	N.C.
	Catharine	30			Ark.
	Mary E.	10			Ms.
	Calvin Belcher, Sr.	66	none		Maine
	Emily H. Sullivan	7			Ms.
	Louisa C. "	3			"
	Martha C. "	9/12			"
	Calvin H. Belcher	21	Overseer		La.
41-41	Josiah P. Woolfolk	39	Planter	10000	Ky.
	Caroline	27			Ms.
	Charles W.	5			"
	Elijah W. McCullen	18	Overseer		Ky.
42-42	Henry T. Branch	30	"		Va.
	Martha J.	16			Ms.
43-43	Samuel G. Parks	36	Planter		"
	Rebecca	40			La.
	Thomas G.	14			Ms.
	George Ann	6			"
	Josephine	3			"
44-44	William Featheringale	28	Labourer		Ky.
45-45	Walter McKaughn	35	"		"
46-46	John McDaniel	30	"		Tenn.
47-47	James Morris	32	"		Ms.
48-48	Soloman Northam	28	"		La.
49-49	Morrell Heodgedon	30	"	500	Conn.
	Fanny "	35			N.C.
	William Cole "	26	"		"
50-50	John Connor	30	"		Mo.
	Eliza	28			Ms.
	Phobe	8			"
51-51	Burwell Bunn	32	Overseer		N.C.

Census 1850 cont   Issaquena Co. Ms.

#	Name	Age	Occupation	Value	State
52-52	Samuel W. Wells	57	Planter	16000	Ms.
	Martha A. "	33			La.
	Martha J. "	17			Ms.
	James J. "	8			"
	Ferdinand J. Moss	32	Overseer		Ky.
	John F. Chaney	29	Planter		La.
	Catharine Chaney	19			Ms.
53-53	Newitt H. Vick	28	Planter	20000	Ms.
	John W. Scott	35	Overseer		Va.
54-54	Evan W. Shelby	33	Planter		Tenn.
	Mary L.	25			La.
	John S. Joor	5			Ms.
55-55	William T. Barnard	28	Planter	6400	Ms.
	Sarah E.	27			La.
	Henry C.(Harry?)	20	Student		Ms.
	Sarah L.	8			"
	Mary J.	6			"
	William B.	4			"
	Bailey J. Chaney	31	none		La.
56-56	Joseph L. Barnard	26	Planter		La.
	Rebecca F.	23			Ms.
	Henry	1			"
57-57	J.B. Mills	25	Overseer		Ky.
58-58	Richard Rawls	45	"		N.C.
	Charity	35			"
59-59	William B. Macquillen	24	Planter		La.
	Melissa J. "	21			Ms.
	Alberta E. "	3			"
	Joseph R. "	17	none		La.
	John P. "	31	"		"
	John E. Butler	26	Carpenter		S.C.
	Jane C. "	19			La.
	Robt. C. "	20	Carpenter		S.C.
60-60	James B. Woolfolk	34	Planter	3000	Ky.
	Verlinda	20			Ms.
	John H.	2			Ky.
61-61	David D. Jackson	24	Physcian	1300	Va.
	Melissa C. "	19			La.
	Antonia L. Chaney	36			"
	Margaret "	15			"
	Wood S. "	17	none		"
62-62	Green B. Long	48	Overseer	240	N.C.
63-63	William Rushing	55	Planter	3000	"
	James M. "	25	none		Ms.
64-64	Mordecai Powell	46	Planter	20000	Md.
	Emily M. "	38			La.
	Henrietta N.	12			Ms.
	Emily M.	10			"
	Littleton M.	8			"
	Mary Kate	6			"
	Judge J.	4			"
	Hetty Ann	2			"
	Laura Ann	6/12			"
	Albert H.	37	none		Md.
	(next 3 names very blurred)				
	William W. Chaney	22			La.
	Sarah C.C. Chaney	17			"
	John W.	31			Va.

Census 1850 cont.   Issaquena Co., Ms.

65-65	Henrietta E. White	41		5000 La.
	Margaret J. "	16		"
	William I. "	13		"
	Mary E. "	15		"
	Henrietta E. "	10		Ms.
	Leonora O. "	8		"
	John Allen	34	Overseer	Va.
66-66	William Myers	40	Planter	6000 N.C.
	T. Francis Myers	1		Ms.
	Jesse R. Fields	39	Overseer	N.C.
	Margaret J. Fields	26		"
	Elizabeth Fields	15		"
	Martha A. Fields	13		"
	Ellen R. Fields	11		"
	Henry C. Fields	10		"
	Jesse H. Fields	8		"
67-67	Miles M. Messinger	25	Overseer	Mass.
68-68	William W. Yandall	33	"	N.C.
69-69	Joseph N. Moss	28	"	Ky.
70-70	John M. Clark	35	Gin-might	400 Pa.
	Eliza "	22		Tenn.
	Edward D. "	5		Ms.
	December "	3		"
	Almedia "	1		"
	Thomas J. Leigh	49	Overseer	Va.
	Amelia P. "	24		Tenn.
	Alfred J. "	21	Overseer	Tenn.
71-71	Daniel T. Williams	47	Planter	"
72-72	Thomas J. Shelby	32	"	"
	Emily M. "	22		La.
	Evan "	2		Ms.
	Albert C. "	1		"
73-73	Walter McKaughn	38	Labourer	Ky.
74-74	Malachi Bradford	57	Planter	6400 S.C.
	Malachi E. "	18		La.
	Martha E. "	13		"
	Elihu Evans	24	Carpenter	Pa.
75-75	William T. Mills, Sr.	53	Planter	6400 N.C.
	William T. " , Jr.	23	"	Tenn.
	Charlotte "	45		Ms/
	John H. "	22		Tenn.
	Sarah O. "	18		"
76-76	William G. Nolen	36	Planter	3000 Ireland
77-77	Ben B. Fore	50	Overseer	Va.
78-78	James Y. Grigging	34	Clergyman (Meth)	Ms.
79-79	George W. Blount	22	Overseer	N.C.
80-80	John N. Porter	37	"	"
81-81	Charles J. Fore	45	"	Va.
	Ann R. "	40		"
82-82	Michael Everhart	31	Labourer	Ohio
	John Fee	30	"	Ireland
83-83	William T. Lowry	26	Planter	10000 S.C.
	Daniel O'Rourke	22	Labourer	Ireland

p. 130

Census 1850 cont   Issaquena Co.

84-84	Alexander D. Duval	57	Planter	3000	Tenn.
	Margaret "	50			"
	Claiborne A. "	16	none		"
	Gwinette S. "	13			"
	Joseph D. Newsom	22	Clergyman (Meth)		La.
85-85	Dewitt C. Bonham	32	Planter	6200	Pa.
	Mary T. "	28			Ky.
	Rebekah E. "	19			Pa.
	Henry Roberts	29	Overseer		Ill.
86-86	Americe Nicholson (f)	40		10000	Ala.
	Richard F. "	17			Ms.
	Fredonia H. "	15			"
	Victoria H. "	14			"
	Wilber F. "	10			"
	Euralia R. "	9			"
	Eliza H. McNicholson	7			"
87-87	Samuel L. Moore	45	Planter	7200	Ga.
	Rachel "	40			N.C.
	Frank W. "	19	none		Ms.
	William S. "	17	none		"
	A. Thomas "	8			"
	Oliver P. "	3			"
	Robert Fraker	10			"
	Melton S. Haire	28			N.C.
88-88	Mary Green	62			Tenn
	Thomas "	1			Ms.
	Oscar Willis	18	Labourer		Ohio
89-89	Samuel Nelson	51	Planter	10000	Tenn.
	Eunice R. "	41			N.C.
	N. Thomas "	16	none		Tenn.
	John "	14			Ms.
	Sam "	12			"
	James "	10			"
	Frances L. "	8			"
	Eunice A. "	6			"
	Emma "	4			"
	Dick "	1			"
	Theodore H. Beckman	22	School Teacher		Germany
	James Conley	30	Overseer		Va.
90-90	George G. Gregory	42	Planter	4000	Ky.
	Pricilla W.	36			Pa.
	Peter	2			Ms.
	Mary	1			"
91-91	Richard W. Pettway	29	Physcian	1200	Va.
	Julia I.	18			Tenn.
	Thomas R.	4/12			Ms.
92-92	Horatio D. Coffield	27	Physcian	10000	Ky.
	Amanda E.	17			Ms.
93-93	Turner R. Miller	36	Overseer		Mo.
	Alexander A.	11			Ms.

Census 1850, cont.

P.132
Issaquena Co.Ms.

94-94	Elisha North	28	Overseer	Tenn.
95-95	Absolom Williams	35	"	S.C.
96-96	Richard Christmas	45	Planter	N.C.
	Stephen Y.Whitehead	40	Carpenter	"
	Zachariah Leatherman	37	Overseer	Ms.
	Martha B. "	18		"
97-97	John J.Boniel	63	Planter	Ga.
	America A. "	51		Ky.
	James "	12		Ark.
	John R. "	15		"
98-98	Fletcher E.Mayfield	29	Planter	Ga.
99-99	Robert B.Cammack	44	"	Ms/
	Elizabeth "	27		La.
100-100	William Christmas	27	none)married	N.C.
	Mary H. "	18	) w/in yr.	Ms.
101-101	George P. Johnston	23	(blurred)	Ky.
102-102	Patterson G.Scruggs	27	Labourer	Va.
	Mary F. "	22		N.C.
	Anna "	1		Ind.
103-103	John McLaurin	37	Clerk of the Court	S.C.
	Sarah G. "	35		Ms.
	Mary Sophia "	12		"
	Glen-na H.(female)	6		"
	Mary C.Singleton	17		"
104-104	George P.Jones	36	Physcian	Md.
	Martha H. "	28		Ala.
	Mary D. "	9		Ms.
	Maria H. "	7		"
	Martha P. "	5		"
	Charles H. "	3		"
	Laura F. "	1		"
105-105	John H.House	40	Overseer	Va.
	Julia "	28		Tenn.
	Elizabeth "	10		"
	Sam "	8		"
	Henry "	5		Ms.
	Mary "	2		"
	J.G.Miller	27	Overseer	Ala.
106-106	Agnes E.Collins	28		S.C.
	William A. "	10		Ms.
	Mary A. "	6		"
107-107	Eli L.Haygood	26	Overseer	S.C.
	John Williams	30	Carpenter	Ohio
108-108	John Coalter	30	Planter	Tenn.
109-109	Ahab Holmes	24	none	Ms.
	Mary "	18		" !
	George "	1		"
	Hugh Lemon	35	Laborer	Ill.
	James Christmas	21	none	N.C.

Census 1850 cont

Issaquena Co.

110-110	Robert M. Smith	38	Overseer		Ky.
	Serena "	19			N.C.
	Robert M. " , Jr.	2			Mo.
	Walter J. "	4/12			Ms.

The enumerator for the 1850 Census, Issaquena County, was George P. Johnston, Deputy Assistant Marshall, who also enumerated Hinds Co., Ms. His work is very meticulous, and he wrote a beautiful hand.

Census 1860, Issaquena Co., Ms. (Random names)   134

Pg. 1

1-1 Theodore Fitler   45   b Pa.

2-2 N.C. Skinner   35 Phy.   bNC
     Emma Laws   20   Pa.
     Sarah Thompson   31   "

3-3 Thomas Hayes   41   bMs
     Isham Roach   41 Overseer KY

4-4 Richard Christmas   50   NC

- - - - - - - - - - - - -

9-9 Samuel Nelson   61   bTenn
     E.R.   "   50f   Ms.
     N.F.   "   25m   "
     J.W.   "   23m   "
     Saml., Jr. "   21   "
     J.   "   19   "
     F.L.   "   17f   "
     E.A.   "   15f   "
     Emma R. "   13   "
     Mary   "   8   "
     J.T. Pettway   29   "
     Thos. R. "   10   "
     Ida E.   "   8   "
     Sally G. "   6   "
     Laura D. "   4   "
     R.W.   "   3m   "
     Mary R. "   1   "
     E.F. Herbert   21 Teacher Ala.

10-10 S. Leatherman   78   B. Pa.
      S.B.   "   44m   Ms.
      M.W. Lindsey   35f   "
      F.A.   "   16f   "

11-11 Wirt Adams   35   bMs.
      Sallie "   26   SC
      Wirt, Jr.   9   Ms
      Fanny   7   "
      Anna   5   "

12-12 Oscar R. Welles   26 Overseer bNC

Pg. 2
13-13 A. Hundermark   27 Merchant b Seaport of Breman
      Kate   "   22   bLa.
      (Married within yr.)

14-14 Chas. C. Balfour   26   bMs.
      Rosa   "   26   "
      Rosa, Jr. "   3   "

Census 1860, Issa. Co. Ms. cont.

Pg. 2 cont.

```
15 - 15   Jas. C. Barrow      34                       bGa.
          M.M.       "        19f                      La

16 - 16   M. Duval            60f                      bTenn
          C.A.   "            28m  Physcian              "
          J.A.   "            22f                      Ms
          (C.A. & J.A. married within yr.)
          G.S.   "            22f                      bTenn.
          Wm. Murphy          25   Overseer            bKy.

17 - 17   Jesse Bass          35   Overseer            bVa.

18 - 18   Wm. S. Langley      51                       bNC
```

Pg. 3

```
19 - 19   Joseph Spriggs      30                       bEng.

20 - 20   Wm. T. Barham       34                       bVa.
          wife and 4 children
21 - 21   A.M. Guven          43                       bTenn
          wife & 5 children

22 - 22   C.C. Eustis         40f                      bMiss.
          10 children

23 - 23   J.W. Butler         28                       bKy

24 - 24   J.A. Kelly          38 Surveyor & C. Eng. bIll.
          wife & 2 children

25 - 25   D.W.C. Bonham       40                       bPa.
          Mary T.  "          36                       Tenn
          Belle    "          10                       Ms.
          Jennie Cone         20   Governess           N.Y.
          R.Y. Maxwell        27   Overseer            Tenn.

26 - 26   Lucinda Davis       51                       bMs.
          Z.T.       "        11m                        "
          Alonzo Givens       25   Physcian            Mo.
          T.A.       "        22f                      La.
          (Alonzo & T.A. m within yr.)

27 - 27   John H. King        44                       bTenn
```

Pg. 4

```
28 - 28   Frank W. Moore      28                       bMs.
          Mary E.    "        20                         "
          J.E. Nicholson      33   Physcian              "
          M.M.       "        30f                        "
          Laura M.   "         5                       La.
          C.L. Belote         26m  Overseer            Tenn.
```

Census 1860, Issaquena Co.Ms., cont.

P.4 Cont.
```
29 - 29  Rachel Moore          52              b.Ky
         THomas A.Moore        18              Ms.
         Oliver S.Moore        11              "

30 - 30  D.H.Alexander         33              Ms.
         Leonora Z.  "         19              "
         (D.H.& Leonora married within
           year.)
         J.P.G.Holmes          6               "

31 - 31  George N.Parks        23              Ms.
         Georgianna  "         20              "
         King P.     "         1               "
         Susan E.    "         45              La.
         Maggie E.   "         15              Ms.
         Lizzie Brown          13              La.

32 - 32  W.Monk Patterson   30 Overseer        Ms.

33 - 33  O.H.P.Ritch        37 Overseer        Ga.

34 - 34  Jacob Garrett      30 Overseer        S.C.

35 -35   Thos.W.Thurtow     30 Overseer        Ms.

36 - 36  Stephen C.Heard    36                 Ms.
      *  +wife and 4 children

37 - 37  Wm.J.Rowe             42              S.C.

38       Vacant

39 - 39  Robt.A.Furlow         32              Ms.
      *  +wife and 4 children
```

*This is a partial listing.

Census 1860, Issa. Co. Ms, cont. Random names, incomplete:

Pg. 5

40 - 40	S.T. LeMay	41		b NC
	wife & 2 children			
41 - 41	Robt. M. Smith	48		
	(10 in household)			
42 - 42	Andrew Spratt	43	Overseer	bNC
43 - 43	L.T. Wade	41	RE28,520	bTenn
			PE#30,000	
	M.J. "	35f		bLa
	George"	6		bLa
	S.J. "	4f		B"
	Nannie	3f		Ms
	James	6/12		"
	I.Hagerty	48f		Tenn
	A. Hedrick	23m	Clerk	Ms
44 - 44	A.C. Gibson	33		"
	D.B. Wade	34		"
45 - 45	L.L.F. Peet	35	Merchant	Ohio
46 - 46	H.V. Keep	30m		bLa
	L.H. "	46f		"
	A.L. "	2f		Ms.
	Richd. G. Bunn	24	Overseer	NC
47 - 47	A.J. Perry	41		"
48 - 48	N.E. Robinson	43	Overseer	Ms
	O.R. Daughtery	21m	Clerk	"
49 - 49	J.M. Godboll	35		Ms
51 - 51	H.P. Duncan	44		"
	Mary "	30		"
52 - 52	John Heath	38		Ms
	Mary M. "	29		"
	John W. Heath	6		"
P.6	Thos. A. "	4		"
	Nannie	3		"
	James P.	1		"
53 - 53	Wash. B. Farr	44		"
	E.J. "	26f		La.
	A.L. Penny	22f		"
	M.L. Ronaldson	4f		"

CENSUS 1860, ISSA. CO. MS.: Randon names

54-54 A.F.Rhodes 30

55-55 L.C.Hill   40   bMs
     Ann   "   65   Tenn
     E.C. "   29f   La
     G.A. "   11f   Ms
     F.B. "   9m   "
     E.L. "   4f   "
     S.E. "   2f   "
     Susan Taylor 26 Teacher b England

56-56 Joseph Bunn   32   NC
     S.A.   "   27f   Ms

57-57 P.Hamel   44m   Ireland
     (5 others in household)

58-58 George Poosen 21 Clerk   SC
     Daniel Levy   __   Prussia

61-61 R.J.Fitz   50   La
     M.E. "   46f   Ms
     J.W. "   14m   "
     S.Ward   18f teacher La

62-62 W.F.Shannon   38   Ireland
     r.   "   "

63-63 W.H. Ladd   45m Brickman England
     M.E. "   25f   Ark

64-64 Wm Osburn   39 Keeper of woodyard bLa
     Ann   "   34   Mo.
     Jas. B."   11   Ms.
p.7 Wm.J. Osburn   10
     Ben B. "   34 Keeper of Woodyard La
     Jackson "   45 woodchopper   Ark

65-65 G.W.Pittman   26m   bLa
     E.A. "   24f   KY
     A.   "   11/12f   Ms
     J.O. "   13m   La

66-66 E.Morton   33f   Ark
     S.E. "   La
     V.   "   "
     Henrietta Rawls 19   Ark

67-67 S.C.Gilchrist 25m   Ky
     J.E. "   20f   "
     M.C. "   2f   "
     C.C.P."   1   Ms
     G.J. "   17m   Ky

CENSUS 1860, Issa. Co.:Random Names
p. 7 cont.

68-68 T.V.Cooper 30   bOhio
      M.C.   "   23f   "
      M.C.   " ,Jr. 7f   "
      H.   "   7/12m Ms

69-69 G. Harden 30 bVa.
      5 additional persons in household

70-70 Thos. Kershaw 50   bSC
      Anna   "   18   Ms
      Mary   16   "
      Rose   14   "
      ___(?)   12m   "
      Richard   10   "
      Trainy   8   "

71-71 Willis M. Owen 35 bMs

72-72 T.F.Alford   33   "
      John S.Lacey   37   Tenn
      J.Blarrenburger __ Pa.

73-73 Alex Bunn   28   __
      Thos. R. Hotchkiss 21 __

74-74 Andrew Turnbull 59 planter RE 192,500 PE$286,000 bSC

p.8
75-75 J.D.H. Weir 30   SC
      E.G.   "   30f Ala
      Wm.J.   "   5m   Ala

76-76 Wm H.Bunn 35 NC
      4 others in household

77-77 A.Turnbull, Jr. 29m RE37000 PE$20000 bMs

78-78 L.H.Collier 30 Ms
      G.A.   "   17f "

79-79 G.D.Jamison 25, Ms (Married within year)
      R.   "   31f "   "   "   "

80-80 S.M.Spencer 22m Planter   Ms
      J.L. Burns   30m Overseer NC
      G.M.Crume   21m Carpenter Ind
      T.M.   "   24m   "   "
      D.F.Hunt   23m   "   N.Hamp.
      W.D.Smith   45m Sawyer   Tenn

CENSUS 1860, Issa. Co. Random Names, incomplete

p. 8 cont.

81-81 Louis Tillman 44 bVa
4 others in household

82-82
- S.G. Parks 45m RE20,000 PE $31,025 bMs
- T.G. " 25m 200 "
- S.D. " 9m "
- M.J. Sullivan 19f RE3000 PE750 "
- E.A. " 17f " " "
- L.C. " 12f " " "
- M.K. " 10 " " "

83-83 R.J. Turnbull 31m Planter RE37000 PE 30000 bMs

84-84
- M.M. Laughlin 24m bOhio
- E.C. Blake 27m Vermont

85-85
- E. Mount 49 Va
- EE. " 49f Conn
- W.G. " 20m Ms
- M.E. " 18f Ms
- D.B. Obannon 30m Va

p. 9

86-86
- J.R. Chisholm 32 La
- N.V. " 31f Ms
- L.B. Gray 9m La
- A.S. Chisholm 7m "
- H.V. " 1f Ms
- F.M. Phelps 16m La

88-88 J.P. Woolfolk 49 bKy

89-89 D.N. Anderson 49 Va
5 others in household

90-90
- T.J. Shelby 43m bTenn
- E.M. " 33f La
- E. " 12m Ms
- A.C. " 10m "
- T.J. " JR. 8m "

91-91
- H.C. Barnard 30 Ms
- E. " 27f La
- M.E. " 7f Ms
- H.B. " 4m "
- S.F. " 2f "

CENSUS 1860, Issa. Co., Random names, incomplete

p.9 cont.

```
92-92  W.T.Barnard     38   bMs
       E.J.    "       27f    "
       LL(S.L.) "      17f    "
       M.L.    "       15f    "
       W.B.    "       13m    "
       A.Creath        15f    "

93-93  W.W.Brown       35m    "
       R.F.    "       32f    "
       W.H.Barnard     11m    "
       J.L.    "        8m    "
       M.L.    "        6f    "

94-94  F.M.Brewer      30m   Ky
       M.A.    "       34f    "
       M.A.    "        7m    "
       --------------

99-99  W.W.Goodloe     23m   Planter  bAla
       W.H.Cartwright  30m   Overseer  Ga
       S.      "       31f             Ala
       J.E.    "        7m             Ms
       M.A.    "        6f              "

100-100 D.D. Jackson   33   Physcian  Va
        M.C.   "       28f             La
        A.L.   "        5f             Ms
        E.H.   "        3f              "
        D.D.   " ,Jr   9/12             "
        J.M.McQuaid    25m  teacher   Pa.
        ----------

103-103 J.M.Brown      35   Clerk    Va
        J.H.Monroe     28            Ireland

104-104 Geo. Hopper    38   Ms
        4 others in HOUSEHOLD

105-105 R.C.Floyd      41   Ky
        B.     "       55f  Ms
        G.W.Brooks     16m   "
        H.Pittard      35m  NC (Overseer)
        D.Davis        33m        "

106-106 Wm Myers       49   NC
        M.C.   "       26f  Ms
```

CENSUS 1860, Issa. Co, Ms, Random names, incomplete

p.11
106-106: cont.

F.C.Myers	12m	bMs
M.E. "	7f	"
R.S. "	5m	"
W.A. "	9/12m	"
M.E.Mizell	40f	NC
J.T. "	12m	"
M.F. "	10f	"
I. "	7m	"

109-109
Wm Rushing	64m	NC
M. "	26f	Ind
W.B. "	1m	Ms

110-110
W.B.Macquillen	35	La
M.A. "	40f	La
M.A. "	12f	Ms
J.J. Wells	17m	"

p.12

113-113 J.Rutherford 36 Rafting bKy

114-114
G.W.Faison	29	Merchant	Va
E.R. "	19f		NC
R.B. "	21m	Clerk	Va

115-115
W.J.Chaney	31	Physcian	bLa
T.Y. "	24m	"	Ms
W.Walsh	20m	Mechanic	Ky
John Dunn	30	Gardner	Ireland

116-116
W.D.Brown (Exr) (?)	27m	bTenn		
A.V. "	18f	Ms		
W.Brown	7/12m	"		
J.H.Robertson	13m	"		
A.C. "	11f	"		
E.C. "	9f	"		
L.C. "	5f	"		
N.S. Cornell	26m	Method Epis. Preacher	bN.Y	
M.J. "	26f			Mass
A.J.Leigh	28m	overseer	Tenn	

117-117 J.W.Browder 32 Merchant bVa.
8 others in household

118-118
E.J.Harvey	33m	bMs
M.J. "	28f	"

CENSUS 1860, Issa. Co.; Random names, Incomplete

p.12 cont.
```
119-119  J.B.Woolfolk      40m   bKy
         V.    "           30f   Ms
         J.    "            8m    "
         L.    "            5f    "
         R. Raney          21m    " (Overseer)
```

p.13
```
121-121  G.W.B.Messenger   35    bOhio
         S.A.    "         30f   NY
         H.M. Sites        39m   SC

122-122  J.E.Butler   34  SC
         5 others in household

123-123  J.S. Joor    14m  Ms
         G.F. Ring    23   NY (Mechanic)

124-124  E.W. Sites   41   SC

125-125  S.Williams   26m  Tenn
         M.A.   "     26f  La
         Tim Heen     38m  Ireland

126-126  R.F.Eatmond  52   NC
         5 others in household

127-127  S.L.Williams  21m  Ms
         J.I. Rice     35m  NC

128-128  Wm. Gibbons   42   bEngland
         M.E.   "      28f  Ms
         N.T. Wade     39m  Tenn  (Overseer)

129-129  J.M.Clark     43m  Pa
         E.S.   "      32f  Tenn
         E.D.   "      15m  Ms
         D.     "      13m   "
         J.E.   "       9m   "
         L.W.   "       6m   "
         M.M.McDonald  11f   "
         P.P.Leigh     35f  Tenn
         J.Phipps      35m  Pa (School teacher)
         A.A.P.Clark    3m  Ms
```

p.14
```
130-130  J.C.Wright    43m  Ms
         C.S.   "      19m   "
         D.A.   "      17f   "

131-131  B.J.Chaney    40m  La
         C.A.   "      27f  Ms
         J.F.   "      10m   "
         M.A.   "       5f   "
```

CENSUS 1860, Issa. Co., Ms. Random Names, Incomplete

p.14 cont.
```
132-132  E.W.Shelby      42m   bTenn
         M.L.    "       35f   La
         M.B.P.  "        4f    "
         D.F.B.  "        1m    "

133-133  G.W.Johnson     34    ____
         E.A.    "       30f   ____
         4 others in household

134-134  A.H.Sanders     44    NC

135-135  W.M.Powell      41m   Tenn
         N.A.B.  "       39f    "
         D.W.    "        5m   Ms

136-136  W.P. Branch     48    Va
         5 others in household

137-137  B.B.Mills       35    Ky

138-138  N.G.Rutland     24m   NC

140-140  S.J.Eakin       34m   Ala

141-141  C.J.Fore        50m   Va
         B.B.    "       62m    "

142-142  W.H.Rutland     40m   NC

143-143  L.C.Watson      46m   Ms
         B.B.    "       21m    "
         W.T.Blake       29m   Tenn
         Alex McGregor   30    Scotland
```
p.15
```
144-144  J.L.Kingsburg   24    Ms
         M.C.    "       20f    "

145-145  J.S.Clark       45m   Pa.
         M.J.    "       25f   Ms
         Jas.T.  "        5m    "
         Eunice M. "      2f    "
         C.Batts         60f    "
         W.Hopper        32m   Pa
         E.G. Eatmond    19m   Ms

146-146  J.Densmore      50    NY

147-147  F.B.Martin      48    Vt.
```

CENSUS 1860, Issa. Co., Ms; Random names, Incomplete

p.15 cont.

148-148 W.S.Balfour   32m   bMs
        7 others in this household by this name
        G.W. Murphee   37m   bVa
        6 others in this household by this name
        M.A.Matheny   16f   bMs (deaf & dumb)

149-149 Jas. L. Mayfield   46   Judicial Officer   bGa
        J.W.Prescott   27m   Clerk in Circuit Court   bLa
        J.T. Walton   24m   Counsellor at Law   bGa
        Thos. W. Sellers   27m   Judicial Officer   bMs

150-150 M.Hodgdon   42m   bN.H.
        S.H. "   40f   Ky

151-151 F.E. Mayfield   39m   bGa.

Enumerator - Thos. W. Sellers, assistant Marshall

Completed 30th Nov 1860

MEDICAL LICENSES ISSUED IN CHRONOLOGICAL ORDER: 1882-1901 ISSA. CO., MS.

NAME	AGE	PLACE OF BIRTH	NOW LIVING	SCHOOL
1. Halbert, F.M.	27	Miss.	Duncansby (1882) Miss.	Jefferson Med. Philadelphia, Pa.
2. Simonton, James Ross	27	Miss.	Hinds Co. Miss. (1882)	Univ. of La.
3. Parish, Robert Davis	37	Woodville Miss.	Mayersville, Miss. (1882)	U. of Va. & U. of La.
4. Petway, Thomas R.	32	Issaquena Co., Miss.	Mayersville, Miss. (1882)	
5. Winslow, Richard C.	33	Jackson, Miss.		Jefferson Med. Philadelphia, Pa.
6. McGown, Basil Duke	40	Tuscaloosa	Issa. Co.	Ohio Med. College
7. Neal, Thomas L.	26	Clinton, Ms	" (1882)	KY. School of Med.
8. Heath, Thomas Adolph	27	Ms	Wash. Co. Ms	
9. Bunz, Hartwig	35	Denmark	Issa. Co. Ms	Prussia
10. Phillips, Thomas Emmet	23	, Ms	Madison Co. Ms	
11. Ware, Reuben	48	Morgan Co. Ga.	Hinds Co. Ms (1882)	No Medical Education "Eclectic" is his field
12. Lawson, Isaac N.	32	America (?)	Wash. Co. Ms,1882	
13. Warren, B.B.	27	La.	Issa. Co. Ms	
14. Scudder, W.H.	26	Wilkinson Co. Ms.	Mayersville, Ms.	New Orleans Med Col. (1887)
15. Davis, John E.	22	America	Issa. Co. (1889)	

MED. LICS., cont.

NAME	AGE	PLACE OF BIRTH	NOW LIVING	SCHOOL ATTENDED
16. Elliott, S.C. (Pharmist)			Mayersville (1893)	(not named)
17. Cox, James H.	"	"	Duncansby (1893)	"
18. Hazlip, John K. (Pharm)	"	"	"	"
19. Griffing, William A.	"	"	Summit, Ms	"
20. Toy, Clinton	25	La.	Greene Co. Ms.	"
21. Ellis, T.C.W.	24	America	Amite City, La.	"
22. Chilton, Charles Marshall	21	Ms.	Issa. Co.	"
23. Webb, H.D.	26	Ms.	Hinds Co. Ms.	"
24. Pierce, Walten Bell	24	"	Warren Co. Ms	"
25. Gayden, Hugh Dickson	33	Ms.	Rankin Co. Ms	"
26. Quin, Russell Aubrey	29	Ms.	Issa. Co.	"
27. Worthington, Thos. Flournoy	25	Ms.	"	Tulane (La.)
28. Bethea, Robert Eachin	50	S.C.	Lincoln Co. Ms	(not named)
29. Groves, Wallace Wade	52	Ms	Hazelhurst, Ms.	"
30. Parker, Will O.		"	Scott Co. Ms	Morton
31. Lamon, John William	25	La.	Baton Rouge, La.	(not named)
32. Benton, J. Burnet	36	Ms.	Port Gibson, Ms	"
33. McDonald, William Eugene	33	Archibald, Ls.	New York (1906)	"
34. Champenais, Fern	22	Ms.	Meridian, Ms (1905)	Tulane
35. Foster, Robert Heath	22	"	Shiloh, Ms.(1907)	(not named)
36. Thames, John Allen	24	"	Collins, Ms(1906)	Tulane

End of taking transcript...Bk. ?? ... til 1977

MARRIAGES: BOOK A: ISSAQUENA CO.MS. 1866-1870
Partial listing; Indexed; Microfilmed

	MALE	FEMALE	DATE LIC.ISS.
1.	James French	Eliza Clark	17 Aug.1866
2.	Hartwell Henderson	Flora Ann Peterson	1 Sept. "
3.	Mat Burrell	Nancy Banks	5 Aug. "
4.	Loudon Carr	Lizzie Bollinger	17 " "
5.	William Britton	Raney Hinton	28 " 1886
6.	Harper Baker	Maria Dickerson	19 " "
7.	Samuel Lewis	Elizabeth Lewis	8 " 1866
8.	Matilda Bowman	Kackson Brown	8 Sept.1886**
9.	Henry Weisinger	Mary Henry	* " " **
10.	Isaac Britton	Frances Ann Childers	22 " 1866
11.	Robert Lowry	Eugenia Moore	6 Oct. "
12.	Alfred Fisher	Dora Shelby	10 Nov. "
13.	Caleb Smith	Sarah Seixas	27 Oct. "
14.	John Jackson	Sarah Goodson	28 Dec. "
15.	Winfield Scott	Clara Ann Maeberry(Mabens?)	23 Nov. " **
16.	Samuel McGee	Fanny Lee	9 " " **
17.	Edward Brown	Maria Jackson	13 Nov. "
18.	Hector Baldwin	Peggy Boyd	26 Dec. "
19.	Charleston Roberts	Margaret Jackson	28 " "
20.	Charles H.Morris	Mary Childs	2 Jan.1867
21.	George Williams	Mary Mitchell	2 " "
22.	Henry Crumb	Spicey Gibbons	5 Jan. "
23.	Charles Jones	Amanda Smith	5 " "
24.	Jack Tyson	Bettie Wright	2 " "
25.	Semper Gadison	Louisa Williams	1 Feb. "
26.	David Mickey	Clara Ann Taylor	3 Jan. "
27.	Anderson Munor	Susan Reid	31 Dec.1866**
28.	Hiram Hickman	Parthenia Taylor	1Jan.1867**
29.	Mayes Griffin	Clarissa Davenport	
30.	Henry Harris	Ellen Paul	5 Feb.1868

MARRIAGE BOOK B, ISSA.CO.MS.:Indexed, Random Listing for Freedmen and Freedwomen.

31.	Henry Page	Mary Green	4 Nov.1870
32.	William H.Davis	Caroline Gee	4 " " **
33.	Alec Parker	Binky Green(Marr.bds.)	7 " "
34.	Oscar P.Green	Lucy A.Webb	" " **
35.	George Griffin	Sarah Ann Harris	23 Nov. "
36.	Nat Hawkins	Tena Gibson	26 " "
37.	Joe Murray	Becky Lunkins	22 Dec.1871
38.	Evan B.Shelby *	Emma S.Wright	6 Feb. "
39.	Harvey Davis	Celia Spriggs	27 Feb. "
40.	R.F.Bay	M.Ella Myers	6 July "
41.	Osborn Wilson	Mary Johnson	2Sept. "
42.	John Allison	Amanda Wilson	2 " "

* Rites performed by Henry P.Bowen,Min.of Gos.M.E.Church.

** Marriage Bond not returned.

INDEX TO ESTATES: Numbers are Estate Packets (filed in drawers)

Probate Records: Issa Co. Ms.

Alston, P.G.   126
Alexander, D.H.   36
"   , Heirs of, Minors 36
Adams, D.A.   121
Anderson, Alex   60
"   , Ophelia   321/324
"   , Harmon   18
Adams, Randall   210
Armstrong, Josephine L.   348
Aden, H.B.   77

Baker, Joseph   181
Brehur, J.H.   199
Bonley, Leila   222
Banks, Aaron   213
Brown, Charles   266
Birdsong, Frank   271
Brown, S.B.   339
Bland, Elizabeth   327
Barnes, Henry   330
Brown, Emma   332
Baskins, Frank   334
Brown, Geo. H.   302
"   Lucy   302
Barlow, Frank   75
Barnard, Henry C.   6
Boyd, J.L.   10
"   A.P.   11
Buan, B.   18
Branch, Henry   19
Barnow, W.L.   20
Binney, Martha   28
Bennett, Minors   51
Briscoe, Wm.P.   50
Blanton, Oliver   78 *
Barrett, J.E.   47
Bernstein, Elias, est.   67
Beard, Benj.   122
Bell, J.S.   125
Banks, O.R.   158
Brehm, Rebecca   118
Brazil, Albert   140
Brum, Alex   183
Beaker, Minor Heirs   201
Brown, Violet, est.   240
Broma, Fleir (?)   245
Boyd, John W.   254
Binder, Leon   288

Blair, Mila Lachs   300
Bronson, Minie B   306
Collins, Wm. A.   49
Christmas, H.H.   20
Chase, Alexander   79
Coffield, H.D.   74
"   , Amanda   68
Chapman, John L.   109
Calhoun, John C.   112
Clark, J.S.   ?
Chaney, Susan H.   32
"   , Ann L.   46
"   , Jon F.   34
"   , Thos. Y.   18
"   , Margaret   48
"   , C.A.
Crouch, P.W.   23
Creath, M.B.A. & S.   3
Council, W.S.   10
Cullen, E.W.
Cobb, Henry   80
Coker, Jno. H.
Coalter, George   25
Coleman, Angelina   75
Conner, Jn. A.   133
Converse, J.B.   134
Coursey, D.
Cowan, T.B.   169
Cox, J.H.   182
Curd, Elizabeth
Chilton, Mrs. Alice P.
(Will)-198
Curd, David   148
Coleman, Nancy   212
Carter, Louisa   216
Coleman, Wesley, est.   224
Cunningham, Jno,est.   242
Carter, H.C.,est.   235
Cheatham, John   241
Carter, R.T.   275
Chilton,St. Jno.est   318
Collins, Abe   357
Cook, G.   333
"   , Frank   361
"   , Mary Jane   345
Cullen, E.W.   21
Cohn, John W.   51

*: Ermgarde & Oliver Blanton; Lucia, Belle, &Nora Doughtery,dec.
O.R. Daughtery, Guard....Est. of Mary Fitzgerald Daughtery,dec.

INDEX TO ESTATES: ISSA.CO.MS: Cont.

Chapman, Isabella 109
Chilton, H.R. 186

Davenport, Joseph 61
Dunn, Franklin 71
Duval, A.D. ---
Deloach, M.P. 12
Davis, Fielding --
Doughtery, Belle, Nora
et al 78.
Dickens, E.B. Est. 190½
Dorsey, Mary 192
Davis, Winchester 208
Diggs, A.R. 278
" , Alfred 268
Davis, Josephine 320
Dean, James Ann 356
Davenport, E.V. 359
Duval, A.D. ---
Daniel, James W. 37
Deeson, A.G. & M.J. 87
Davis, Yancey 328

Elliott, J.S. 17
" , S.C., Minor 157
Eastman, R.F. 89
Eustis, H.S. --
Everhart, M. 129
Elliott, Walter 95
" , Mrs. Emma
(Chas.) 96

Fox, Henry 82
Fowler, E. 124
Fischel, Lyon 45
" , A.L. & M. 46
Fore, B.B. 12
" , C.J. 16
Foster, Lelia A. & E.
minors 40
Foster, Sarah --
Fulton. R.N. --
Ferriss, Anna M. --
Farr, John H. --
" , W.B. --
Fly, A.D. --
Ford, Manly
Farish, Wm.S. 171

Fitz, John W. 155
Fowler, Sarah (w) 184
Fleming, Nathaniel 220
Ford, Edna (Guardian) --
Farish, Jane L., H.P.
Guardian 217
Freshwater, Peter 256
Fields, Drury 243
Fleming, Kinworth 270
Foe, Henry 279
" , " 188
Foster, Nannie E. Est. 280
Farish, Robert D., minor 222
Farish, Thos. H., minor 221
Farish, F. Powers 223
Ferguson, Gabrell 335
Freshwater, Peter 368
Farr, John & Robert ---
Furlow, Robert N. --
Ferriss, St. Clair --
Foster, Nannie E. 280
Ford, West 365

(Note: From this point, many of the boxes are unnumbered)

Gray, Stephen --
" , Jno. W. --
" , Samuel B. --
Gregory, G.G. --
" , Peter --
" , Peter & Mary
minors ---
Garrett, Jacob --
" , M.R., minor --
Gwin, A.M. --
Garner, H.C. ---
Griffin, Jno. & Mary --
Green, E.H. 39
" , Annie & Sarah 107 & 108
Grace, J.C. 80
" , Eva & Louis 99
Gilkey, Ada L. 72
" , Eva, Loyd, Laura 94
George, H.P. & James M.
Parks 24
Grooms, Pane & Viney 35

INDEX TO ESTATES: ISSA. CO. MS.; cont.

Griffin, Alfred __
Gamble, J.T. __
Grambling (Heirs) 147
Grant, (Heirs) __
Grace, Geo. C., Minor 98
Goodwin, Jn. L. 151
Grant, Amos 138
" , Mary 146
" , Lenora 145
Green, Henry 161
" , Taylor 184
Grant, Lawrence H. 144
Green, L.S. 219
Gilkey, Mary E. 233
Green, ___ 177
Gilkey, A.S. (Adm) 229
Grant, Lenora, Guard. 145
Gray, Jno H. 238
Gubbs, W.G. 287
Gano, Robert 329
Grant, Thos. J. 143
Green, Jolen 167
Grant, James __
Goshea, Liz. 352
Graves, Geo. 353

Harwood, Agnes E. 56
Hollberg, Robert & Ida 27
Hays, Thos. W. 134
Hardin, Ira 57
Heyman, A. 69
Holmes, R.B. 50
Hester, C.A. 54
" , Jno. __
Heath, Jno. W., 23
   Minor,
Heath, Thos. & James 22
Henderson, H. 18
Harris, J.R. __
Hennessy, Jno. 48
Hampton, Wade __
Howard, S.D. __
Hill, H.R.W. 65
" , Isaac C. __
" , Frk., B.G. __
A. Lizzie, et al 67
Halloran, James __
Hardin, Alma & Ida __
Hamel, Kate & Wade H. __
Hogan, Wm. __
Hamel, Patrick __

Higgins, R.G. (137 ?)
Hicks, W.P. 135½
Hays, J.P. 138½
Harden, Nancy __
Heath, John 174
Hill, Henderson 200
Harris, John __
Holmes, Mackley 205
" , Chas. (Minor) 209
Henderson, Geo. 268½
Hennessey, Adaline 246
Holmes, Margaret Hughs 203
Howard, L. est. 252
Holland, Clara 244
Hart, Anna M. Est. 316
Holmes, Angeline est. 326
Hailburton, Robert est. 130

Irving, John est. 115

Jeans, Wm. __
Johnson, James 59
" , Moses 84
Jackson, Andrew 42
Julienne, L. __
Joor, George __
" , Jno. S. (Minor) __
Jones, Geo. P. __
Johnson, C.S. est 18
Jeffords, Mrs. N.P. 228
Johnson, Henry 231
" , A.G. 225
Jones, L.J. 232
Jenkins, Geo. 250
Jones, Penella 230
Jackson, Matthew 247
Jinkins, Eliza 274
Jackson, Posey 337
Johnson, Sam 340
Jordan, York J. 312
Johnston, C. 166
Jones, Rachel 308
Johnson, Wesley 310
" , Wm. est. 349

Knight, Geo. & Mary 55
Keep, H.V. 106
" , Anna L. __
Killian, Max 159
Kellog, M.B. 172
Killian, Va. 313

INDEX TO ESTATES: Issaquena Co.,Ms.cont.

   Keep,Mrs. Sallie B.   331,106

  Luhm,A.G. 97
Lallien,John 2
 Leatherman, Samuel 9
 Leighton,T.J. --
 Ledbetter,H.V. --
 Lax,Aaron & wife (Ayora Lacks,sp.?) 34
 Lynch,J.C. 138
 Lucus, I. (Pet. for Adm.of Est. of I.Sterch) 173
 Lucus, I. App.Levee Commissioner
 Lynch,Jas.P. ---
 Lighes,Rial ---
 Lynch,Mattie T. ---
   "   , Ruby 138
 Lawson, L.E. 257
 Love, Dave 289
 Laesen,Morris 303
 Logan,Mary 360
 Lee,A.M. 360
 Lee,Sam 185
 Lypscomb, Ben 362
 Lee,Lizzie B. 366

ABELL: James 36,74,76,81,82, 84,86,88; Nannette 27,88.

ABRAMS: H.M. 18.

ABSON: Andrew 43.

ADAMS: Anna 134; Caleb 50,54; D.A. 149; Fanny 134; Sallie 134; Saml. 68; Susan 31,50; Randall 134; Wirt 134; Wirt Jr. 134.

ADEN: H.B. 149.

ADESON (ADDISON): Dick 45.

AIKEN: Mrs. Josephine 57; W.B. 58.

ALDRIDGE:(ALDRICH): Alfred 3, 104; A.D. 44,48; Annie 104; Bettie A. 40,46,95,105; Fannie 104; Frank 104; Hall 104; L.D. 46,48; Limon G. 94,105; Lyman 105; Mary 104; S.G. 40; Thos. 104; William 104.

ALEXANDER: A.F. 28; Clara 99; C.I. 85; D.H. 136,149; F.P. 28,29,31; Hester 99; Jacob 52,97,99; Leonora Z. 136; Ludwig 34; Rachel 55,99; Soloman 43; Theo. 71; Virgil 148.

ALFORD: T.F. 139.

ALLEN: Claudia 64; John 47, 130; Henry 113; Margaret 113; Mary 18,64,113; Robt. 64; Robt. M. 124; Rich. 64; Sarah C. 18,64,113; Susan Banks 98; Wm. C. 16; Wm.Geo., M.D. 98.

ALLING: Chas. 4.

ALLISON (ALLISTON): John 148.

ALSBROOK: Willis 8;

ALSTON: Mary 64; P.G. 149; Robt. 18.

AMES: Lucy V. Semple 47; Rev. Edward R. 82.

AMOS:Sarah 70; Wm. 70.

ANDERSON: Alex. 149; Harmon 149; Lars. 37; Lewis 20; Lomax 35; Lorenzo B. 108; Mary M. 30; Mrs. O.C. 117; Nellie 35; Saml. 15; Sarah 20; W.E. 117.

ANDREWS:Benj. 28; C.C. 45; G.49; J.T. 29.

APPERSON: E.N. 37.

ARCHER:Alice 56; Annie M. 57; Jas. 51; R.T. 46; Stevenson 51,57,88; Stevenson, Jr. 56.

ARMALL: Lula 55.

ARINFIELD:John 111.

ARMSTRONG: Josephine L 149; Thos 16.

ARRINGTON: Stephen 1,2, 10; Wm. 5.

ARTHEN: Isaac W. 9.

ARNOLD (ARNOLS): Jas. M. 3; J.O. 125; Lenora 55. Pricilla 55.

ASEEY: Saml. 117.

ASH: Morris 18, 31.

ASHBROOK: Moses 20.

ASKEW: Eliza 74.

ATCHESON: Elijah 7.

ATKINS: John 56.

AUGUSTUS: Glenn 50.

AULT: Phillip 2,5.

AUSTIN (AUSTEN) : Hugh 5, Wm. J. 111.

AXMAN: Chas. 55,56.

B

BACON: Wm. 19.

BADGER: C.W.46.

BAGLEY: A.P. 22; Arthur P. 85.

BAILEY: Benj. 11; G.M. 48; J.B. 26,32; Jethro 67; Jos.67; Milton 41; S.P. 29,40; P.T. 31; Wm. 19

BAIN: James 126; Mary 126; Patterson 4,46; Robt. 126; Wm. 5,67,74.

BAINBRIDGE: E.T. 52.

BAKER: Cornelius 7,13; Harper 148; H.L. 45; Joe 118; Jos. 149; Lucy 118; Martha T. 26; ---54.

BALDWIN: Hector 148; Mattie B. 58; 54.

BALFOUR: Chas. C. 134; Rosa 134, Rosa Jr. 134; W.S. 145.

BALL: G.W. 24; H.W. 56; J.P. 48,49,52; W.R. 58.

BALLARD: Jonathon 2,92.

BALLOU: Thos C. 51.

BANKS: Aaron 149; Nancy 148; Nannie R. 58; O.R. 149.

BAREFIELD: Eva L. 57; Hugh 74; Stephen 75; Susan 75.

BARHAM: Wm. T. 135.

BARKER: Andrew S. 80w; Eliz. Hazard 80; Jacob 18,80;

BARLOW: Frank 149.

BARNARD: Corinne 102; E.J. 141; Helen 52; H.C. 106,129, 140,149; Henry 106,129; J.L. 106,129,141; J.S. 106w; Jos. 106; Mary Jane 106,129; M.L. 141; Rebecca 106, 129; Sara Louise 106,129,141; S.F. 140; Thos. 52,102; Wm. Bailey 106,129,141; W.H. 141; Wm.T. 45,106, 107,117,129,141.

BARNETT (BARNET): J.W. 18, 106,110; Rich. 10; T.W. 110.

BARNES: Henry 149, H.W.(M) 96; Jenne E. 96.

BARNOW: W.L. 149.

BARNWELL: Robt. 61; Ed. 61; Wm.N. 61.

BARR: Wm. 63,65.

BARRETT: Catherine 50; Henry 50; J.E. 149; Mrs. T.T. 55; Wm.C.2,65.

BARROW: A.H. 106,123; Jas. C. 135; Jos. J. 123; M.M. 135; Wm.J. 123.

BARRY: Ada Quay 56,57.

BARTLEY: Emily M. 91; W.T.91.

BATEMAN: Mary 72.

BARTON: Lucy H. 21; Wm.P.21.

BARWICK: E.M. 51.

BASKINS: Frank 118,149.

BASS: Chas. D. 55; Council R. 1,12,14,15,28,61; Jesse 135; Jno. M. 106,111.

BATE: H.C. 28; Miss 28.

BATT (BATTS): C. 144; John 29.

BAUER: Wald. 57.

BAUGH: Archie 34.

BAY: R.F. 148; S.T. 51.

BEALL: Henry R. 18; Isaac 1, 14,66,70;

BEAKER: Minors 149.

BEARD: Benj. 149; E. 117; Rich 111.

BEARDSLEE: Neta 58.

BEASLEY: Louisa 103.

BEAVERS: Henry 113; John 113; Margaret M. 113; Wm. 113.

BECIE: Susan 79.

BECK: Alex. W. 38; Frankl. 22.

BECKMAN: Theodore H. 131.

BEDFORD: T.C. 42.

BELCHER: Calvin 2,3,6,7; Calvin Sr. 106,128; Calvin H. 128.

BELKNAP: Wm.B. 8.

BELL: Alice V. 57; D.B. 51, 52; John M. 1,39; J.S. 149; Jane 83; John 83; L.A. 56.

BELOT: C.L. 135.

BENJAMIN: Emanuel B. 56.

BENNETT: Albert G. 64; Cath. 41; Charlotte H. 64; Christ. 64; Henry 64; Marg. 64; Minors 149; Rebecca 64; Wm. 5.

BENSON: A.C. 42; L.S. 56.

BENTON: Dr. J.B. 117,118; Thos. H. 118.

BERNSTEIN: Elias 149.

BERRY: 49; John C. 64.

BERTINATTIE: Eugene P.28, 29,33; Joseph 28,29,33.

BETHEA: Robt. Eachin 147.

BEUSMAN (BEUSEINEN) F.M. 124.

BEVEL (BEVIL): Sarah 116; Wm. E. 116.

BIDDLE: Jno. A. 22,27.

BIGGS: Zach. 3.

BINDER: Leon 149.

BINE: Andrew 49; Wilton 40.

BINNEY: Martha 149.

BIRDSONG: Frank 118,149.

BIRKHEAD (BINKHEAD): 31,36.

BISHOP: R.J. 57.

BLACK: Emily 52; Henry 99; John 19; Moses 52; Sarah 21,97w.

BLACKBURN: David Flournoy (Flemoy) 12,13,16,22,60,61, 62,73,85,88,106,107; E.C. 56; E.M. 85; Geo. F. 18, Geo. T. 81,83,85,91,92; Louisa 91; Mary Belle 91.

BLACKMON: H.G. 35.

BLACKMORE (BLACKMOOR): Thos. 22; Thos.J. 89.

BLAINE: Jas. 11.

BLAIR: Meta Lach 118,149;

BLAKE: E.C. 140; W.T.144.

BLANCHARD: John R. 30.

BLAND: Doff 100; Eliz. 118, 149; Featherstone 1; Jas.2.

BLANTON: A.M. 89; C.M. 80; George L. 101; Georgia 101; Harriet B. 5,11; Idea H. 101; John H. 1,12,16, 61; Lolla 101; Martha 101; M.R. 32,36; Orville 101; Orville M. 31, 32,36,81,101; Willie 101; W.C. 32,34; Wm. C. 79; Wm.W. 5,11.

BLARRENBURGER: J. 139.

BLOOM: D.S. 64.

BLUE: Daniel 11.

BLUM: Saml. 55.

BODDY (BODDIE): Martha E. 117; V.B. 57.

BODLEY: Thos. 65; Wm. 10.

BOGART: W.8.

BOLLING: A.H. 56.

BOLLINGER: Lizzie 148.

BOLTON: M. 107; Wm. 101. Wm.H. 39,40.

BONHAM: Belle 135; Dewitt C. 131,135; Jas. 65; Mary T. 117,131,135; Rebekar E. 131.

BONIEL: America A. 132; Jas. 132; John J. 132; John R. 132;

BONIEY: Lelia 149.

BOOKOUT: Benj. R. 3,4,11, 18; Georgia 58.

BOON: Dollie 58;

BOORAINE: Thos. L. 6.

BOOTH: E.G. 36,49; Martha 127; V.S. 12.

BORSURER: Michael C. 102

BOSWELL: Wm.H. 8.

BOTTS: Elizabeth T. 94; Elizabeth 42,102; John M. 18,81,82,94; Jos. B. 82.

BOURGES (BURGESS): A.B. 25; E. 50; Francis A. 23,24; John R. 24.

BOVARD: Ellen E. 126; Laura R. 126; WM. A. 126.

BOWEN (BOWNE): Grant A. 77; Henry P. 148; Saml. 16.

BOWERS: 54.

BOWLING: Barton 100.

BOWMAN: Matilda 148.

BOWS: Kerran 9.

BOYCE (BOICE): Felix H. 46,89,94,96; Virginia L. Brooks 89; Wm. M. 10.

BOYD: Alex.P. 117,149; Henrietta 65; James L. 117,149; John 52,102, 118,149; John Wm. 98; Mary A. 117; Peggy 148; Thos. P. 9,60,68; Wm. 60; Wm.W. 117.

BOYLAN: Adelaide 117; James 117; John H. 117; Wm. 117; Wm.W. 117;

BRADFORD: Daniel 10; Eliza 83; M. 106,130; Malachi E. 130; Martha E. 130; Simon 83; Wm. 78.

BRAGG: Jos. 16.

BRANCH: Henry T. 149,128; Martha J. 128; W.P. 144.

BRANTON: J.E. 56,57; Peter R. 56,57.

BRASHAW: Loman 11.

BRASHEAR: H.C. 56.

BRAZIL: Albert 149.

BREHM: Rebecca 149.

BREHUR: J.H. 149.

BREWER: F.M. 141.

BRICKELL (BRICKWELL): Helen 21; L.Miller 55; W.E. 21.

BRICK (BROECK): Patsy 30; Rich. T. 30,49.

BRICKER: Jacob 31.

BRIDGE (BRIDGES): Corriner 118; Ed. 28; Matt. 3.

BRIEN (BRYAN): Wm.H. 19.

BRIGGS: David F. 16,61;

BRINKERHOFF: Wm.C. 116.

BRISCOE: Ann 107; Emily C. 23; Jas. E. 106,107; John M. 44; Lizzie 23; Mary 107; Mason 107; Sidney 23; Thos. 50; Wm. 107; Wm.P. 106,149.

BRITTLE: J.W. 107.

BRITTON: Isaac 148; Wm. 148.

BRODNAX: Adele 21; Ed. 21; Mary T. 21; Roberta 21; Wm. 21.

BROMA: Fleir 149.

BROMFIELD: John 99.

BROMLEY: Mattie A. 56.

BRONNER: Flue 118; Triffie 118.

BRONSON (BROUNSON): Edna 57; Ephraim 55; Minnie B. 149.

BROOKE (BROOKS): Bettie 46; G.W. 141; Jos. M. 87, 89; 54; Lucy 46; Virginia 23; Virginia S. 87; Wm. R. 7.

BROWDER: Eliz. 20; Jas. W. 20, 81,142;

BROWN: Amanda 50; A.V. 142; C.A. 31; Chas. 118,149; Daniel 1,46; Edward 148; Eliz. M. 126; E.W. 47; Emma 149; Geo. H. 149; Jas. 43,47,50,126; Jas. G. 35; J.W. 69; Kackson 148; Lizzie 136; Lucy 149; Marg. 101; N.I. 55; R.F. 140; S.B. 149; Shepherd 19,33,64,73; Violet 149; W.142; W.D. 117, 142; W.S. 126; W.W. 140.

BRUISE: Wm. B. 67.

BRUM: Alex 149.

BRYANT: Wm. 113.

BRYSON: 15.

BUAN: B. 149.

BUCHANNON: Griffin 45; Jas. 45; Lillian Mae 58.

BUCK: Chas. L. 20,24,54; Elza. 69; J.S. 48,69; R.S. 41,54.

BUCKLEY: Benj. C. 9; H.S. 45; H.W. 44; Rich. 9.

BUCKMAN: Colin 103; Willie 103.

BUCKNER: Amanda 105; Davis 105; D.M. 46; D.W. 94; Fielding 46; H.S. 40,49; J.M. 96; John T. 23; Kate 35,39; Mrs. Rachel E.M. 85; Sarah F. 35,36; Thos. H. 2,8,16,36,65,95; Wm. 105.

BUFORD: Sallie J. 39.

BUIST: Geo. 64.

BULL: Saml. B. 56; Wm. 64.

BULLITT (BULLET): Alex. C. 35,94w,95; Irene S. 95; Irene Williamson 94; Wm. 5;

BUNN:(BURM): Alex. 139; B. 44; Burwell 117; Jos. 138; S.A. 138; Rich. G. 137; W. H. 25; Wm.H. 117,139.

BUNZ: Hartwig 146.

BURCH: Geo. W. 36.

BURDETTE: Emma 103; Fanny 103; Manuarve 103; Marshall 52; Rich. 49,103; Willie 103.

BURFORD: Geo. 22; T.A. 58.

BURKE: Glendy 1

BURNEY: Mary 20; Robt. W. 20.

BURNS (BIRNE) (BYRNE): Ed. 25,30; E.P. 36,39,41,42; Geo.P. 3,49; Jas. 59; J.L. 139.

BURRELL: Matt 148.

BURTON: C. 56; Edna 58; Florence 58; John 21,96; Sten 56; Wm. 21.

BURUS (BURRUS): Mrs. W.D. 55.

BURWELL:54; Bunn 128; Eugenia 121.

BUSH: David 7.

BUTERO: Mary 56.

BUTLER: Frances 71; Jane C. 129; John E. 129,143; J.W. 135; L. 107; Robt. C. 129.

BUTTS (BIETTS): Eva 107; J. 106, 107; Jno. 87; J.M. 107; Mary 107.

BYAS: Clark 100.

BYME: Edward P. 85.

C

CAFFAEL (CAFFAL) CAFFALL): Chas. 92; Lewis 92;

CAGE: Chas. C. (Judge) 89.

CALAHAN: Jno. 46.

CALHOUN: A.B. 57; John C. 43,149.

CAMERON: Eliz. 66; John R. 47.

CAMMACK (COMMACK): Eliz. 132; Jas. 27; Robt. 113,132.

CAMPBELL: Alex. 111; Chas. 15; Geo. W. 72; Henry 95w; Jane W. 20,26; John M. 9; Jos.H. 20,72; Lila 95; Luther 55; Marg. 18,20,23, 24,25,28,32,47,72,102; Mary S. 20; Martha G. 20; Nedham 20; Rich. 72; Robt. J. 8; Stella 20; Susan 95; W.A. 20; Washingtonia 20; W.L. 26,27; Wm. 72; Wm.R. 4,15, 18,20,72,91.

CANNON: E.A. 80; W.B. 56.

CANTY: Ed. 48.

CARPENTER: Andrew 16; Jno. M. 14,15; Horace 9.

CAPERTON: A.C. 30.

CARLIN: H.T. 16.

CARNEAL: Thos. D(Major) 80.

CARR: J.M. 96; Loudon 148.

CARRICO: R.P. 37.

CARROLL: Mother Columbo 43.

CARSON: Andrew 2,19,20,24, 26,27,29,34,36,38,51,62, 64,69; A.B. 86,87,88; Sarah 20; Saml. 64; Thos.D. 20.

CARTER: Alf.G. 2,4,7,12,15, 18,31,65,68,69,79; A.R. 26; Alfred Z. 79; E. 45; Eleanor - Ellinor 45,102; Eliz.102; E.L. 37,39,59; Eliz. L. 79; H.C. 149; John A. 59; John 2; Lou. 149; Matt. 71; Mary E. 37; R.B. 27; R.M. 26,28,45,68,79;

R.T. 98, 149; Robt. H. 18,27,34, 37,79,102; Spencer 148; Wm. 45; Wm.G. 102.

CARTHWAIT: Jere 4.

CARTWRIGHT: J.E. 141; M.A. 141; S. 141; W.H.141.

CASE: Fred. 2,18.

CASON: A.B. 86,87,88; Benj. 19.

CASTLEMAN: Chas. F. 127; David F. 127; Hannah E. 127; Louisa F. 127; Marg. J. 127; Mary M. 127.

CASWELL: John 57; Ruth 57.

CATTIN (COTTIN): Jas. 80.

CAUGHEY: John J. 81; Mary H. 81; Saml. N. 19.

CERNIGLIA: Rose 56.

CHAFFIN (CHAFFEE): Edw. H. 1; John 49.

CHAMBERLAIN: Aaron 9.

CHAMPENAIS: Fern 147.

CHAMPION: Wm. 116.

CHANDLER: Wm. 69.

CHANEY: Mrs. Ann S. 107,108,113; Antonia L. 63,129,149; A.T. 108; Bailey J. 129,143; C.A. 143; Cath. 129; I.F. 108; J.F. 106,108,116, 129,143,149; Jas.J. 63; J.T. 108; M.A. 143; Marg. 63,108,113,129, 149; Sarah C.C. 129. Sarah H. 106, 149; Susan H. 107,149; Thos.Y. 118, 142,149; W.J. 142; Wm.W. 129; Wood S. 63,129.

CHAPMAN: Jno. 6,10,12,13,14,15,16, 18,20,21,62; John L. 149; Isa.149.

CHARTARD: Charley 102; Mary 102.

CHASE: Alex. 149.

CHEATHAM: John 149.

CHEW (GHENN): Augus. 104, Marg. 104; R.H. 28.

CHEWING: Jas. J. 4,7.

CHICK: Alfred 29.

CHILDERS: FRANCES A. 148.

CHILDS: Mary 148.

CHILTON: Alice P. 118,149; Chas.Marshall 147; H.R. 149; John M. 12; St.John 118,149; Wm.D. 65.

CHISLOM: Anthony 118;A.S. 140; J.R. 140; Kate 56; N.V. 140; Pauline 56.

CHISM: Mattie 118.

CHRISTMAS: H.H. 118,149; Jas. 132; Mary H. 132; Rich. 132; Wm. 132.

CHURCH: Catherine 68; Ed. 68,70; Ed.B. 65,67,68,70; Marcia 1; Maria B. 67,68, 70; Wm. 68.

CHURCHMAN: Jno. 18.

CLACK: A.R. 56.

CLAIBORNE: Mrs. Ann 60,61.

CLARK: Almedia 130; Edward D. 130,143; Eliza. 130,143, 148; Eunice M. 144; Dawson 46; Dec. 130,143; Dr. Jas. 11; Fred 69; Geo.W. 65; Jas. T. 144; Jno. 5,49,69; Hno.M. 130,143; J.E. 143; J.S. 25,144,149; Martha 1, 49; W.B. 55;54; Mary 100; M.J. 144; L.W. 143.

CLARY: F. 45; W.A. 45.

CLIFTON: 3.

CLORE: David L. 21; Henry 21.

CLOUSTCH: W.G. 57.

COALTER:G. 107; Geo. 108, 149; Jno. 107,108,132; Judge 1,4,8.

COBB: Henry 108,149.

COCKE (COCKS)(COX): Alf.G. 5,7,9,10,16,60,62; Ella 92; Ellen 40; Jas. 3,4,6,10,11, 14,15,8,9; Jas.H.147,149; Jno. 92; Jonathon G. 126; John G. 7,8,9,10,11,59,60, 61,62,67; John H.1,3,4,8, 10,14,15; J.J. 41,73; J.R. 40,50,53; Katy 92; Louisana 59; Phillip 5,6,7,9,11,12, 13,59,60,62,71,67,69; Thos. I. 3; S.C.77,78,92,93.

COCHRAN: Louisa 69; Wm.R. 62,69.

COFFER: Jos. 93.

COFFIELD: Amanda E. (Mrs.) 118,131,149; H.D. 108,113, 114,131,149; Lura 55; S.A.P. 113.

COFFMAN: A.P. 57; Jacob 79; Lewis 79; Mary 79; Nancy 79.

COHN (CAHN): B. 52,57; Freida 55; John W. 149; Josie 55; Phillip 100; Soloman 56.

COKER: JNo. H. 149.

COLBURN: 27.

COLE: Eliza G. 123; J.B. 51.

COLEMAN: Angelina 149; Chapman 9; Ella 56; Jas.12; Jno B. 7; Nancy 118,149; N.D.3; Wesley 149; Wm.11.

COLLIER: G.A. 138; Jas. R. 94; J.N. 128; L.H. 139.

COLLINS: Agnes E. 112,132; Abe 149; F.B. 81; F.H. 12, Jeremiah H. 87; J.W. 78,87; Mary A. 132; Merian A. 60; Wm. A. 132,149; Wm.L. 87; W.S.25; WM.W.2,6,11,14,59, 60,70,71;

COMEGY: B.F. 38.

COMMODORE: Jas. 39.

COMPTON: Jeff. 94; Jno. 94; Mary 94; Pickens 94w.

COMSTOCK: E.J. 26,35; Evil-en 35.

CONE: Jennie 135.

CONDY: Thos. D. 18,61,64.

CONLEY: Geo. C. 131.

CONNELLY: Sarah J. 123.

CONNER: Eliza 128; John 128; John A. 149; Phobe 128.

CONNERLY: David W. 8.

CONVERSE: J.B. 149.

CONWAY: Ellen 28.

COOK: Caroline 108; D.D. 44,45,46,48. Ed. 26; E.G. 32,40; Frank 149; G. 149; Mary Jane 118,149; Wm. 48; 54.

COOLEY: 3;31;

COOPER: E.J. 95; Ellen 21; E.S. 53; H. 139; Jacob 118, Jos. 21; M.C. 139; M.C.Jr. 139; Robt. 9; R.L. 95; R.S. 53; T.V. 139.

CORBETT: Wm. 84.

CORDELL: Jos. 62.

CORNELL: M.J. 142; N.S. 142.

COSETT: Geo. 3; Fred A. 3; Pearl S. 3.

COTTINGIN: Jas. B. 68.

COTTON: Saml. 14.

COUNCIL: Washington S. 108, 147;

COURSAN: C.H. 55.

COURSEY: D. 149.

COURTNEY: Jane E. 102, Jno. 102; John T. 30,35,39,43, 44,49,82,91.

COWAN: T.B. 118,149.

COWDEN: John 70.

CRAIG: John A. 19; Saml. 12; Susan 19; T.J. 39.

CRANE: B.R. 47.

CRAWFORD: Wm. 63

CREATH: (CRATH): Alberta 26, 107,108,124,140; Albert G. 15,107,124; D.H. 107,124; Endora (Eudora) J. 107,124; Mary B. 107,124,149; Shallina Y. 107,124; Shanline 107.

CRECHLOURS (CRECHLOW): Sarah 113.

CREGAN: Francis 85

CRENSHAW: Sarah D. 44.

CRONLY: Louis 12;

CROSS: Jerome 46.

CROUCH: A.P. 114; Peter 107,112,149.

CROW: A.J.H. 22,25, 67,84; Andrew 78; Henry 9,67.

CRUMB:(CRUME): G.M. 139 Henry 148.

CRUMP: 26.

CULLEN: E.W. 149.

CUMMINGS: W.H. 55.

CUNNINGHAM: Benjamin 19, John 118,149; John Peavie 7,61,65,73,76; Richard M. 18,76.

CURD: Elizabeth 118, 149; David 118,149.

D

DABLEGREEN: Chas.G.42.

DABNEY: Edward 28.

DAMERON: Robt.C. 126.

DANGERFIELD: Henry 59.

DAN: Della E. 58.

DANIEL-(DANIELS):38; Lizzie 55; James W.150;W.E.75,81.

DASCHIELE: Jere.Y.7,14.

DAUGHTERY (DOUGHTERY): Belle 150; Nora 150; O.R. 137.

DAVENPORT: Clarissa 148; E.V.150; Joseph 150; Rich. 15; Robt. 42, 94.

DAVID: Jane 50.

DAVIDOW: S. 55.

DAVIS: D. 141; Fielding 118,150; Felix 10; Harvey 148; H.P. 64; Jas. L. 56; Jeff. 47; Joseph 29; Josephine 150; John B. 1,5,43; John E. 146; Lula C. 56; Lucinda 118,135; Mary 84; Ned. 45; Rebecca 29; S.M. 118; Winchester 150; Wm.H. 22,148; Wm. 50; Warren 57; Robt. 50; Yancey 150.

DAVISON (DAVIDSON): Anna L. 120; John 96; Robt. 67; Minnie 58.

DAWSEY: John 50; Rachel 50.

DAWSON: J.D. 61; F.A. 43; Henry S. 4,59; Thos. F. 58.

DAY: L.E. 55; Matt. 12; Sam.104

DAYLEY: John 23.

DEAN: Arthur G. 56; Ann 118, 150; James 118,150.

DEESON: A.G. 150; M.J. 150; Wm. 111.

DELANEY: 5;

DELOACH:(DELOCH)Mathison (Madison) P. 108,109,150.

DEMAN: Thos. W. 127.

DENSMORE: J.144.

DENSON: John E. 91.

DENTON: Gabriel 19.

DESAVIER: Gisso 42.

DESOUTHERN: John 38?.

DICK: Benj.S. 115; James 110.

DICKENS: E.B. 150.

DICKERSON: Maria 148; A.G.86.

DIGGS: Alfred 150; A.R. 118,150.

DILLINGHAM: A.R. 42; J.40; JOHNP. 32; Nancy 1,5,6,7, 13; W. 42.

DINKINS: Mary E. 98;R.T. 98.

DINWIDDIE: Robt. C. 64.

DIXON (DICKSON): 54; Edwards 52; Harry S. 37,39; James 39; R.L. 35,39,42,87,91; Thomas 10.

DOBBINS: Mary 22.

DODDS: Cecil E. 126; Cornelia 126; Elizabeth T. 126, Mary A. 126; Nancy Y. 108, 126; Wm. 72,108,126.

DONALDSON: Saml. 60.

DOREMUS: Thos. C. 1.

DORIC: Dr. John 84. (See Downs)

DORR: Francis 16, Saml. 16.

DORSEY: Mary 150.

DORSON: Nancy 43.

DOUGLAS: Kate N.95; Kate R. 95; Robt. F. 95; W.H. 95,96,

DOVER: John 45.

DOWNING: Jas. 65; Jos. 68; John R. 11,14,62,65,66; Geo. 29,65,66.

DOWNS: Jas. R. 90; Lettitia Vick 90; Dr.John 84.
DOYLE: John 37; Mary A. 70.
DRABELLE: S. 40,53.

DREYFUS (DREYFIS): Albert 118,150.

DRINKARD: Frances 101; Geo. 101.

DRISKELD: Cyrus 5,10,11.

DROMGOOLE: Sarah 61; Wm. 2, 3,10,13,14,15,61.

DRONE: Rich. 30.

DUDLEY: C.W. 36,38; Charlie 92; Emma 92; Johnson 92; Lillie 92; Margaret A. 91, 92w; Wilkins 92; Victor 92; Willie 92.

DULANA: John 10.

DULANEY: Benj. 59; Daniel 59; Alf. 59; E. 59; John P. 59; G.S. 59; Gertrude 59; H.P. 59w; Rebecca 59.

DUNBAR: Albert W. 8; John R.W. 15.

DUNCAN: Henry P. 118,137; Jessee I. 47; Saml.P. 118; Stephen 36,118; Mary 137.

DUNLAP: 54; John H. 19; Sarah V. 19,21; Susan V. 19,21.

DUNN: Betty A. 74,87,90; Byron 104; Chapin 74; Edward 3; Emma 57; Finlay 74; Franklin 150; John 142; John N. 74; Harriet T. 90; Mary 87; Mrs. E.A. 89,90; Marion 58; Orville B. 90; Sarah R. 90; Saml. R. 1,5, 11,12,14,15,16,74,81,87w, 89,90;Thos. W. 74,15; Thos. K. 90; Wm. 87; Wm. Blanton 87.

DURFEY: Robt. W. 74,84.

DUVAL: Alex. D. 108w,131, 150; Margaret 108,118,131, 135; Claiborne Alex. 108, 131,135; Gwinet S. 108,131, 135; J.A. 135; Mary C. 108; Matilda N. 108.

DYER: Flora A. 96w.

E

EASTIN: Emma 50.

EASTMAN: R.F. 150.

EATHERLY: W.R. 56.

EATMOND: E.G. 144; R.F. 143.

ECKFORD: Hattie 58.

ECKSTONE: Clara 58; Mark 58.

EDE: Joshua 55.

EDGAR:84; Archibald 28.

EDWARDS: Arthur M. 113.

EGG: Joseph 8,14,43.

ELDER: E.J. 42.

ELLIOT: A.F. 33; H.H. 48, 52; Mrs. Emma (Chas) 150; J.S. 150; Samuel 101; S.C. 147,150; Theod. D. 2,28,30; Walter 150; W.S. 64.

ELLIS: A.L. 58; Catherine 101; Eli 58; T.C.W. 147; Wm.L. 3,7, 19,58.

ELLSWORTH: 58.

ELY: Wm. 68.

EMANUEL: Morris 10.

EMERSON: J.H. 58.

EMMONS: Eliza 51,104.

ENDARQUIRE: 33.

ENLICOTT: Thos. M.(W). 1,5,6,7,8,9,13,14,15,16,59,62,66,71.

ERWIN (ERVIN): Andrew 70; Bettie J. 29,92; Henry C. 92; John 38; Marg. E. Johnson 92; Victor 38; Wm. 38.

ESTILL: C.R. 33,34,39; Jas. M. 11,34,39.

EUSTIS: C.C. 119,135; Horatio G. 119; H.S. 150.

EVANS: Elihu 130; Emma 35; Jno.H. 40; Lon.D. 35; Macklin 13,16,62,65,69; Mary A. 69,72;

EVERETTE: John B. 72.

EVERHEART: Michael 130,150.

EVERMAN: 39; W.A. 40,50,53.

F

FAISON: Ellen 20; Geo. 20; E.R. 142; G.W. 142; R.B. 142.

FALCONER: 54; C. 74.

FALL: Caldonia 100; E.A. 32,40; Geo. R. 32,40,94.

FALLON: Chas. 73.

FARISH: 51; F. Powers 150; H.P. 150; Jane L. 150 Robt. Davis 146,150; Thos. H. 150; W.S. 119,150.

FARLEY: 36.

FARMER: Houston 48.

FARR: E.J. 137; J.H. 109,150; John F. 109; John 150; Mary A. 109; Robt. 150; W.B. 109,119,126,137,150; Wilson 1.

FARRELL: Michael 88.

FAUST: Aug. B. 60; Sarah 60.

FAWN: John 45,46.

FAYSSOUS: Callender 119.

FEATHERINGALE: Wm. 128.

FEATHERSTONE: Rich. 2.

FEBIGER: J.C.,Jr. 52.

FEE: John 130.

FEIDMAN: Rebecca 102.

FELLOWS: Cornelius 33.

FELTENBERA: Henry 100.

FENTON: Jas. E. 5; Lucy 82.

FERGUSON: E.W. 36; Gabrell 150; S.W. 36,40,42,50,51,53,54; Cath. 94; Saml. W.94

FERRIDAY: Wm. 5.

FERRIS: Anna M. 150; St. Clair 150.

FIELDS: Harris J.20,81; Henry C. 20,81,130; Drury 150; Ellen R. 130; Eliz.

130; Margaret J. 130; Martha A. 130; Jesse R. 77,81,130; Jesse H. 130.

FIFE: James 60,61.

FILIMAN: Lewis 72.

FINKLEY: John L. 68.

FINLAY (FINDLAY): Nora 101; Betty D.101; Eliza A. 101; Eliza Burk 90; Ann B. 33,91; Benj. F. 18; Ann P. 86; Helen M. 86,101; John 83,101; John L. 18,22,27,68,77,79,81, 83,86,87,88,89,91; Mary N. 101; Pricilla W. 101; Sam D. 101; Thos. R.101.

FINNEY: Wm. 18.

FIRTH: Thos. B. 3.

FISCHEL: A.L. 150; Lyon 150; M. 150.

FISHER: (FISCHER) Alfred 148; Emily 6; John 6; John S. 49; Geo. D. 41; Sidney 6; Thos. 13.

FISK: Alvarez 21, Stewart W.21.

FITLER: Theodore 134.

FITZ: R.J. 69,127,138; Martha E. 127,138; John W. 127,138,150

FITZGERALD: John 126

FITZPATRICK: Ann L. 20; J.L. 20

FLAGG: Wm. 69.

FLEMING: Kinworth 150; Nat. 150; W.R. 19.

FLORENTINO: Leo 56.

FLOUACHER: Lee 55.

FLOWERS: Jas. A. 84.

FLOWERY: Mattie B. 57.

FLOURNOY: E.J.36,41; C.M. 66; David 66; Betsy 66; Matthew 66; Francis 66; V.M. 66.

FLOYD: B.P. 58; B. 141. Collin 92; R.C. 141.

FLY: A.D. 150.

FOE: Henry 150.

FOLKES: James 19; Miles C. 6,15; Saml. 6.

FONTAINE: N. 42;

FOOTE: John T. 35,38; H.W. 51; 54.

FORD: Nicholas 3, Robt. 42; Edna 150; Manly 119,150; West 150.

FORE: Ann R. 130; B.B. 150; Chas. J. 108,109, 111,119,130,150.

FORTSON: John T. 111.

FOSTER: Ambrose J. 21; Eliz. A. 21; Anna M. 38, 125,150; E. 150; John T. 119,125w; Tillman 125; Sarah 106,109,150; Lelia 125,150; Robt Heath 147; Nannie E. 150; E. 150.

FOWLER: E. 150; Sarah 119, 150.

FOX: A.S. 91; Burrell 76. Henry 150

FRAKER: Robt. 131.

FRAME: Joe 58.

FRANK: W.S. 41.

FRANKLIN: Wm. J. 21; Robt. 45

FRAZIER: Alex. G. 42,92; Edwards 92; Wm. 10,60,67

FREEMAN: John D. 12.

FRENCH: James 148; Matilda 37; Saml. G. 37

FRESHWATER: David 93; Peter 119,150.

FRIAR: (FRYER): Georgianna 56.

FROST:5.

FULTON: Adelia 78; Annie 22, 93; G.A. 49,51; John 9,67, 78w; Minnie A. 51; R.N. 150; Winnie 49; T.K. 12; Zenas K. 9; Sara Jane 78.

FURLOW: Robt. N. 150; Wm. J. 136.

G

GADISON: Semper 148

CAINES: Abner 48; A.L. 35; A.S. 43; Julia 99.

GANO: Robt. 151.

GALLOWAY: Lewis 21,28.

GAMBLE: J.T. 151; Fred 58; Felix 65,68.

GANT: Wm. 33

GARLAND:J. 63; Saml. 63,64.

GARNER: H.C. 150.

GARNETT: R.C. 58.

GARRETT: R.D. 18; Mary E. 84; Salina 84.Lizzie 119; Jacob 136,150; M.R. 150.

GARY:(GARRY): Patrick 75, 80w; Bernard 80; John 80; John Jr. 80; Thos. 80.

GASCOIGNE: Jas. B.10; Chas. 10.

GAUTREY: Ann 94; Atkins 94w.

GAY: 41; Wm. 64,65,69. Caroline 102.

GAYDEN: Hugh Dickson 147.

GEE: Caroline 148.

GENERIS: 28;30; E. 59.

GEOGHEGAN: C.F. 100; C.T. 39,42.

GEORGE: H.P. 150; John W. 15

GIBBONS: M.E. 143; Spicey 148; Wm. 117,143.

GIBBS: C.L. 49; R.W. 49; J.J. 55.

GIBSON:A. 24; A.C. 137; Catherine 116; Nancy 65, 66; Tena 148.

GILBERT: Phil A. 66.

GILCHRIST: C.C.P. 138; J.E. 138; G.P. 138; M.C. 138; S.C. 138.

GILES: Julia 44; Perry 44.

GILKEY: A. 67; Ada Logan 98,119,150; A.J. 98; A.S. 151; Andrew J. 98; Eva 150; Laura 150; Loyd 150; Mary E. 98,119,151.

GILLESPIE: Christopher 27, 29,33; Wm. 48.

GILLILAND: Ed.C. 57;

GILMAN: B.L. 56.

GILMORE: S.R.9; Elea.62.

GINGUARD: (GUIGNARD):Jas. S. 24,31,72.

GINSBURGER:Helen 57; M. 45,46, 50,57; Julia 100; Mark 100; Sarah 58, 100.

GISH: Christopher 79; Lewis K. 79; Susan 79; Wm. 79.

GIVEN: (GUVEN): Alonzo 135; A.M. 119,135; T.A. 135.

GLASS: Jas. 6.

GLASSCOCK: Robt. 126

GLENN: Jas. 126; Mary 126.

GODBOLL: J.M. 137.

GODBOLT: Jas. 16.

GOLDSMITH: Rachel 56;

GONSDALE: N. 29; F. 29.

GOOCH: 4.

GOODLOE: W.W.141.Arch. W. 11.

GOLDMAN: J.A. 50; H.C. 55.

GOODMAN:Thos 3; Lewis 46.

GOODRICH:48.

GOODSON: Sarah 148.

GOODWIN: Albert G. 62; Jn.L 151.

GORMAN: 58; Elijah 69; Felix 69; Mary 69; Sarah 69; Starling 69; John A. 58; Mamie C.A. 58.

GOSHEA: Liz 151.

GOTTLICH:Henry 55.

GOURVILLE: Geo. 50.

GOUTER: Jno. D. 34.

GOZA: S.Dempsey 88.

GRACE: Eva 150; Geo. C. 151; J.C. 150; Louise 150.

GRAHAM: G.B. 26; Pinky 55.

GRAMBLING: (GRAMLIN): Adam R. 94; A.D. 94; Jno. L. 94; Heirs 151.

GRAMMER: Wm. H. 56.

GRANT: Daniel 22,25,93; Jno. 22; Rich. 8; Amos 151; James 119,151; Lawrence H. 151; Lenora 151; Mary 151; Taylor 119; Thos. J. 150 Heirs 151.

GRAVES:(GRAVAIS):Geo. 119; 151; Wm. C. 28; Eliz. 79, Henry 79

GRAY:Hester 50; Wm. 50; Jno. H. 151;Jno. M. 109w, 150; Jno. M. Jr. 109; L. 109; L.B. 140; Nancy T. 109; N.V. 109; Mary Leah 109; S. 109,150; Samuel Bailey 109,150; Sarah Ann 109; Stephen 150; J.B. 92.

GRAYSON: A. 37.

GREARY: (GREASY) (GREANY): T. 48;53,36;49.

GREENE:(GREEN): Abe 57; Annie 150; Binky 148; Duff 26; E.H. 150; Francis 119; Henry 151; Jolen 151; J.R. 58; L.S. 151; Mary 131,148; Oscar P. 148; Sarah 150; Taylor 151; T.B. 107,109; Thos. 131; Thos. M. 38; Wm. H. 68.

GREENFIELD: Thompson 33;

GREENLEE: C.G. 85.

GREENWOOD: Thos. 1; Gustave 34.

GREGORY: G.G. 109,131,150; Mary Dunn 109,131,150; P. 40; Pricilla W. 109,131; P.W. 40; Peter 109,131,150.

GRIFFEN: (GRIFFIN): Alfred 151; Dennis 64,66,69; George 148; John 150; Hines 119; Mayes 148; Mary 150; Frances 24,65; Fannie 94w; J.L. 96.

GRIFFING: Wm. A. 147.

GRIMES: Thos. 2,8,9,61; Wm. 39

GRISHAM: Leon M. 119; W.D. 119.

GRISWOLD: Edwin 96; Jenne E. 96; Wm.H. 96.

GROOM: Pane 150; Viney 150.

GROVES: Wallace Wade 147. J.R.28;J.S. 28.
GRUBS: Loyd 46; W.G. 151.

GRUNWELL: L.F. 55.

GUION: 5; Jno. 72.

GUSTINE: Saml. 6.

GUY: Jas. 9; Jno. H. 119.

GWIN: (GWYN): Wm M.(W). 3, 6,41,80.

H

HAGAN: Hiram 106,110; Henry 110; David 58,110; Martha 110.

HAGERTY: I. 137.

HAIG: Geo. 18.

HAILBURTON: Robt. 151.

HAILE: Amanda 44; Calhoun 44,82; Geo. 62; Jno. 82.

HAIRE: Melton S. 131.

HALL: Fred 47; G,R, 85; Wm. E. 14.

HALBERT: F.M. 146.

HALLAM: Jas, D. 9; J.V. 2.

HALLORAN: Jas. 119,121,151; Pat. 119.

HALSEY: Ann D. 34,39, 52; Dr. Seymour 34.

HAM: Jackson M. 70;

HAMEL: Jas.H. 127; Kate 151; Lavinia 127; Mary E. 127; Patrick 127,137,151; Wade H. 151.

HAMER: Malachia B. 11.

HAMILTON: Jas. S. 40, 42; Lucy 28.

HAMMETT: Ed. 27,44,88; E.M. 88,90; Evelina 27; Jas. 88; Rich. 11,14; Robt.C. 88; W.H. 88w.

HAMMONS: Lucy 58.

HAMPTON: Christ. F. 21, 22,36,90; Jas. 20; Octavia 20; Wade 21,22, 36,37,38,72,90;Wade Sr. 22,78.

HANAWAY: Elleta 102; John 102; Maggie 102.

HANDLZER:J.W. 42.

HANDY: Edwards 83; Jno. 64.

HANNA: Jno. 32.

HANSER:Phillip 47.

HANWAY:(HAMWAY): B.53, 40; Christopher 55; Jno. 50,53; Mary 53.

HARBISON: Saml. 49.

HARDAWAY: Benj. 28; Zin 33.

HARDEMAN: D.7,15,19; Wm. 26.

HARDEN: G. 139; Ira 151; Mattie 55; Nancy 151.

HARG: Susan 64.

HARING: Cornelius 2,5,9,11; John 95; L.J. 55.

HARPER: Jas.T. 19; Jesse 19.

HARRINGTON: W. 85.

HARRIS: A.W. 56,73; Daniel 21; Eliz. 21,78; Geo. C. 45; Henry 40,148; Jas. L. 48; Jas. M. 15; Jas. R. 119,151; J.E. 43; John 151; John F. 95; John I. 95; Laura D. 21; Martha 40; Sallie 78; Sarah Ann 148; J.P. 76.

HARRISON: David 23,107; Emma 23; Jas. O. 13,23,49; Jas. P. 23; J.B. 55; Harry 46; Minnie C. 55; Nannie V. 56.

HARROD: Smith 57.

HARROW: J.W. 46,51.

HART: Anna M. 151; Chas M. 21; Jos. 47,53;

HARVEY: Belinda 62; E.Jones 106,116,128,142; Eleanora W. 128; Evan L. 62; Jas. R. 62, 128; M.J. 142.

HARWOOD: Agnes E. 120,151; Jas. H. 62; Sam. B. 11; Thos. 62,71.

HASKINS: Atty. 112.

HASLEN: Peter 50.

HATTER: Mollie 58.

HAUGH: Jos. 73.

HAUN: Jackson N. 16;Sol 55.

HAWES: M.E. 51.

HAWKINS: Nat. 148.

HAY (HAYS): J.K. 2,39; Jos. 44,49; J.P. 151; Thos W. 151.

HAYCRAFT: W.A. 27,28,29, 36,40,101,88.

HAYGOOD: Eliz. L. 132.

HAZLIP: Jno. K. 147.

HEARD: 43; Minerva A.127; Minerva L. 127; Nathan A. 127; Jos. C. 127; Julia W. 127; Stephen C. 136.

HEATH:Jas. P. 137,151; Jno. 137,151; Jno.W. 41, 120,137,151; Mary M.137; Nannie 137; Thos.A.137,146, 151.

HEBB:Jno.L. 56.

HEEN: Tim. 143.

HEDRICK: A.137.

HELM: 56.

HENDERSON:Elliott 25; Geo. W. 64,151; Hartwell 148,151; Jno. 19; S.J. 36; W.J.38.

HENNESSY:Adaline 151; Dennis M. 120; Marg. Adaline 120.

HENRY: Mary 148.

HENSICKER: D. 96.

HERALD: Jas. G.2.

HERBERT:E.B.134.

HERNDON:L.L. 22.

HERRON: Andrew J. 86; Andrew S. 86.

HERRING: Reding B. 16; Saml. 16;

HESTER: C.A. 151; Jno.8,110,151.

HEYMAN: A. 151.

HEXTER: Belle 55.

HICKMAN: Hiram 148; Louisa D. 39.

HICKS: D. 53; W.P.151.

HIGGINS: R.G.151.

HIGGS: Ed.E. 58.

HILDEBRAND: Saml. 15.

HILL: Ann 62,110,115,119,126, 138; B.G.151; Chas. 103; E.L. 138; Elenora 120; Emily C.119, 120,126,138; F.B. 138; Frk. 151; Glenara A. 126,138; Henry R.W.110,151; Henderson 151; Isaac C. 62,72,109,126,151; Jas. Dick 110; J.C.110,111, 112,138; Jno.A. 110; Lizzie 151; Mary 103; Mary M. 103; N.42; Oren H. 6,64; Parley 2; S.E. 138; Thedona 103; Thos. 103; Thos. H.33,37,91, 103; T.W. 110; W.R.110; W.D. 96.

HILTON: Chas. 65.

HILZIMN: Percy T. 57.

HINES: (HINDS): Geo. 120; Howell 34; Mary A. 41,47, 53; Thos. 32,41,42,48,105.

HINTON: Raney 148; Robt.1.

HIRSCH: Hattie 57; Julia 57; Rosa 55.

HOBBS: H.W. 95.

HOBSON: Jos. 22.

HODGEN: (HOEDGEDON): Fanny 128; M. 110,128,145; S.H.145; Wm.Cole 128.

HOFFMAN: 31;36.

HOGAN: Sallie 94; Sallie Isabell 94; Wm. 151.

HOLD: Wm.D. 4.

HOLDEN: (HOLDER): Jos.8; W.G. 51.

HOLLAND: Clara 151.

HOLLBERG: Ida.151; Robt.151.

HOLLENBECK: H.P. 42.

HOLLEY: P.W. 44.

HOLLINGSHEAD: J.V. 2.

HOLLIS: Alfred 50; Henry T. 127.

HOLMAN: Alf. 58; David 37; Lydia 50.

HOLMES: Ahab 132; Angeline 151; Chas. 151; Edwin 101; Geo. 132; J.P.G. 136; Mary 132; Mackley 151; Marg. H. 151; R.B. 151.

HOLT: A.C. 21; Jos.H.1, 4,12,13; Jno. A. 65; Jno. B. 65; Wm.D. 4.

HOOD: Eliz.W. 18,19,55; Mary Ann 18,19; Thos.H. 18,19,37,56; Wm.H. 18,19; Wm.N. 37.

HOOPS: Passmore 5.

HOPE: W.C. 57.

HOPKINS: Wm.A. 42.

HOPPER: Geo. 141; W.144.

HORD: Lewis 23,24; Mary I. 85; R.H.18,23,35,36, 43,85.

HORNE: Geo.W. 3.

HOROWITZ: (HORWITZ): Mich. 18,23,76.

HORSCH: David 57.

HOTCHKISS: Thos.R. 139.

HOUN: Henry 68.

HOUSE: Eliz. 132; Henry 132; Jno.H. 132; Julia 132; Mary 132; Saml. 132.

HOUSTON: Meredith 50.

HOWARD: Katie E. 57; Jos. 52; L.151; S.D.110,151.

HOWE: R.D. 41.

HOWELL: C.T. 21,22; J.M.51; Rich. 61; Wm.W.11.

HUBBARD: Willis 45;

HUDSON: Bawley 68

HUGGINS: 54; E.Clarence 95, 86; Wm.D. 126.

HUGHS:(HUGHES): Atty.3; Jeff.J.19; Jas. H. 112; Jno. W. 29; Lucia C. 112; T. 119.

HULL: Oliver 16,18,22.

Frederick 8; Gabriel 2,8; John 8,37,82,86,89,91; J.V. 82; Jos. G. 75; Laura 81, 89,92; Mary 43; Nancy Jane 84; Theodoric J., Jr. 82, 85,86; Thos. 89; Theo. Jeffrey 2,74,75; Thos. J. 8,24,60, 74,89,91. Thos.V. 75,76,82,84, 88,89; Theodoric Edward 75; Theodoric T. 75.

JAMISON: G.D. 139; R. 139.

JAYNES: W.G. 55.

JEANS: Wm. 151.

JEFFORDS: 54; Chas.S. 120; Mrs. Nancy P. 120,151.

JEFFRIES: Sallie T. 58; Wm. T. 56,58.

JENKINS:(JINKINS): Eliza 151; Geo. 151; Harvey M. 4,10; John P. 115; Wm. 8,16,70,71.

JENNIFER: B.J. 120.

JENNINGS: Thos.R. 83.

JETER: B.E. 55; E.E. 57; Katie 58.

JEWELL: J.D. 47,48,51; W.A. 47,48; 49.

JOHNS: Thos. H. 28,34.

JOHNSON:(JOHNSTON): Ann 65, 70; Betsy 66; Betty W. 89; Benj. 91; Bartley 28,30; Capt. 39; Chas.F. 91; Claudius M. 91; Elizabeth J. 91; Eliz. Tilford 91; E.T. 35; Ellen 47,49,51; E.J. 49; E.P. 29, 31,65,66,74,78,89,93; E.P.Jr. 92,93; Henry 8,19,91w,151; E.A. 144; Boston 100; Clarissa 99; C.S.151; A.G. 120,151; C. 151; Henry J. 91; G.P. 111, 114,116,132,133; G.W. 144; Helen L.86; Jas. 2,16,70,151; Jos. 19,64; J.W.89;92w; J.S. 29,41; Junius L.(S). 29,30,

32,55,92,93; Marcus 25; Marg. J. 91; Martha 48; Matthew F. 49,50,91; Mary 148; Moses 151; Mrs. Nanette 57; N.B. 34,49; Lycurgus 86; Rueben 48; Robt. 44,62,66; Robt.A. 91; Robt.R. 91; Saml. 151; Van 57; Watt 33; Wesley 151; Wm. 41,69, 151; Wm. Henry 47,49; W.N. 46,53.

JONES: Benjamin 16; Chas. 148; G.P. 111,132,151; Chas. H. 132; H.J. 58; Jos. C. 34; Joel 44; Jesse 11; Katie 120; Laura F. 132; L.J.120,151; Lewis S. 117; Mary D. 132; Mary J. 56; Maria H. 132; Martha H. 132; Martha P. 132; Panella 151; Peter Stokes 120; Rabun 57; Rachel 151; Saml. E.9,13; Sarah Jane 117; Thos.H. 88; T.J.58; Wm.A. 60; W.D. 85; 54.

JOOR: Catherine P. Shelby 107,124; Geo. 7,107,111, 124,151; John S. 107,114, 124,129,143,151.

JORDAN:(JOURDAN): C.E. 57; E.M.58; Lydia 50; Napoleon 50; York J. 151.

JOYNER: Eli 78; John 78; Turner 77,78w.

JULIENNE: L. 151.

JUREY: & Harris 35; Farley 36.

K

KANATSER:Jos. 55.

KAUSLER: Geo.S. 48.

KATZ: Simon 81.

KEATING:Robt. W. 4,5.

KEATON: R.W. 5.

KEENE: A.C. 67; W.H. 92.

KEEP: A.L. 137,151; H.V. 120,137,151; L.H. 137; Miss Sallie B. 120,152; Oliver H. 120.

KEITH: J.H. 58.

KELLOG: M.B. 151.

KELLY: A.D. 29; C.J. 56; J.A. 135; J---D. 83; Wm.F. 33.

KELSEY: Lydia 73.

KEMPT: Rachel 47; Wesley 47.

KENNEDY: G.H. 34; Kate M. 30; Thos.J. 30.

KEONE: Eliza 50.

KERSHAW:(KIRSHAW) Anna 139; Ann 24; Emaline 60; Chas. 60; Fanny 60; Frances R. 60; Geo. T. 24,28,60; Henry 60; John 60; J.P.C. 28; Mary 60,139; Mary Jane 60,76,86; Mattie 60; Mrs. Newman 60; Newman 60; R.C. 28; Thos. 4,6,8,9,10, 12,14,15,16,18,23,24,28,31, 32,60,76,86,139; Rich. 139; Rose 139; Trainy 139.

KEY: Thos. 50.

KILLIAN (M): Max. 120, 151; V.A. 120,151.

KILPATRICK: Ebenezer 32; Eliha 32,65.

KIMBALL: Laven 15,34.

KINCHEN: Mary 57.

KING: Amelia 78; Jas. 30; Jno.H. 135; Jos. 83; Robt. W. 83.

KINGSBURG: J.L. 144; M.C. 144.

KINKEAD: Geo.B. 63.

KIRK: A.M. 35; 51; John 1.

KLEEBER: Mrs. Mary F. 57.

KNIGHT: Geo. 151; Mary 151.

KNOX: Ambrose 8,18,22,85w, 90; Andrew 7,8,9,10,12,15, 16,22,23,24,59; Eliz. 85; Eliz.Marg. 85; High. 24; John S. 16; Marthia Lowry 85; Mary B. 85; Thos. 85; W.B. 73.

KREGER: Anna 58.

KUNAN: Hugh 3.

L

LACEY: F.Ida 55; John S. 139; Thos. 69.

LACHS: Meta Blair 120.

LACOSTE: C.A. 24.

LADD: M.E. 138; W.H. 138.

LAFOE: Mrs.N.A. 56.

LAKE: W.A. 5.

LALLIEN: John 152.

LAMB: Georgia 57; Neesom 15,16; Parcena 56.

LAMBERSON: R.T. 55.

LAMON: John Williams 147.

LAMPKINS: Saml. 45; Sidney 45.

LANCASTER: Alonzo 70.

LANE: J.H. 3; Levine 90; Walter 90.

LANERMAN: C.J. 56.

LANGLEY: Alf. 69; Wm.S. 135.

LANKFORD: F.C. 56.

LAPSLEY: Catherine 83; Robt. A. 83.

LARRAINE: J.G. 57.

LAESEN: Morris 152.

LASATER:(LASSETER): Martha 116; Jas.R. 116;

LASHLEY: Arnold 22,23,24,25, 26,27,42; G.56; Robt. 25; R.M. 37.

LATHAM: Haney 33; Harvey 28.

LAUGHLIN: M.M. 140.

LAW:(LAWS): Jesse E. 57; Emma 134.

LAWLER: J.L. 58.

LAWSON: E.A. 43; Isaac N. 146; J.B.M. 43; L.E. 152; Frances Ann 77; Frances 77; Saml. 77; Wilhemina 77; Wm.H. 1,77w.

LAX: Aaron 152.

LEATHERMAN: Martha B. 132; S.B. 134; Saml. 120,134,152; Zachariah 132.

LEDBETTER: Homer V. 111,112, 152.

LEE:(LEIGH): Catherine Sarah 75; Eleanor P. 70,76; B.M. 32; A.M. 152; Amelia P. 130; Alf. J. 130,142; Harry P. 39,44, 75,76,77; Jno.M. 75,76,77; Kate 26; Lizzie B.152; Matt. 26; Nathan W. 75,76,77; Nellie 101; P.P.143; Sam 152; T.J. 112,130; Thos.R. 41; Thos.L. 1; Wm.H. 26,28,32,33,75.

LEIGHTON: T.J. 152.

LEMAN: 54.

LEMAY: S.T. 137.

LEMLE: Jennette 55.

LEMON:(LEMMON): H.F. 27; Hugh 132; Robt. 57.

LENGSFIELD:(LINGSFIELD): (LONGSFIELD): 44,45; Aug. 99. Eliz. 99; Henry E. 99; Ignacion 99; Julias 99; J.J. 48; Julius 48,49,50, 99; Laurs 99; Lizzie 99.

LESLIE: P.Homer 110.

LESTER: Mrs. Walter A. 56.

LESASSUR: Chas.J. 55.

LEVALLY: 38.

LEVERETTE: Joan 104.

LEVY: Chas. 120; Daniel 138; Hulda 99.

LEWELLYN:(LLEWELLYN): T.M. 57; Jno.R. 6.

LEWIS: Chas. 57; C.M.39,41; C.W. 42,51,52; Eliz. 148; Eugenia 57; Saml. 148; Wm. 5.

LEY: Florida 62,68; Wm.62.

LIGHES: Rial 151.

LIKENS: Catherine 71; Endora 73; Jno.H.22,73; Kate Knox 73,84,87; Marion 73; Myra 73; Thos.J. 16,61, 62,65,67,71,73,84,87,107, Wm.R. 73.

LILKENS: S.H. 80.

LINDSEY: Nimrod 7; Nimrod T. 88,93; H.C.31; F.A.134; Mrs. Ida B. 120; M.W. 134,

LIPPINCOTT: Eliz. 84.

LITCHFORD:(LITCHFIELD):M.H. 32; W.H. 48.

LITTLE: Alfred 29; B.M. 29; Emily 29; Jno. 29; Saml. 29; Wm. 29.

LITTLETON: Lula 57.

LIVINGSTON: J. 38; Mattie 57; Robt. 57; S.24.

LOCKE: Jas. 4.

LOCKLAND: Nelly 66.

LOCKRIDGE: L.A. 86.

LOFTON: Eldridge 128; Evan S. 128; Lucinda 128; Mary A. 128; Wm.B. 128; Walter C. 2, 8,9,12,13,15,128.

LOGAN: 33;74; Daniel 33; Mary 120,152.

LOMBARD: Coote 51.

LOMAX: W.W. 95,96.

LONG: Green B.2,129; Jas.46; Parks B.9.

LONH: Green B. 16.

LONGLEY: Alf. 2,19

LONSDALE: F.W. 33,46; Fitz Wm. 92,93; H.H. 46; Henry T. 33, 92; Jane T. 46; Nannie J.46,92. Henrietta T.92; Maggie 92; T.46.

LORILLARD: Eliz.K.S. 124; Ernest 124.

LOVE: Bessie 58; Dave 152; Marg. C. 58.

LOVELL: Jos. 27.

LOWE: 25,64; E.F. 25.

LOWRY: Agnes Eugenia 111; Eliz.Caroline 111; J.G. 58; Lucia Cornelia 111; Robt.37, 148; Susanna Cushia 111; Wm. 111,112; Wm.T.111,112,130.

LUCAS: 49; I. 152.

LUHM:(LUMM): A.G. 152; Katie 120; Mary F. 120; Otto A. 120; Robt. J.120; Robt. H. 120.

LUNKINS: Becky 148.

LUSK: Lou 56; N.L. 56.

LUTHAN: Jno. 101.

LUTTRING: T. 95.

LYONS: Martha E. 58.

LYNE: Thos. 8,12.

LYNCH: Jas.P. 152; J.C. 152; Mattie T. 152; Ruby 152; Gov.Chas. 5.

LYPSCOMB: Ben 152.

M
MACK:Isaac 40

MACKLIN:B.32; G.B.32; Fred.M. 32.

MAEBERRY: Clara Ann 148.

MAGEE: Wm. 112.

MAITLAND:Robt.L. 121

MANCASTER:(MUNCASTER): C.W. 12,14.

MANGUM: W.W. 96.

MANLOVE: 88

MANN - MAN: AAron 40; Daniel P. 69; Geo.W. 69; Nancy G.69; P.L. 58; Tennessee W. 69.

MANNING: Peter 42.

MARBLE: Martin 27.

MARR:Claudia V.20; Dan 74; Jane 20; Nicholas 20; Sallie 20; R.H. 20.

MARSH:Robt. 23,25,36,121.

MARSHALL: Florence 38; Henry 121; Wm. 38,42,45,52; T.A.&M.M.54; Smedes & Marshall 5.

MARSTON: Jas. 20.

MARTIN: Clarinda 40; F.B.144; Dr.Joseph 88; H.G. 111; M.J. 88; Thos.J.,Jr.33.

MASON: C.L. 121; Thos. 7.

MATHENY:M.A. 145.

MATTHEWS: Ann 31; Eliza A. 18; Jas.T. 18; Jos. T. 37; Jos.J. 41; Mrs. R.C. 58; Wm.L. 57.

MAULDING: James B. 60; Wesley 19.

MAXWELL: Jas. A. 12; Low.P.12; R.Y. 135.

MAYER:Emil 121; Henry L.121

MAYES - MAYS - MAY: Daniel D. 1; Jas. 8; M.A. 31; Robt.B.1.

MAYFIELD: Abby 55; F.E. 132; 145; Jas.L. 3,121,145; J.E. 108; M.A. 112.

McALLISTER:- McCallister: Augustus 8,20,105; Augustus W. 34,65,68,69,75,80,89;Caroline 105; Charles 105; Gervais 105; Jane Knox 110; Louisa 105;Wm.110.

McCABE: Jane 104.

McCALES:Ed. 32

McCARROLL:Green 16,67.

McCAUL: Geo. 56.

McCAULEY: Catherine 86.

McCLUSH: Frank C. 58.

McCOY:Fred 57;T.W. 57.

McCOYIM -COYIN - COWYAN: Walter 112.

McCRAE: Carroll 100.

McCULLEN: Elijah W. 128.

McCULLOUGH: John 2; Robt. 2.

McCUTCHEN::John M. 91; Susan 67.

McDANIEL: John 128.

McDONALD:M.M. 143; Wm.E. 147.

McDOWELL:E.P. 37,38.

McFARLAND: 49; Nancy 74.

McGARTH - GRATH:A.E. 48; Alice 105; Billy 105; C.48; Caldwell 105;Julia 105; Mary 105.

McGEE:Samuel 148.

McGINTY: Z.C. 30.

McGOWN: Basil Duke 146.

McGREGOR:Alex 144; F.A.43.

McGUINIS:John M. 43.

McGUIRE:Joseph 21; Rosend 21.

McHATTON: Chas.G.24,25,27,29, 32,41,43;Jas. 23,24,27,28; Fenelon 28.

McKAUGHN:Walter 128,130.

McKEE:Sarah 57; Robt.W. 56.

McKEONE:Patrick 52

McKINNEY:Brander 18; Jno.F. 10.

McILOAM:Mattie 102; Marg.102; Roger 102.

McLAUREN:Glenna H. 132; J.110, 112,132; Mary Sophia 132; Sarah G. 132.

McLEAN: Dan 58.

McLELLAN: Annie 103; Emma 103.

McLEOD: Norman 43.

McLEMMON - McLeman: Jefferson 20; Jno.D.20; PriceP.20; Saml.E.20.

McMAHON: Daniel 9; Wm.C. 5.

McMEEKIN -(McMEEKEM): John 84, 87; L.D. 37.

McMURCHY: Geo. 9; John 9.

McMURRAY: J.J. 44.

McMURTREY: Vincent 7; W.W.96.

McNAIRY: Eliz.P. 108.

McNEELEY: J.L.49;54; J.S.94; John 101.

McNICHOLSON: Eliza H.131.

McNUTT: Alex.G. 5,15.

McPHILTERS: Wm.A. 46.

McQUAID: J.M. 141.

McQUILLIAN: Alberta E. 129; Cynthia A.112; Jos. 112; Jno. P.129; Jos.R. 129,M.A. 121;142; Melissa J. 129; R.121; Wm.B.112, 129,142.

McRAE: A.L.45.

McRAVEN: Jas. H. 24.

MᶜRoberts: Elijah 127.

MEADE: Christ. 55.

MEANY: E.A.5,11,80.

MEARS: Jno.L. 90.

MELIAN: Albert 29; Wm.F.26; Wm.P.24,26.

MELTON: Carrie R. 57.

MERCER: Corbin W. 101, Jno 101.

MERCHANT: H.R. 46,53; N.95.

MERIWEATHER: N.M. 33.

MERRILL: Willie S. 95.

MESSINGER - MESSENGER: G.W.B. 121,143; Miles M.130; S.A.143.

METCALF:(e) Albert 102; Albert Hammet 88; Cleve 102; Drucilla 102; F.A.37,88,90; Frederick 102; Frederick,Jr.102; Geo.102; Harley 58,102; Jno.A. 102; Martha 102; M.P.88; Sally 102.

MEYER: David 58.

MICKEY: David 148.

MIDDLETON: R.N. 124.

MILLER: Agnes 59; Albert 5,14; Alexander A.131; Anderson 2,7, 10,15; Betty J.89; Eliz. 121; E.W.55; Feldon 101; Harvey 35, 56,57,59,89w,104; H.C.49; J.117; Jas. 6,63; Jane 60; J.A. 12,18, 23,33,41,46,47,53,77; J.G.132; Jno.C.59,60; Laura 59; Lewis 121; Maggie 35; Maggie J. 104; Malvina 35,104; M.Georgie 53; Robert 85; Robert D.6; S.S.57; Turner R.131; Violet 110; Wm.2,7; 54.

MILLIKEN: Daniel 73; Jno.73; J.Minor 73,74; Jos. 73; Mary 73,74; Mary Ella 73; Saml. 74.

MILLS: B.B. 144; Charlotte 130; J.B.129; John H. 130; Sarah O. 130; Wm.T.Jr. 130;68.

MILLSAPS: Barton H. 128.

MILTON: Julius 45.

MINOR: Robt. 121;w.j.93.

MITAN: Chas.H.65.

MITCHELL: Amanda 121; Jas. 79; Lydia 94; Mary 148.

MIZELL: I.142; J.T.142; M.E.142; M.F.142.

MOBLEY:54

MOFFETT:Robt.A.9.

MOLOWY:Wm.J. 96.

MONROE: J.H. 141.

MONTGOMERY:Alex.B.7,8,11,18
22,47,87;A.P.35;Davis 5,7,
8,65; Davidella 47;E.A.39;
Eliz.65; Emeline 105; Hellon
105; James 82; Pinkey 105;
Saml. 105; W.B.36; Wm.29,
34,39,44,82; Wm.P. 29,35,
82,84,87,92; 54

MOODY:54

MOORE - MORE: Alex. 121; A.
Thos.131,136; C.S. 19; Eugenia
148; Frank W. 131,135; Isaac
52; Jane M.28; Jeff W. 38,
95; Jesse 81; Laura May 121;
Mary E. 135; Oliver P. 131,
136;Rachel 121,131,136; Mrs.
R. 112; Saml.L.112,131;Wm.S.
131; Wm.W. 121.

MORELAND:

MOREHEAD: 54

MORGAN:C.E. 40,41,42,46;
Emma 38; Dillie May 58;
Geneva 55; Maria S.46;
Oliver T.31.

MORRIS:Chas.H. 148; D.52;
Henry 19,22,25,26,27,,4,92;
James 128; J.J.99; M.M.99;
Mary 22,25,26,27; N.B.98;
Steve 65; Thos.W.2;W.J.121.

MORSON:Arthur 59; Kate 57.

MORTON:Cornelia 82; E.138;
E.E.47; James 82;V.138;
Washington 121.

MOSBY:Eliza G.90w; G.S.91;
James W. 90; Montgomery 90;
Pauline P.90.

MOSLEY:A.W. 121; Alfred W.
69,91; Isaac R. 91; John H.
91; Lucy 121; Y.S.33; 75.

MOSS:Ferdinand J. 129; Henry
M.128;Jos.N.130;T.J.34.

MOTT:R.112; ___ 15.

MOUNT:E.40,140;E.E.140;
M.E.140; W.G.140.

MOURAS:D.T. 50; G.W.50.

MOYSE: Alphonse 55.

MUIR: H.P. 44

MULCHER: Emeline T. 97.

MULLEN: Bertie 56; R.M.56.

MUNOR: Anderson 148.

MURDOCK: Alfred 20; W.B.44,47.

MURGEE: Mattie 55.

MURLELL: Catherine 50.

MURPHEE - MURPHEY - MURPHY:
Emeticus 127; G.W. 145; Jas.
W. 92,45,49;J.R.42;M.16; R.B.
45; Wm. 135; ___ 81.

MURRAY: Chas. 59; Joe 148.

MUSGROVE: Edgar B.57;

MYRES: F.C.142; M.C.141;M.E.
142;M.Ella 148;R.S.142;T.
Frances 130;Wm.16,62,110,112,
130,141;W.A. 142; W.S.57.

N

NARY:Marg. 37.

NEAL:Sarah 78; Thos.L.146.

NEBLETT:Ann S. 96; Sterling
30,96; Wm.J. 96.

NEELSON: C.P.56; Henry A.8;
Mary E. 56.

NELSON:Archie 49; Aug.J. 96;
Bettie H. 49; Dick 131; E.A.
134; Emma 131,134; Frances L.
131,134; Henry A.8; James 131,
134; John 100,113,131; John H.
52,87;J.L.1,35,36; John S. 88,
91; John W.112; J.W.134;Laura

NELSON:CONT. Laura 100; Martha 100; Mary 100,134; Mary Louisa 112; Mary L.S. 112; Nathan T.47,48,112; Newman 100; N.J.35,39,76, 81,89,91,92; N.Thos. 131,134; Sam 131,134;54; Samuel 112, 113,121,131,134;T.C.112; Thos.112,113;

NEWMAN: Alex.F. 11,36,37, 57;A.W.36;Martha O.46;Robt. C.57;S.B.18,46.

NEWSOM:Dred 50, Jos.D.131.

NICHOLS:W. 80.

NICHOLSON: Americe 131;Dr. 73;Euralia R.131;Fredonia H.131; J.E.121,135;Laura M. 135;M.M.135;Richard F.131; Victoria H. 131;Wilber F.131.

NIXON: John M.1.

NOLEN: Wm.G. 130.

NORMAN: Betsy 53; Granville 53; Jos.120;Julia Luhm 120.

NORTH: Elisha 132.

NORTHAM: Soloman 128.

NORTON: E.E. 39; Hewitt 32, 39,53.

NORVELL: Hannah 83; Moses 83.

NORWOOD: John 27.

NOYES:Appleton 42.

NUGENT: Wm.L. 86,87,88,89, 90,92;Wm.S.83,84,85.

NUTT: Mary D.121; Nancy 64; Virginia 64.

NYES: N.G. 18,19.

O

O'BANNON:Obannion: A.H. 79; D.B.49,140.

O'CONNER: Tim 52.

ODEN: Walter E. 56.

OFFULT - OFFUTT: Alfred 32; B.A.48; Geo.50;Z.C.39.

OGLESBY: J.T. 56.

O'HEA: Rich.A. 52.

OLMSTEAD: D.G. 93w; Marcellus 93.

ORGLER: Etta 55.

O'ROURKE: Daniel 130.

ORRICK: N.C. 35.

OSBORNE - OSBURN: Ann 138; BenB.138; Jackson 138; Jas. B.138; Wm.138;Wm.J.138.

OSGOOD: Dr. 69.

OTIS: Mary G. 58.

OURSLER: Belle 56;L.J.58.

OVERTON: John P. 5.

OWENS:Abrams 127; Elvira H. 127;Emily A.127;Wm.M.139.

P

PAEPCKE: Eliz.Julia 121; Herman 121.

PAGE: D.C.16,61; Henry 148.

PARBERRY: J.W. 49.

PARKER: Alex 148; Howard 102; John 35; Roberta 35; William 102; Will O. 147.

PARKS: Ann 114; Amanda 113; George Ann 128;Georgianna 136; George N.61,63,113,114,126,136; Geo.N.Jr.113,126; James M.150; Josephine 128; J.W.25;King P. 136;Louisa 114;Martha Kate 114; M.E.114,126,136;Mary J. 114; Rebecca 128;Saml. G.113,114,128; 140;S.L.140;Susan E.113,126,136. Thos.61,63,113,114;Thos.G.128,140.

PARMELE:Freeman 7, Truman 13.

PARTEE: Chas.W. 43;Lizzie A. 43;Sam 45.

PATERFIELD: Allie 99.

PATTERSON: Emma 58;Jas. 25;Jno. 25;P.B.56;W.Monk 136.

PASSENGER: Mrs. Mary J. 58.

PAUL: Ellen 148.

PAXTON: Alexander 103; Andrew 103;Andrew,J. 21,29,85;Andrew Jr.103; Cornelia 103;Hannah 103; Hannah M.103;John Gallatin 85; Lucy 103; Nannie 103; Wm.103; ___ 4; ___ 54.

PAYNE: Thos.J. 1.

PEACE: Frances A.123;Marinda L.123; Willis 123.

PEALY: Elijah 22.

PEARCE: Jonathon 88.

PEEBLES - PEOPLES: Harriet 48; Henry 21; Levi 48.

PEEL: Dempsey 127.

PERT -PEITE: Alex. 15;L.L.F.137.

PELHAM: John B.2,87; Thos.D.86w.

PELWAY:Thos. 99.

PENCOFFS: Chas. 57.

PENDER: Cora 58.

PENDLETON:John T. 66.

PENNY;A.L.137; Amelia 100; Benj.F.88,100; Carrie 100; Thos.18; W.J.88;W.T.84,85.

PENRICE:Alice 68; Amelia 105; Amelai E. 48; Cordelia A.60; Elizabeth 60,62;Frances 2,4, 7,9,60,62,63;James 71; John G.61,62;John L. 48,79,82,87; John S.2,79,13,14,18,22,23, 25,26,31,59,68,79,84,105; Jos.B.2,60,71; Susan E.60,62; Thos.S.16,71;Wm.2,4,11,13;Wm. J.2,14,60,61,62,63;Wm.L.60.

PEPPER: Frank 58.

PERCY: Annie 99;Chas. 22,68, 69,70,80; Chas.B.80;Ellen 22; Ellen M.80;Fannie 30;Fannie E. 90,99;Henrietta 22,80; Josiah 22,80; J.Walker 22,70,75,80, 90w,99;J.W.76;77,78,80;Ladie 99;Leroy 99;Leroy P.90; L.P. 22,30,70; Maria 30,61,68,90; Robt.H.70,80;Thos.G.22,61,68, 70,80;Wm.A.22,30,70,80,85, 90, 99;54.

PERKINS: Caroline 20;Daniel 20.

PERRY - PEERY:A.J. 137; Carrie 58;Crockett 15;Sam 48.

PERVIS;Jos. 2,8.

PETERS:Bettie T.96; Harriet H. 96;Julia H. 96;Matthew L.96w; Minnie 96; Mollie 96.

PETERSON:Flora Ann 148.

PETMAN: Phebbia 57.

PETTWAY;PETWAY : Ida E. 134; John R.117;J.T.134;Julia J. 121,131.Laura D.134;Mary Caroline 117;Mary R. 134;R.W.111,121,123, 131,134;Sally G.134;Thos.R.131, 134,146.

PEYROMEAUX - PEJRONEAU:H.W.19.

PEYTON: E.G. 41,50.

PHARR: Albertus 126;E.A.114; Elias 113,115,126;Elizabeth 126;Henry 113;Henry N(W?)113; Hester 113; Hampton 126;James 113;Jane M.113;Margaret B.113; Mary Eunice 107,113;Mary 113; Robt. 113;Saml. A.113;S.Eliz. 114,115;Theresa J. 113;Ursilla M.113,126; Walter N.113.

PHELPS: A.J. 30,39,53;Alonzo 104;F.M.140;Henry V.104;Jas. 65;Jas.H.104;Mary 30;Mary B. 104;Nannie W.104;Wm.G.45,104;54.

PHILLIPS - Philips: Alias(?)4; A.J.45;Geo.F.58;Jas.W.20; Thos.Emmet 146.

PHILLIPSON: Theod. 42.

PHIPPS: J.143;Rich.B.98.

PICARD: Amelia 99; Aron 99; Belle 99;Hattie 99;L.52; Saml. 99;S.43,45,46,48.

PIERCE: J.C. 47;Jon. 39; Walter Bell 147.

PIERSON - PEARSON -PURSON: John F.1,John Reed 55

PILES: J.W. 52.

PINCKARD: Bailey 84; Geo.M. 8,26,65;Sarah A.26;Wm. 26.

PINCKNEY: Ned121.

PINDELL - PENDELL: Henry C. 86;Mrs. Jas.A.86.

PITTARD: H. 141.

PITTMAN: A. 138;E.A. 138; G.W. 138;H.P. 121;J.O.138.

PLATT: Lewis C. 115.

PLANT:Fred 8,10,11,12,13,14, 15,60.

POINDEXTER: Ann 33;HEnry 10; R.68;Thos.68.

POLK: Thos.G. 32.

POLLOCK: W.A. 43.

POOLE: R.P. 55.

POOSEN: George 138.

POPE: Frances A.70;Leroy 70; Wm.H. 69,70.

PORTER: E.H.36; J.R.55;T.F.42.

PORTERFIELD: Dock 47;Nellie 47;Wm. 52.

PORTMAN:M.B.47;W.B.38.

POWELL: Albert H. 129;D.W. 144;Emily M.129;Geo.P.86,85; Henrietta 129;Hetty Ann 129; Ira M.91,85;John M.62;Judge J.129; Laura Ann 129;Littleton M. 129;Mary Kate 129;Mordica 12,65,113,129; N.A.B. 144; Nancy I(J?) 86,89;N.J.89; Thos. 41; W.M. 144.

POYNT: Jas.P. 39; Jno.B.39.

PRATT: Jos. 5,8,15.

PRENTISS: S.G.15.

PRESCOTT: J.W.144.

PRESTON: Ginas 93;Zenas 121.

PRICE: John M. 82; Maria 83; Mary Louisa 82,87; Wm.T.6,7, 9,11,12,13,14,15.

PRINCE: James 69,71,76; Wm. Berry 107; Wm.J. 11.

PUGH: Robt. 41,42.

PURNell: W.S. 67.

PUTNAM: H.R. 42.

Q

QUATTLEMAN:A.M. 56.

QUIN:Russell Aubrey 147.

R

RABB - ROBB:Ann 74;Eugene A. 50;Gab.23,72;J.H.96;John 4,5,8,74.

RABHUN:A.H. 58

RADJESKY - READJESKI:Arabia 99;Ella 99;J.41,42,44,45; Jacob 99;Jos.99;Lemon 99; Lewis 99;Racheal 99;

RAGAN:Thos.3
RAGLAN:Nellie 58

RAINEY - RANEY:R.143;Saml.46.

RANDALL:Wm.E.8.
RANDOLPH:R.26;W.F.34,45.

RATLIFF:R.L.58

RAWLS: Charity 129;Henrietta 138;Rich.129

READING:Abraham B.1
REDD:Thos.21;Thos.S.85

REDHAMMER: Jas.16

REID - REED:54;Dottie C.58; Jane 45;Robt.45;Susan 148.

REINHOLD:Frank O.58
REISINGER:Jacob 48;Marietta 48

RENSHAW:Thos.50

REYNOLDS:Geo.W.1,2,3,4,5,6,8,9,10,11.

RICE:J.I.143

RICHARDS:Ed.63

RICHARDSON:Col.E.96;E.48,52; John E.6,8;Leonard 51;M.E.51;

REICHMAN:F.C.57.

RIEVSON:Bail 45

RIGGS:F.W.58

RING:G.F.143;Jos.N.55.

RITCH:O.H.P.136

RITTER - Riter;Ida Pitt 122;Phillip 56.

RIVES:Mary W.38;O.C.38,50,81,90.

RIVERE: J.F.58

ROACH:Benj.19,23,28,29; David 19;Eugene 19;Jas.W.19;I.F.76;Marg.49;Mahala P.H.122,125;Mrs. James 125.

ROBARDS - ROBARD - ROBIRDS; Chas.L.25,26,31,74,76,79,54; Willis 23,66,69;Wm.D.122; Wm.H.15;Wm.L.72.

ROBERTS:Charleston 148; Henry 131.

ROBERTSON:Alex.61;Alta Calif. 128,142;C.K.61;E.C.142;Eliz. 70;J.H.142;Jos.5,16,62;Jos. H.128;J.W.114,121,128;L.C. 142;Leanah 121,128;Olive V. 128;Patsy 83.

ROBINS:Thos.E.10

ROBINSON:D.C.47;Harry C.58; Jeremiah 29;John N.20;J.S. 33;Mrs. Rebecca L.55;N.E. 137;W.W.49.

RODEN:Minnie G.56

RODES - RHOADES - RHODES: A.F.138;C.V.68;Walter 66.

RODEWALL:Eliza 18;Fred W.18 Henri.18;Henry 18;John D.18

ROGERS:J.E.44;M.B.11

ROLLISON: Jos.T.126; Sarah A. 126.

RONALDSON: M.L.137.

ROOD: Harvey 2,5,9,11.

ROSS: Jno.M.62,64; Joslin 69; Mr.6; Wm.B.14,62,64.

ROSSMAN: L.A. 55.

ROTCHFORD: Phillip 33.

ROTCHILD: Louis 57.

ROTH - RATH: Chas.81; Isaac 71, 81; Jacob 21,22,81,87.

ROUSE: Lawson 34.

ROUT - ROOT: Cynthia 81; G.W.81; James R.81; Thos.81; Vol.81; Wm.81.

ROWAN: Eliz.I.55,63; Eliza 63; Ester 63; John A.63,64; Marg.63; Martha E.63; Sarah 63; Susan 63, 64.

ROWE: Wm.J. 136.

ROYALL: T.F.27,30.

ROYCE: Eada Luhm 120.

ROYSDAN: DeLa.F.2.

RUCKERS: Jesse T.4; Sarah H.65, 70; Wm.B.65,70.

RUCKS: Amanda 32,103; Arthur 77, 80,81,89,90,103; Benj.103; Grant 103; Grant B.32; Henry 32,74,89, 90,94; Henrietta 77; James 32,47, 48,77,89w; James,Jr.89; James T. 25,28,32,74,89,90; Jane T.25; Lewis Taylor 32,33,77,89,90; Louisa 77; Maria Louisa 77; Mary 103; Mary M.25,32,47,89; Marion 77; Melvian 90; M.S.32; Sally 32, 56,103; Sarah 103; Sarah J.94; Saml. 103; S.E.32; ___18; ___54.

RUDD: Alex. 19.

RUPP: John 102.

RUSHING: James M.55,129; M. 142; Wm.16,63,112; 121,122, 129,142; Wm.B.142.

RUSK: Wm.L. 13,15.

RUSSELL: Robt. N.1; Robt.H. 2; Thos.A.66.

RUTHERFORD: Calvin M.11; J.142; R.S.56.

RUTLAND: W.H. 144.

RYAN: Wm.126.

S

SAINT: Douglas 81

SAEZIER: Anna Louise 58.

SAMUEL: Abraham 7,11,15; A.J.2.

SANE: John A. 2.

SANDERLING: Mary E. 57.

SANDERS: Aaron H. 128,144; Eliz. 101; Elly 101; Jno.O.1,7,14,15! Louisa E.66; Martin R. 101; Vincino 101; Wm.P. 29.

SANFORD: Julia A.96w; Sarah Eliz. 96; Wm.Peter 96.

SATTERWHITE: Wm. 94.

SAUNDERS: V.L. 48; ___27.

SAWYER: Abner 8; Ed.G. 57; Tully 11.

SAXTON: Erastmers 3,6; Sam 3,6,14.

SCARBOROUGH: ___54.

SCHUYLER: Phillip A. 82,84w; Wm.C. 84.

SCHWARTZ: Amo Elisee 85.

SCOTT:Annie 57; Calhoun 24, 82; Caroline S. 95; Chas.52; F.E.24;Guignard 22,24,74,82; H.P.122; J.58,74; John 114; John A.22,29,34,48,72,82;Jno. W. 129;Mahala 52;Pamela E.43; Robt.B.95; R.W.32;Sarah 24,34; S.P.92; Stephen 44; Thos.J.12; Willie S. 56; Wingfield 148; Wm.S.(L?) 2,7,13,43,59.

SCRUGGS: ___ 54; Anna 132; Mary F.132;Patterson G. 132.

SCUDDER:W.H. 146.

SEALES:Chas.J. 64.

SEARCY:Dailey 47.

SEIXAS:Sarah 148.

SELBY: ___ 44.

SELIG - SEELIG - SALIG:Ferdinand 99; Moses 48; M.Salig & Co. 39,41,42; Norris 77.

SELLERS:Alice G. 127;Amelia A. 127;Ann 62; Andrew 66;Benj. Menus 62,63,110,114,115,126; Cornelia 63; David 62;Edward B.127;Edward R.63,110,111,126; Elberta 126;Emily 63;E.W.109; H.Clinton 126;Isaac 62,63,110, 114;Isaac F.126;Jas.T.126;J.115; Joana 122;J.W.109; Silas 62; Thos.62,63;Thos.W.110,111,126, 145;Wm.63;Wrenna Breathette 62, 63,114.

SEM: Thos.J.58.

SEMPLE:Lucy V. 51.

SERIO:C.J. 56.

SESSIONS:Egbert 6;Dan.71;R.122.

SEYMOUR:Nathaniel 6.

SHAEFER - SHAFFER:A. 55; Clarissa 23;Henry 23.

SHALL:Geo. 25; J.A. 58;Susan 102.

SHALLIS:M.H. 111,114.

SHANNON:Ed.S.2;R.138;Rebecca S.41;W.F.138.

SHANNAHAN: D.42;T.M.49.

SHARKEY: Green P.24;Tallula 24.

SHEARER:Letitia J. 20;W.B.20.

SHELBY:Albert Creath 125,130, 140; Ann 101;Bettie 47,49; Catherine P.124;Creath 107, 124;Dora 148; D.F.B.144;Emily M.130,140;Evan 9,16,105,107, 124,130,140;Evan B.125,148; Evan Jr. 105,130;Evan W.111, 112,114,115,129,144;Flournoy 105;Katy 105;M.B.P.144;Marg. 105;Mary105;Mary L.129,144; Mollie Kate 125;Robt.105;Robt. Prince3,7,9,10,12,13,15,73, 106,107,115,124w,125,128;R.T. 106;Thos.31,35,47,49,68,69, 88,89,107,124;Thos.Jr.140; Thos.J.107,122,124,125,130,140.

SHELTON:Nelson 15.

SHEPHERD:--42

SHIELDS:Fay 57;Mary W.56; Thos.B.15.

SHINDLER:Jos.87.

SHIPP: Wm.5; ___ 37.

SHIRLEY:Adam 2,4,6,8,10,11,13.

SHOAF:H. 115;Jacob 115.

SHORT - SHART:Absolom 18;H.1.

SHREWSBERRY:Chas.S.82;Ellen 82,87.

SHRICK: Lisette 57.

SHRIMPSKI:Shall 23.

SHRODER:J.A.C.51.

SIAS:Oliver Sr.122.

SIGLER:Geo. 3,6.

SILLERS:Wm.67.

SIMONTON:Jas.Ross 146.

SIMPSON: J.J.44;O.P.122;
Mrs.AnnaM.84.

SIMRALL:JohnW.G.82.

SIMS -SIMMS:Chas.21;E.R.31;
G.G.40;J.H.21;J.T.28;Nancy
31;R.G.36,48,49;R.L.21;Thos.
Y.61;Wm.H.1;W.R.21,31,58.

SINGERT:Phillip 32.

SINGLETON:Ann J.9,12;John G.
12,13;Mary C.132.

SITES:E.W. 143;H.M.143.

SKIENE:Benj.6;V.V.6.

SKINNER:Kate B.122;N.C.90;
134;N.D.50;Saml.P.56;Trim L.96

SLATER:Henry 8.

SLEMONS:Wm.62

SMALL:Jas.S.86.

SMART:T.W.57.

SMEDES:Abram 21,A.K.26,69;
Chas.21,28,45;Geo.3;Henry 12;
Martha 21; __54,72;Thos.21.

SMITH:Atty.Webster & Smith1,3;
Abram F.6,11,12,13,24,26,54,
59,62,65,69,71,73,76,86;A.C.
35;Aleck127;Amanda148;Andrew
W.91,93;Mrs.C.C.40;Caleb148;
Catherine W.91;Clinton 127;
Ellen42;Fannie 102;Fannie L.
94;Francis 60;Geo.101;Harrison
78;Henry 19,102,127;Irene95w;
Isaac(Mrs.)94;Jane 127; Jane
P.101;Jas.D.36;J.M.32;John84;
John C.O.81;Jos.42;Lucinda91;
Marg.127;Mary E.57;Minerva G.
114;Rachael 78;Robt.B.91;R.M.
113,114,115,133,137;Robt.M.Jr.
133;Sarah133;Serena133;Sidney
84;SidneyR.19,36;S.Myra30,35

SMITH:cont.Thos.127;Thos.J.52;
Thos.M.84w;Walter J.133;W.D.
139;Wm.F.24,26,27,28,29,31,33,
48;Wm.Henry78;Wm.45,84;Wm.T.63.

SMITHHURST:John M.93.

SMYTHE:Jennie 57.

SNODGRASS:John 8.

SPEARMAN:Patsy 95.

SPEARS - SPEER: Abram 3;Geo.3.

SPENCER: Selden 122;S.M.139.

SPIARS:Marshall M.122.

SPRAGUE: __11;E.M. 44.

SPRATT:Andrew 137.

SPRIGGS:Celia 148;Jos.135.

SQUIRE: __4.

STAFFORD:Wm.R.116.

STAMPLEY:D.Y.74.

STANDARD:C.W.46,52;L.50.

STANTON:Amos 122.

STARKE: __43.

STEED - STEELE: Claiborne4,6,10.

STEIFF:Jos.110.

STEIN:Ruth 55.

STERLING:Mary 56.

STEPHENS - STEVENS:Judge Stephen
C.82;Thos.T.9,10,11,13;Will H.
48,53.

STEVENSON:E.E.51,58;Thos.67.

STEWART - STEWARD:A.T.37;Chas.D.
97;Jennie99;John Black 97;Willie
S.57;Wiley 107;Wm.W.21.

ST.JOHN:Wm.25.

STOCKETT: T.G. 28.

STOCKMAN: Jas.6.

STOKES: Julius C. 57.

STORMS: Asa 46.

STONE: Alf.57,58; Alice H.57; C.S.45; Dr.Walter 45; Jas.45; 104; Kate 45,53; Mary W.104; Oliver 45; Wm.P.6,15; W.W.45.

STOUT: John 57.

STOW-STOWE: John 61.

STURDIVANT: M.P. 58.

STURGIS: Emma L. 120.

SUGGETT: David 8,14,16,72.

SULLIVAN: Catherine 128; Emily Ann 113,140; Emily H. 128; J.J.113,115,128; Louisa C.128,140; Martha C.128; Martha Kate 113,140; Mary Eliz.113, 128; M.J.140; S.A.114; Saml.N. 108,114; Saml.W.2,60; Susan A. 126; Vans.M.14,15.

SUMMERS-SOMMERS: Adams 34; Chas.100; Adam.S.5; Wm.78.

SUTTON: Benj.H.97; Emma Wilsie 95; J.M.68,96; Junius M.97; Laura 97(w); R.H.37; Sarah C. 55; Sarah Eliza 95; Stephen T. 95; Thos.J.97; Wm.95(w); --1.

SWAN: Frances Ann 81; John C. 81; John Raliegh 81; Mary J. 81; Pamelia B.29,81.

SWANSEY: Alfred 50

SWANSON: James 114,115.

SWEET: Sophia 122.

T

TALBOTT - TALBUTT: Chas.B. 88; Davis 81; L.M.93; Wm.3,8.

TALLEFERRO: Jas.F.21.

TAMPLIN: Marg.V.41.

TANDY: --13.

TANNER: Saml.61

TARBE: John 11.

TARLETON-TARELTON: --39.

TARUM: T.W. 58.

TASLEY: Alex 11.

TATE: John 3; Robt.3,10.

TAYLOR: Clara Ann 148; Diana 122; Eliz.29; Henry 44; James Hunt 62; Jesse 68; Mrs.J.S.122; J.T.41; Lydia 73; L.L.22,26; L.S. 29; Parthenia 148; Peter 51; Saml. 26,32,33; S.S.38; S.T.41,42; Susan 138; Susan P.44,29; Thos. 68; Wm.68,111,115,122; Wm.Henry 62.

TEMPLE: Archie 122.

TEMPLETON: Saml.8.

TERRY: Amelia S.95; Wm.H.95.

THAMES: John Allen 147.

THANLEY-THOMLEY: J.E.115,122.

THEOBALD: Adelia 67; H.B.32,34; Saml.32; Sarah 67; Thos.66,67;

THOMAS:
G.W.53; Horton 48; John H.11; Lewis 51; Mary 101; O.D.51.

THOMPKINS-TOMPKINS: Geo.M.63; Wm.77; --61.

THOMPSON-THOMSON: Jennette 58; J.M.122; Lewis 19; L.W.45,86; Manluis V.8,12,15,16,19; P.47; Phil B.42,65; Sarah 134; S.R.47; S.W.38; Volney 19; Wm.45; A.T.84; C.C.84; Mary 84.

THORNEY:J.E.116.

THORNHILL: __30.

THRASHER:J.B. 67.

THRELKELD: David H.10;Jos.C.70.

THURTOW:Thos.W. 136.

TIBBETTS:Steph.M.7;Steph.W.7.

TIDWELL:A.E.114,116;Edmund 127; Jesse 68;Madison 68;Milton 68; Mary F. 68;

TILLMAN:A,M. 127;Lewis 127; Louis 140.

TILLOTSON:W.W. 56.

TINKER:Jos. 30.

** TOOF: __33

TORREY:Geo. 35.

TOUSIMAN:F.M. 58.

TOWSEY:Erasmers 7,13;Erastus 9,11,12,15.

TOY:Clinton 147.

TRABUE:- TRABUL:Robt.W. 83.

TRAVIS:E.R.116

TRIGG:Abraham 101;Ellen G.58; Nelson 50;Susan Q. 101;Wyndham R.41,89,94.

TRINGLE:Mary 84.

TRIPPE:James 15;John F.15.

TUCKER:Claudia 18;Jos.18; Thos.M. 2.

TUDWELL:R.J.115.

TUFTS: __31.

TUPPER:C.H. 31.

TUREY:Farley 29.

* TONNAR: 120.

TURNBULL: Andrew 2,4,14,18,43, 59,60,64,98,115,116,124,125, 139;Anne 115;Anna 124;Andrew Jr.139;Catherine Van Rensselaer 124;Catherine 115;Chas.11,13, 16,59,61,69;Cornelia 115,116; Chas. Frederick 98,123;Fred. G.1,5,6,10,13,14,15,16,59,60, 87,89;Gracia 43,124;Heonard Eliza.122;John 5,7,10,14,15, 16,59,60;John Jr.1;Lewis 115, 116,123;Mary 124,89;Mary Ann 59;Mary Rubin 123;Matthena 115; Robt.J. 43,59,60,61,115w,116, 122,123,124w,125,140;Robt.J.Jr. 124,125;Robt. 7,115,116,124; Sinclair 115,116;Wm.B.59.Wm.59.

TURNER:Annie P. 56;Geo.63; Henry 64; Newman 46;Saml. 15.

TURPIN:(daus.)4;David 12.

TUTT:Wm.G. 65.

TYREL:E.P. 28,33.

TYRNER: Wash. 48.

TYSON: Jack 148.

U

ULIN:F.Y. 41.

UPSHAW: __54.

UHL:Joseph 58.

V

VALENTINE:Mark 12.

VALLIANT - VALIANT: Denton 65; Denton H. 79;Elihue 65;Frank 32,33,42,45,48,65,90,100;Franklin 79,94; Fannie 100;Henry 100; Jane 65;Janie 100;John 100; June C.79;Leroy 100;Leroy B. 32,45,79;Levy 65;Marion 32,100; Mary 56,100; Martha 65; __54.

VANARSDALE:A.M. 47.

VANDERPOOL:Beech 4;John A.4.

VANDYKE:Harriet 84.

VAN EATTON: H.S. 42.

VANNAMER:R.E. 55.

VAN NERMAN:Nina 55

VAN NORMAN:T.B. 58.

VANONUM:Mary W. 97.

VANVECOVEN:Chas. 55.

VAN WICK: Absolom 1.

VARNER:James 116;John 116;Jos. 116;Mahaly 116;Martha 116; Minerva Jane 116;Saml. 116w; Sarah 116.

VENABLES:N. 20; Tenn. 20.

VERDELET:Harry 40.

VERNON: Chas. 27,28,30.

VERSER:WM.R. 9.

VEXTER:Belle S. 55.

VICK: Geo.A.C.86,88;Henry 19,66;Henry G/86w;Henry W. 86,88;J.W.90;Mary B.86,88; Newitt H.1,7,129.

VIEGO: Donna J.C.69.

VILEY:John 28,37;Willa 66.

W

WADDINGTON:Geo. 124.

WADE:D.B.137;Geo.137;Jas.137; L.T.137;M.J.137;Nannie 137; N.T. 143;S.J. 137.

WADELL:Geo.C. 26;J.A. 56.

WAKEFIELD:Marshall 98.

WALCOTT:Charley 104;Jas.E.104; Robt.H.104;R.W.38;Theodore104; Theodore G.31,36,47,51,104.

WALKER:Chas. G. 1,2;E.G.1; Freeman 22,24,25,29;F.W.123; Gracie 56;Jas.22,24,25,29; M.H.27,29,41,90;Marg.83;Robt. W.83;Sarah 29;Peter M.29,41, 90;Sarah 29; Wm.1;Sister 83.

WALL:Ella 46.

WALLACE: Jas. 21;Robt.21;Wm.43.

WALLIS:E.A.22,25,83,84; Jas. 83;Marion M.83,84.

WALSH:W. 142.

WALTER:Harvey 30;M.F.20; __54.

WALTON: J.T. 145; Mrs. Grace M.124.

WARD:Emily 66;Geo.9,19,28,35; Geo.V.78,88;Jeremiah 75; Jeremiah S.75; John W.44,70;Junius 37,78;Mrs. Junius 78;Robt.J.9; R.J.Jr.89;Sarah Ann 70;S.138; Thos.6.

WARE:Jas. D.64;Nathl.61;Reuben 146;Thos.4.

WARFIELD:C.56;Thos.B.1,7,12,36, 37;Thos.33;Wm.P.7.

WARNER:Annie Mae 57.

WARREN:Agnes 30,42;B.B.146; John F.42,94;Nelson T.37,38; Phil 31;Robt.H.13;Stephen 85; Wm.30,31,42,53.

WASSON: B.F. 58.

WATKINS:Wm.S. 112.

WATSON: B.B.144; Harriet 123; L.C.144;Wm.2.

WATTS:Addie 56;Given 33; John 1; Miss 89.

WASHINGTON: John T. 57.

WEATHERBEE - WETHERBEE: __33; Percie B.58;Hiram E. 101.

WEBB:Chas.4;H.D.147; John A. 57;J.G.55; Lucy 148.

WEBBER:L.L.46;L.T.49,51; Maud 55;S.T. 44.

WEBSTER:Eliz.48;J.D.48,95; Isaac 11;__1;__3.

WEEKS:Alex B. 127;Wm.W.57.

WEEMS: S.B.46.

WEILENMAN:Martha J. 55.

WEINBERG:Sara 56.

WEIR:E.G. 139;J.D.H. 139; Wm.J. 139.

WEISS - WISE:Birdie 58;Isaac 85;Jacob 55;M.B.57;Morris 34; Reanna 95;Solomon 95.

WEISINGER: Henry 148.

WELLS:Eleaser H. 2,5,9,11,12; Jas.J.129,142;M.A.116,129; Martha J.129;Oscar R.134; Saml.M(W?)106,116,117,129; Thos.L.116.

WERLES:J.D. 49,53.

WEST: Amelius C. 47;John B. 83;Sallie 52;Winstone E.51.

WHATTLEY:Green B. 71.

WHEAT:Emma 58.

WHEATLY:Emma W. 52;W.B.40,48,52.

WHITCOMB: C.S. $&,%!.

WHITE:Abe 51;C.48;Charlie 99; Emily 28;F.J.58;Franklin 28; Henrietta E.116,130;Jas.M.15; Laura 99;Leonora O.130;Marg.J. 130;Mary E.130; N.S.84;S.48; Sally 51;S.F.36,50;Stuart 35, 94;Vandke 28;Wm.116;Wm.I.130.

WHITING:Jas. 10.

WHITMAN:Rowland M.1,3,5,14.

WHITNEY:D.B.43.

WHITEHEAD:Mary 78;S.Y.117,132.

WHITTEN:John Jr.63;Melissa O.63.

WICKLIFFE:Aaron 20,26,32,86.

WILES:W.W.Jr.55.

WILEY:James 126.

WILKES:John 124.

WILKERSON: E.39;Robt.2

WILKINS:Gov.M.115,116,125.

WILKINSON:Jas.C.14.

WILKOSKI:Annie 100;Frances 100; Julius 100;Lewis 100;

WILLIAMS:Absolom 132;Catherine 70;Chas.123;Daniel 42;D.T.117, 130;Eliz.66;Geo.66,148;Henry 45;Jacob 123;Jas.123;J.B.45; J.N.28;John 123,132;John G. 117;John W.9,45,51;Jas.23; Louisa 148;M.A.45,143;M.E.28; M.C.109,117;Nancy 45;R.116;S. 143;S.J.117;S.L.143;Teda 123; Thos.J.45;Virginia S.95;

WILLIAMSON:Archer 58;R.P.55.

WILLINGHAM:J.H.116.

WILLIS:A.36;A.B.57;Joel H.88; Kate 58;Oscar 131;Robt.L.55; Willie 40.

WILLS: J.Q.46.

WILMOT:Mans.42.

WILSON: Amanda 148;Andrew L.8; Anna 105;A.L.89;Bettie Ann 89; Bettie B.105;Cornelius 41; Henry F.7;Lea 102;Mary Wells 105;N.W.45;Osborn 148;Thos.W. 89,94;V.W.27;W.T.80,81.

WILZINSKI - WILZINSKY:J.95w; Joseph 96,100;L.52,53;Leopold 96,100;Nathan 95;S.51.

WINCHESTER: __54;Samvilla 83; Valeria 83.

WINGATE:H.66; Mrs. Penelope 66.

WINN:Edmund 38;Orsamus 27.

WINSLOW:O.53;__49;Richard C.146.

WITKOWSKI:G.95;L.95.

WOODBURN:Ellen 82;John 82;J.L. 24;Jno.R.24,52;John Rector (Ruter?)82,84,87;Isaac Leonard 82,87w; Mary M. 82.

WOODS:Andrew 83;Houston B.57; Jas.83;Jane 83;Jos.83;Josephine 83;Julia Hannah 83;N.M.2; Robt. 83w,84;Robt.Jr.83;Sarah B. 83.

WOLFE - WOOLFE:Chas.W.38;96w; Soloman 11.

WOOLFOLK:- WOOLFALK: Caroline 128;Chas.W. 128;J.143;Jas.63; Jas.B.129,143;J.E.123;John H. 129;Josiah P.9,10,15,128,140; L.123;Verlinda 129,143.

WORDEN:Geo. 38;Julia R.38.

WORTHAM: __51

WORTHINGTON:Amanda 45,93,104; Ann 78,81,86,105;A.W.20,37; Carrie 102;Carrie J.55;Edw.T. 30,43,104;Elisha 80;Eliz.104; Eliz.P.47;Fannie 102;Fannie M.55,93;Geo.102;Geo.T.94; Isaac 16,63,70,78,80,81,86, 105;Josephine 29,43;Mary 102, 104;Mary G.93;Pose 102;Sallie 104;Saml.64,78,80,81,93w,104; S.G.52;Thos.104,105; Thos. Flournoy 147;Wm.102,104;Wm.M. 93,95,104;Wm.W.30,31,47,78,80, 81,95;Wm.H.78,81,86,93.

WRIGHT: Aaron 48;Bettie 148; C.E. 123;C.S.143;D.A.143; Ed. A. 8; Emma S. 148; Joe 52; John T.11; J.S.143;John L. 14;John H.14;Hamilton 28; R.I.123;Thos. 63.

Y

YANDALL:Lunsford P.10;Wm.W.130.

YEATMAN: __49.

YERGER:Alexander 32;77,103; Campbell 26,101;Carrie 57; Edwin 103;Eliz.103;Eliz.B. 32,89;Harry 34,104;Hal 35, 38,39;Harvey 34,104;Henrietta 32;Jacob S.104;Jacob 30;Jas. 47,72,75,103,81;Jas,C.80; Jas.H.75,77,80,93;Jas.R.89; Jennie 101; John K.1;J.S. 26,56,90;Judge Wm.90;Maria 103;Maria L.32,38;Malvina H.32; Mary 35; Mary H. 101; O.S. 58;Sallie 34,35,104; William 32,74,101,103;Wm. A.101; W.G.26;William S.32.

YOUNG: Louisa M. 18.

Z

ZUNTS: James 22.

www.ingramcontent.com/pod-product-compliance
Lightning Source LLC
Chambersburg PA
CBHW030552080526
44585CB00012B/344